Threads of Life

Clare Hunter

Threads of Life

*A History of the World Through
the Eye of a Needle*

Abrams Press, New York

ABRAMS The Art of Books
195 Broadway, New York, NY 10007
abramsbooks.com

To the NeedleWorks team, board, volunteers and
communities; Anne Munro, champion of communities
and banners; and Glasgow's Thursday Group,
who share my love of sewing.

Contents

Acknowledgements

In August 2013, when I was browsing the books in the Edinburgh International Book Festival's tent, I discovered a rose crafted from newsprint. Attached to it was a handwritten paper tag. On one side was the message 'A Gift for You', and on the other '. . . freedom, books & the moon. Oscar Wilde.' I took the rose to the counter and asked its price. The assistant said it was free, one of fifty left that day by an anonymous paper artist who had been depositing beautifully crafted homages to literature in libraries and art venues since 2011. It was a gift.

At the time, I was wrestling with a decision: whether to apply for the creative writing course at the University of Dundee. I decided the rose was a sign, a talisman. I sent off my application the next day. I made a pact with myself that day in Edinburgh that, if I was ever published, I would tell this story so that the leaver of the rose would know that her kindness had made a difference.

For help with research I would like to thank: Claire Anderson; Liz Arthur; Ellen Avril of the Herbert F. Johnson Museum of Art; Ruth Battersby Tooke of Norfolk Museum Service; Harriet Beeforth and Vivian Lochhead of the People's History Museum, Manchester; Jean Cameron; Eileen Campbell; Ian and Thalia Campbell; Sally and Anthony Casdagli; Dr Annette Collinge of the Embroiderers' Guild; Common Ground; Andrew Crummy; Ginnie and John Cumming; Laura Dolan and Dr. Adele Patrick of Glasgow Women's Library; Cat Doyle and Jocelyn Grant of the Glasgow School of Art Archive; Alison Duke, Dr. Carol Hoden, David Mendez and Carolyn Walker of the Coram Trust; Kerry Harvey-Piper, Charlotte Hall and Shannen Long of the Peace Museum, Bradford; Ann Hill; Claire Hewitt; Cristina Horvath of Biggar & Upper Clydesdale Museum; Alan Jeffreys of the Imperial War Museum, London; Professor Janis Jefferies of Goldsmith's College; Elizabeth Kemp; Alison King; Elspeth King of the Stirling Smith Art Gallery and Museum; Ryan Mackay and Anne Munro of Pilmeny Development Project; Sue Mackay of the Thackray Medical Museum, Leeds; Olivia Mason; Rachel Mimiec; Moniack Mhor; Frank and Jane Mood; Deidre Nelson; Emily Oldfied of the British Red Cross Museum and Archive, London; Hannah Frew Paterson M.B.E.; Kathrin Pieren, Joanne Rosenthal and Alice Quine of the Jewish Museum, London; Lauren Purchase of the National Poetry Library; Janet Richards; Lindy Richardson of Edinburgh College of Art; Joanne Rosenthal and Eveline Sint Nicolaas of the Rijksmuseum, Amsterdam; Irene Spille of Stadtverwaltung Worms; Danielle Sprecher of the Quilters' Guild Collection; Bruce Steinhardt of Art and Remembrance; Jayne Stewart of The Hunterian, University of Glasgow; Dr. Jill Sullivan of the University of Bristol Theatre Collection; Emily Taylor of the National Museums Scotland; Hilary Turner of the Bodleian Libraries, Oxford; Rebecca Quinton of Glasgow Museums, Burrell Collection; Annette Weber of the University of Heidelberg; Gill Williams of Fingask Castle; Susan Kay-Williams of the Royal School of Needlework; Rev'd Gillean Craig of Kensington Parish, London and the Women's Library, London.

For being patient readers and giving advice and encouragement: Jake Arnott, Ewan Armstrong, Simon Callow, Sophy Dale, Robert Dawson Scott, Janice Forsyth, Catherine Jeffrey, Anne Higney, Roger Hill, Ed Hollis, Rosslyn Macphail Clare Manning and Louise Welsh.

For permission to use quotations: Mary Myams's sampler: Courtesy of the Jewish Museum, London; Extract from 'Carry

Greenham' by Peggy Seeger and published by Harmony Music is reproduced by kind permission of the author and the publisher; Lorina Bulwer's sampler: Courtesy of the Thackray Medical Museum, Object number LTM: 598.001; Louise Buchholtz's sampler: Courtesy of Norfolk Museum Service, Object number: NWHCM: 1965.332.1, Extract from the Billet Book courtesy of the Foundling Hospital, which continues as the children's charity Coram, Ref: 15700-15799 Feb. 23rd 1760; Quotes from Ernest Thesiger courtesy of the University of Bristol Theatre Collection Ref: PFT/000065; Extract from Hymn of the National Celebration Skirt, Withuis Jolande (1994) Patchwork politics in the Netherlands, 1946–50: women, gender and the World War II trauma, *Women's History Review*, 3:3, 293–313, DOI: 10, 10.180/09612029400200057; Extract from Menzies Moffat poster courtesy of the Biggar & Upper Clydesdale Museum; Extract from Ann Macbeth courtesy of Glasgow School of Art Archive, Ref. No: GSAA/EPI I/9/2/1.

For much needed early encouragement: Alison Bell, Jennie Erdal, Lucy Jukes; and Kirsty Gunn, Eddie Small and the late James Stewart of University of Dundee's M.Litt in Writing Practice and Study.

To Creative Scotland and the National Lottery for support with the funding of my research.

To my faithful and never-doubting agent Jenny Brown of Jenny Brown Associates and my editor Juliet Brooke at Sceptre without whom this book would have been far less interesting, and all her supportive colleagues.

Lastly to my long-suffering husband Charlie and my uncomplaining children Kim and Jamie who will no longer need to ask when *The Book* will be finished.

Beginning

You cut a length of thread, knot one end and pull the other end through the eye of a needle. You take a piece of fabric and push your needle into one side of the cloth, then pull it out on the other until it reaches the knot. You leave a space. You push your needle back through the fabric and pull it out on the other side. You continue until you have made a line, or a curve, or a wave of stitches. That is all there is: thread, needle, fabric and the patterns the thread makes. This is sewing.

I

Unknown

Sometimes I dream about textiles. A quiver of moonlit banners drift colour streams across a mirrored lake. Yards of soft-sheened silk are flung by villagers edging a river bank, cast into the water's flow, the people watching silently as the cloth, ripple-etched, is carried out to sea.

Most of my dream settings, however, are more prosaic; a deserted warehouse, a musty charity shop in which rails of clothes stand abandoned. I trail my hand through long-forgotten fabrics – crêpe de chine, duchess satin, tulle net – grazing my knuckles on a crust of beading, smoothing down languid lengths of fringing, stroking the braille of lace, drumming my fingers along a rhythm of pleats: small collapses of spent glory, discarded, uncherished, their makers unknown.

When I wake, it is always with a sharp pang of loss, more acute than might be felt for actual textiles. Because the textiles I touch in my dreams have never existed. There is no hope of their re-discovery.

I am on a train out of Paris, the hem of the city unfolding into a pretty patchwork of rural France. I'm on my way to Bayeux, where its celebrated tapestry is on permanent display. The tapestry is a rare survivor of medieval stitchery, now championed as a precious cultural relic deemed worthy of special safe-guarding by UNESCO's Memory of the World Register. But it wasn't always so well protected. Indeed, for its first 500 years it languished in obscurity, its exposure limited to an annual outing as ecclesiastical decoration for the Bayeux Feast of Relics, when, for a few days, it would be looped around the nave of the cathedral as a reminder to the congregation of the triumph of right over wrong, of a French victory over the English.

The Bayeux Tapestry tells the story of the Battle of Hastings in 1066. It is an embroidered narrative cloth with fifty-eight numbered scenes depicted in linen cloth and wool yarn, the simplest of materials. At its heart, it is a morality tale: a warning of the cost of betrayal. It tells how the English Harold recanted his oath of allegiance to the French William and seized the throne of England for himself; how William retaliated, prepared for war, defeated Harold's army and conquered England. A wrong righted, arrogance and greed avenged.

Images of the Bayeux Tapestry are embedded in our popular culture. It has become an iconic illustration of medieval life in Britain, its stitched narrative reproduced in countless books, on greetings cards and as needlework kits. It is much beloved by cartoonists amused by the incongruity of medieval stitchers and sharp contemporary comment. All of this has won it familiarity, an affection of sorts. But although I have read about it extensively and seen numerous printed versions of it, I only know the tapestry one frame at a time. I have no sense of what impact it will have when I see it in its entirety, no real understanding of its scale or its tangible presence.

When I arrive at Bayeux station, the Musée de la Tapisserie de Bayeux seems disappointingly close. There is only a road to cross, a few hundred yards to walk, a conker-crunching stroll through a tree-lined carpark to reach the museum's entrance. I had hoped for more of a pilgrimage, a little more time to savour the quest.

I buy my ticket and snake through a surprisingly lengthy maze of red-corded barricades used to corral the swell of visitors in high season. The Bayeux Tapestry is a popular tourist destination, attracting close to 400,000 visitors a year. Even today, on a cold October morning, there is a queue. The girl at the desk hands me an audio guide and instructs me about its function keys, but in truth, I'm not listening. I am like a greyhound waiting for the retort of a starting pistol. I am ready for the off.

A long, dark room is illuminated by a gleam of cream, a river of textile that stretches as far as the eye can see and flows back on itself again. I forgo the audio guide; this is to be an encounter between me and the tapestry. I want it to be my guide, to hold me back or beckon me forward, to insist on discovery at its own pace.

The thrum of audio commentaries intrudes, and while I can block out its babel of different languages, I can't avoid the sonorous soundtracks, the chanting of medieval songsters whose voices follow me – rising and falling, rising and falling – to chorus my meanderings. For the Bayeux Tapestry invites promenading. I stroll along its banks, surprised at how easily, given its vastness, it draws you in to its smallest details: the pattern on a cushion, the emblem on a shield, the liquid spill from a pitcher.

It begins grandly with an ornamented, turreted palace with lions growling below on the border: a symbolic portent of warring kings. Edward, his name writ large above his sewn portrait (the soon-to-be-dead King of England), is counselling his brother-in-law Harold about his mission of peace with France. Seventy metres later, it ends tragically: the border is strewn with the war-dead and there is a final distressing image of a naked and cowering English soldier clutching the torn-off branch of a tree as his only defence.

Unfolding between these two scenes are tales of feasting and farming folk, of spies and ship building, of hunting and harvests, of nobility on horseback and slain unarmoured archers, and of slaughter in the rough fray of battle. Its narrow frieze, only fifty centimetres high, has stylised sentinel trees to separate scenes. Embroidered borders provide an emotive and satirical commentary that amplifies meaning and mood in a procession of symbolic motifs and cameos of everyday life. Text travels across its surface in bold stitching to chronicle characters and events, and the visual story is punctuated by boasts of learning and travel: borrowings from Nordic sagas, images copied from illuminated manuscripts, designs culled from Greek and Roman sculpture and illustrations of some of Aesop's fables, including 'The Fox and the Crow' and 'The Wolf and the Lamb'. This is not just one story. This is a complex, multi-layered series of historical, biblical, mythical and cultural narratives, some of which we can still decipher, but much of which is long lost. We can no longer interpret all the tapestry's double meanings, unravel its intellectual challenges or unpick all the creative connections caught within its coloured threads.

It is generally agreed that the tapestry was designed by a man. The vivid illustrations of war preparations, the knowledgeable portrayal of horses and the detailed attention to weaponry all point to a male provenance. Recent research by the historian Howard B. Clarke of the University College in Dublin strengthens the case. He identifies Abbot Scolland, who died c.1087, the head of the illuminated manuscript scriptorium at St Augustine Monastery, as its likely designer because many of the tapestry's images seem drawn from life or memory and are closely connected to places and people associated with the abbot. Bishop Odo, the half-brother of William the Conqueror, is thought to have commissioned it, although some scholars believe that Queen Edith, the wife of the dead King Edward, was its commissioner, pointing to the earlier precedent of a donation by the widow of the English Earl Brythnoth of an embroidered hanging depicting his achievements, given to Ely Cathedral in AD 991. Conquered Saxon women sequestered in English nunneries are thought to have sewn it. This has been disputed by those who argue a French origin, proposing that the tapestry was created in the textile workshops at the Norman monastery of St Florent of Samur; that the yarn used has similarities with that spun in the Bessin district of Normandy; or that Queen Mathilda, the wife of William the Conqueror, who was known for her embroidery, was its principle author.

What is irrefutable is that English embroiderers were renowned for their craftsmanship in medieval Europe at the time, a reputation endorsed by William of Poitiers, chaplain to William the Conqueror, who reported that 'the women of England are very skilful with the needle'. If, as is widely believed, the tapestry was sewn by different hands, then the involvement of women from the nunneries in and around Winchester and Canterbury (there were seven within a day's ride of each other) seems plausible. Some are known to have housed celebrated workshops of fine embroidery supported by church and royal patrons. The proposition that the embroidery was executed by women of varying skill again points to these nunneries as the origin of creation since, in the eleventh century, they were not merely a cloistered retreat for women with a religious vocation, but also a safe house for others who needed a respectable haven, such as the unmarried daughters of nobles given, sometimes unwillingly, to God, widows lacking male protection, poverty-stricken girls and those whose mental or physical disability made them vulnerable in the wider world.

On the other hand, the Bayeux Tapestry is not typical of English embroidery of the period. It has none of its magnificence wrought in silk and metallic threads, nor its complexity of stitches, although the use of such materials and methods on a tapestry of this scale would have been prohibitively expensive. Controversy and conjecture continue. For all the intensive study, the origins of the Bayeux Tapestry remain a mystery, its provenance speculative, its stitchers unknown, its nationality unresolved, its present sequence questionable, its narrative considered incomplete.

During its first five centuries of oblivion, it was only

mentioned once, in Bayeux Cathedral's 1476 inventory: a perfunctory entry that describes it as a very long and narrow embroidery with images and inscriptions of the Conquest of England. In 1792 it was nearly destroyed, seized by zealous French revolutionaries who thought the old cloth would make an excellent cover for their military wagon. Its reprieve was short lived. Two years later it was saved again from being cut up to make a fetching backdrop for the Goddess of Reason float in a local carnival.

It was the tapestry's story rather than its stitching that saved it; its political rather than cultural worth, its propaganda value. Napoleon was its first champion. He commandeered the tapestry as a talisman and used it as a rallying cry when he had his ambitions fixed on England. He put it on public show at the Musée Napoleon in Paris in 1803, where it proved to be a popular exhibit. But the sudden appearance of Halley's Comet in French skies quenched his enthusiasm. It was an echo of the comet stitched on the tapestry itself: a star tailed in streaming flames – a phenomenon witnessed in England in the Spring of 1066, a mere four months after Harold seized the throne. Below the comet on the tapestry's bottom border lies a beached fleet of phantom ships. Both are omens of impending disaster. Napoleon dispatched the tapestry back to Bayeux.

During the Second World War the tapestry was moved for safekeeping to Mondaye Abbey near Bayeux, then relocated to the Château de Sourches. When Germany invaded France, Heinrich Himmler, leader of Hitler's SS guards, appropriated the tapestry for German appreciation. He organised private views for his inner circle and tasked the Ahnenerbe (the bureau of German ancestral heritage) to document it exhaustively. Over 700 photographs were taken, two documentary films were made, watercolours were commissioned and a 95-page description was written.

As the Allied troops advanced on France, Himmler set in

6

motion Germany's *coup de grâce*: to raze Paris to the ground. But he safeguarded the tapestry. In June 1944 he had it secreted in a basement of the Louvre. Even then, he was troubled. Hitler's deputy sent Himmler a coded order instructing its immediate export to Germany. The code-breaking centre at Bletchley Park in England, intercepted the message: 'Do not forget to bring the Bayeux Tapestry to a place of safety.' But Himmler had left it too late. When his SS guards arrived to take possession of the tapestry, the Louvre was already in the hands of the French Resistance. The Bayeux Tapestry stayed in France.

The Bayeux Tapestry has not only been saved but reinvented over its long life. Originally called *La Telle du Conquest*, it was re-christened *La Tapisserie de Reine Mathilde* after the wife of William the Conqueror, who, some proposed, had had a hand in its creation. By the nineteenth century it had become known by its current name. Of course, it is not a tapestry. It is an embroidery. But the misnomer elevated it from the indignity of any association with women's needlework, which, over the centuries following its creation, had become an increasingly de-valued art form. In 1738 the English traveller John Breval dismissed it as a 'most barbarous piece of needlework.' In 1843 John Murray III in his *Hand-Book for Travellers in France* described how the tapestry was subject to 'the fingers as well as eyes of the curious' and derided it as being 'rudely worked with figures worthy of a girl's sampler.' Other nineteenth-century critics found its stitchery primitive, its cream ground too empty, the whole effect lacking finesse. Even the great English writer Charles Dickens was dismissive, describing it as the work of 'feeble amateurs.' While its antiquity secured it as a work worthy of scholarly interest and curatorial care, its re-invention as a tapestry distanced it from criticism, inferring the skilled craftsmanship of professional male weavers whose guilds ensured they had the monopoly on the production of large-scale tapestries. This tale of war became widely accepted as an arte-fact of male history, of masculine creation.

Indeed, the tapestry is concerned with the world of men, albeit translated through the feeling hands of women. That world is its stage. It is a drama of war with a male cast – huntsmen, soldiers, kings – and events located at court, at sea, on farms, in foundries. There are no scenes of home, no flowers in the muddied fields, no apparent insight into women's lives.

Within its depictions of 632 men, over 200 horses, 55 dogs and more than 500 other animals and birds, there are only six women. They include Queen Edith lamenting her husband's death; a young woman being caressed or more probably struck by a cleric; a mother holding her son's hand as they flee from a burning house; a naked woman turning away from a nude man advancing on her with an erect penis; another naked woman holding a lamp in argument with a naked man who is bran-dishing an axe. The women are vulnerable, much smaller than their male companions. They are shown as diminished. They all seem powerless.

There is also the suggestion, however, that parts of the tapestry were drawn by hands other than those of its main designer, and that female stitchers inserted images of their own making, evidenced by less accomplished draughtsmanship. It is perfectly possible, through the long years of its making, that there would have been opportunities for covert additions, the chance to slip in a personal testimony of life after invasion, or even to document abuse.

Whether they inserted unsanctioned motifs and cameos or not, the presence of the embroiderers is palpable, held fast in their stitches. It is there in the diversity of needlecraft, the same stitches executed with a variance of skill. And it is there in the telling humanity of small errors or expediencies: a sudden shift to linen thread when the wool yarn ran out; a horse sewn in green thread; some armour etched in cross stitch rather than the more challenging chain stitch by some less accomplished stitcher. There are sections overlooked, a wrong stitch employed: mistakes, inconsistencies, omissions which lead us back to them, those stitching women – skilled, undoubtedly, but tired, hurried, careless at times. It is there in their awareness of the expense of their materials, the labour involved in hand-dyeing and hand-spinning wool. They attempt small economies as in their use of satin stitch which is sewn without looping the thread on the back, to save on yarn; a thread of colour allowed to travel to this place and that until it was all used up, servicing an eye, a letter, an element of chain mail before it reached its end.

As I scan the tapestry, lingering over its scenes of monarchical triumph and military devastation, I feel pulled into its story. It is as if, in its many reproductions, it has withheld its spirit, determined to disclose its fully tactile self only to a live audience. It is its needlework that brings it immediacy: characters, events and emotions animated by the skilful, imaginative deployment of coloured threads and surface stitches. This is its potency. It is the needlecraft that captures texture, rhythm, tone, personality, the sewing that traps its appeal.

These women had to be inventive. They had only four colours – red, blue, green and yellow – and the ten hues their dye afforded, to tell their tale. They chose their four kinds of stitches to make the most economical use of the wool, just four to create a masterpiece. With their limited palette and stitch repertoire, they conjured an illusion of depth which they emphasised by colouring a horse's forelegs differently from its back, by outlining each separate element in a different colour than the one used to fill in its shape: even the smallest pieces were worked this way. Sailing ships, galloping horses, advancing soldiers were given the illusion of speed by dramatic changes of colour that introduced a sudden energy. The hands of a pleading prince or praying priest were etched in black to accentuate the emotional import of their gestured language. They located the action of war and its preparation in the specifics of place – the sturdy ramparts of a palace, the tumble of a stormy sea, the furrows of ploughed fields – each evoked by a change of pattern or an alteration in the direction of stitches.

The embroiderers manipulated the curve of thread, the length of their stitches, the tightness or looseness of their thread (its tension, in other words) to capture the emotions of characters. This is very difficult to achieve with wool yarn. It has a slight burr that makes precision challenging. Despite being an embroiderer, or maybe because I am one, I am taken aback by their artistry. I had presumed I would find something rougher, simpler, a dutiful retracing of a drawn design in thread. But this is so much more. This is a human chronicle kindled into life through a long-practised knowledge of sewing.

Here too are the embroiderers' own responses to what they sewed, to the scenes they had to revisit: tenderness in the stitching of a hapless group of unarmoured archers battling for survival beneath the thundering hoofs of horsed nobility; empathy for the yowling dog guarding King Edward's deathbed; sadness in the gloom of the stilled fleet of ghost ships beached below Harold shortly after he gains the throne: all set among the poignancy of loss in the borders' motifs of fettered birds, hunted deer and predatory beasts. They elicit an emotional response, encouraging humanity across the centuries. That is the power of these stitchers, who, with just needle and thread, wool and linen, captured human experiences which, 900 years on, still move us.

Others followed them. Through the centuries there was a succession of stitchers, those that came after, intent on the salve of repair. Their nurture is equally visible in the 500 or so patches and darns that lie scattered over the tapestry's surface, in the newer stitches that replace what had worn away: marks of its restorers, menders and carers, the marks of time and of other hands willing it to survive.

I spend nearly three hours with these needlewomen, trying to enter their world through how they sewed, noting their attention to weight, movement, texture, expression, character, emotion, place; trying to understand the choices they made – this pattern, that colour, this stitch – how they made their story tangible, truthful and intimate.

Eventually I succumb to the audio guide. The plummy-voiced narrator is fulsome in his adjectives: 'picturesque, delightful, quite perfect, most impressive, truly magnificent.' But not once does he mention the women who embroidered the tapestry. I visit the accompanying exhibition. There are displays of hanks of hand-dyed wool, a replica of a small section of the underside of the tapestry and an explanation of the stitches used; there are information panels and three-dimensional displays exploring the art of illuminated manuscripts, the making of medieval villages, the craftsmanship of welding armour, but the art of the sewing itself isn't discussed or interpreted. Apart from a panel lamenting the lack of information about the embroiderers, the sewers are totally absent, even in the documentary film shown in the museum's cinema.

Suddenly I am seized with fury at the injustice. All those hours of labour, all that deployment of a practised skill, women's inventiveness and imagination, dismissed as if it did not matter. Nowhere is there conjecture about these women's lives. There is no description of their working conditions, no enthrallment at their expertise.

The sewers would have sat, hour upon hour, month upon month, year upon year, bent over a long rectangular frame, facing each other. Some had to sew upside down. There would have been pressure, an overseer pushing their work on. There would have been moments of crises, when they ran out of one colour and had to make do with another, when sections didn't match up and they had to camouflage an unsightly join, perhaps by inserting another tree.

The sewing was laborious: one hand above the frame, the other below, catching the needle on its exit and pushing it upwards again, on and on: tedious, exacting, monotonous. Their bodies would have ached with the constant arching over their frames; their eyes smarting with the gutter of fire smoke and candlelight, wearying in the poor light from small windows on winter days, the demands of unrelenting focus. It would have been a chore.

Even if we don't know who they were, we know what they did. We can see their skill, appreciate their craft and admire their contribution. These, at the very least, should be acknowledged. Instead, the embroiderers are banished from the story of the Bayeux Tapestry as if their part in its creation was marginal.

This is not the fault of the textile curators who care for our textile heritage. It is not to criticise the guardians of the Bayeux Tapestry. They have inherited the historical and social value placed on the tapestry, not as a triumph of women's needlework but as a chronicle of war, of French victory, of political propaganda and as a visual archive of medieval life. There have been investigations into the processes used, speculation about the identity of the sewers and academic study of the tapestry's anomalies in design, but none has led to precise information. Without that, a curator's interpretation is compromised and any conjecture risks criticism. And so, as with many other pieces of our textile heritage, avoidance is preferable. Embroiderers remain uncelebrated because they are largely anonymous, and while their needlework might be of historical value, donated to and collected by museums, without the necessary provenance, their creators cannot secure a part in its story.

For centuries, this was the fate of women embroiderers. They were robbed of their power. This is the history of needlework.

From the late seventeenth and into the next century, sewing moved into the home, to the domestic sphere, annexed from the public realm of work, economics, heritage, politics and power. There were small insurrections: women using needlework to claim their place in the world, stitching down political comment or a feminist complaint, documenting their experiences through domestic sewing, but they were rare, and their small flames of defiance all too easily disregarded. By the nineteenth century, needlework had been irretrievably demoted, and domestic embroidery was seen as a decorative frippery – just women's work.

Yet in 1816, for the tapestry's 750th anniversary, the London Society of Antiquaries commissioned its historical draughtsman, Charles Stothard, to produce a drawn replica of the Bayeux Tapestry. It took him two years. Despite his detailed illustrations, the society found that the flatness of ink failed to catch the captivating essence of the original. So it took a wax impression of its surface, which was cast in plaster to trap the tapestry's texture and the resonance of its stitching. Clearly, it was its sewn persona that made it unique. But even then, there was little curiosity about the women who had crafted it.

The spirit of the Bayeux Tapestry, however, lives on. In 1885, The Leek Embroidery Society in Staffordshire made an entire replica of the original tapestry sewn by thirty-five women. The society's founder, Elizabeth Wardle, felt that 'England should have a copy of its own.' All displays of genitalia in the original had been decorously draped in the design the society received from South Kensington Museum so as not to offend the feminine sensibilities of its makers or viewers. In 1997, its last missing eight feet of original narrative was re-imagined by the embroidery artist Jan Messent using, as far as was possible, similar materials and techniques. On it she stitched William's final triumph: the bestowal on William of the keys to London by the vanquished nobles, and his coronation in Westminster Abbey.

In 2012, another version of the missing end panel was made in the Guernsey island of Alderney as part of the 950th anniversary celebrations of the Battle of Hastings. This was a community project in which the stitching was undertaken by 400 participants under the direction of local resident Kate Russell. It too depicted William's coronation and was shown for a while alongside the original tapestry in Bayeux. And there have been other tapestries, other stitchers, across time, who have been inspired collectively to create their own sewn narratives. The Overlord Embroidery is a commemoration of the D-Day landings on the Normandy beaches in the Second World War: an eighty-three metre tribute to the fighting forces. It was commissioned in 1968 and sewn by members of the Royal School of Needlework with materials sourced from the uniforms of serving soldiers, seamen and airmen. The 120-metre long Keiskamma Tapestry of South Africa was created by Xhosa women at the start of the millennium to document their and their country's history, and was unveiled on International Women's Day in 2006. It is now wrapped around the walls of the country's Parliament as a reminder of the human gain of racial equality. The Bayeux Tapestry's most recent reinvention was in 2017, when it was used as the template for a new tourist attraction in Northern Ireland. *The Game of Thrones Tapestry* went on display at the Ulster Museum in Belfast to celebrate and chronicle the HBO television fantasy drama of the same name which has been watched by millions worldwide. Embroidered on Irish linen, the tapestry recreates, in seventy-seven metres of needlework, each twist of betrayal and the many battles that punctuate the eight seasons of nail-biting adventure.

And the spirit of the Bayeux Tapestry is there in The Great Tapestry of Scotland, stitched by over a thousand women – and a few men – narrating the chronicle of a nation. Designed by the inventive and community-arts-bred artist Andrew Crummy in 2013 as a homage to the Bayeux Tapestry, it is also sewn on linen in wool threads. In its 160 panels it captures the human history of Scotland with a democratic and empathetic eye. It threads a journey through the Scottish psyche, exploring what has shaped its national identity: its outer islands and inner cities, croft life and industrial trade, intellectual enlightenment and variety theatre, poetry and music.

Its sewers could employ a broader palette of coloured wools and a wider repertoire of stitches than their medieval counterparts. Industrialisation and the invention of synthetic dyes has allowed them a vastly more extensive colour scheme. Their knowledge of stitches stretched across the world and across time and they used it imaginatively. Textures rise from the surface in hundreds of different kinds of embroidery techniques: wool thread manipulated, woven, twisted, flecked, couched, knotted, looped, animating each story with the heartfelt, often heartached, narrative that lies behind each panel.

The sea is rendered local through intimate knowledge: thick in sewn braided waves; gently flowing in waved rows of running stitch; deep in stretches of navy and aquamarine; striped in undulations of mottled blue; still in an expanse of grey satin stitch; threaded lightly towards the shore on single strands of wool or patterned with light eddies of tangled colours. Using just a needle and thread each group has interpreted their own intimate sea, bringing alive its presence in their specific locality.

I made a small contribution, which was more prosaic than any of the rippling seascapes. I was assigned a footballer in a panel that celebrated Scottish hope and glory in the game. As I repeated the stitches of those medieval needlewomen, I discovered that the wool yarn was contrary, constantly snagging in complaint at my rough skin or a ragged nail; fluffing in protest at anything demanded of it beyond the simplest of stitches; weakening and breaking on its fold at my needle's eye. I had only one footballer to memorialise and yet I found him exasperating. He took inordinately more time, patience and care than I had supposed. And I lauded those unknown Bayeux Tapestry needlewomen, who spent years taming their wool yarn, getting to know the pull of it, its strengths and waywardness, and persuading it to yield to their demands.

When I went to see Scotland's tapestry, I wandered through the galleries feasting my eyes and nourishing my love of sewing. I stopped admiringly in front of a panel dedicated to the Scottish novelist Sir Walter Scott, his head phrenologised into the building blocks of Abbotsford, the magnificent house he built in the Scottish borders, each block inscribed with his book titles. The woman next to me gave a sigh: 'too much cream,' she lamented. It was the same criticism levelled at the Bayeux Tapestry itself by Victorian critics used to a cram of stitchery. 'You can tell that some people were better at the stitching than others. The quality's so . . . varied.' She said this with another regretful sigh, as if it were ever thus, an inevitable national weakness. But to me, as I told her, that was the joy of it: the evidence of all those different hands coming together to create a stitched masterpiece redolent with variety. It was the same joy I had taken in the Bayeux Tapestry.

On panel forty-four of the tapestry is Mary, Queen of Scots, the Queen of Scotland from 1542 to 1567, surrounded by miniature sewn motifs of her needlework. She holds an embroidery frame in her hand, and from it a single sewing thread connects her to the stitched legend of her life, which is played out within the frame of her body. She lived at a time when embroidery was one of the most potent forms of Renaissance communication, when it was valued as a transmitter of intellect and emotion, when it was a conversation between people and their God, the church and its congregation, ruler and subjects. Back then, needlework had power and its embroiderers had value. Back then, sewing mattered.

2
Power

It was Mary, Queen of Scots who marked the beginning of my attention to history. At my convent school, she was a rare heroine among the textbook tales of battling kings and male inventors. Unlike the devout missionaries or caring nurses we were exhorted to admire, Mary held sensual and sexual allure. Her portraits and the melodramatic paintings of her life captured her material world: the luxury of velvet glinting with silk thread, the richness of tapestries caught in the flicker of candlelight. Even in captivity she was depicted in stubborn splendour, capped in a coif that shimmered with pearls and clothed in a dress of lustrous black silk, behind which a gossamer veil floated like a waterfall.

Her story has been unpicked time and time again in novels, films, plays, operas, documentaries, biographies and countless academic tracts, her life forensically examined to excavate new morsels of evidence and shed more light on her character and her choices. Queen of Scotland at only six days old, she was already a political pawn. From her birth in 1542, King Henry VIII of England pursued his ambition of a marriage contract between Mary and his own son, Edward. When Scotland refused, Henry began his so-called Rough Wooing, a seven-year war on Scotland. At the Battle of Pinkie Cleugh in 1547 the Scots were defeated and thousands were slain. Afraid that the five-year-old queen would be forcibly abducted, Mary was smuggled out of the country by her Scottish nobles and taken to France as the prospective wife of François, its young Dauphin. There she grew up in what was said to be the most brilliant of the Renaissance courts. She was feted and indulged and when she was seventeen, she married her Dauphin in a head-swimming show of pageantry. But just eighteen months later her glory days were over. The Dauphin had died.

Left without a husband or a role in France, Mary went home to take up her Scottish throne. Her seven-year reign in Scotland was catastrophic, blighted by intrigue, religious distrust, disastrous marriages, miscarriage and murder. She lost the loyalty of her nobles. She lost the love of her people. She lost her throne, her only son and her liberty. And she lost her head when she was executed in 1587 on the command of her cousin, Queen Elizabeth I of England.

It is strange, however, that among the tangled threads of her life, so avidly tugged free by biographers and historians, one remains scantly mentioned. For Mary was an embroiderer and not a highday or holiday stitcher, for her embroidery had a purpose. It was her agent. It was to become her emotional and political representative.

In France, Mary would have been tutored in plain sewing such as hemming, seaming, darning; the basic skills required of every girl, even queens. In the sixteenth century, power was precarious, particularly for women. Queens had to be prepared for a sudden fall from grace: the failure to provide an heir or the elevation of a mistress could see their influence wane and their position alter. They needed to be armed with the tools of survival.

During her thirteen years in France, Mary learned horsemanship and falconry. She was taught to play the lute and sing virginals, how to write poetry and compose arguments in prose, and was tutored in French, Italian, Spanish, Greek and Latin. But another essential part of her education was the artful language of embroidery, learned under the influence, but probably not the tutelage, of her prospective mother-in-law, Catherine de Medici. An entry in the French court's ledger when Mary was nine years old records the purchase of two pounds of woollen yarns for her to 'learn to make works.' Embroidery was the visual language of the French elite. It was a culture of sophisticated visual communication, of symbols and personal ciphers. Textiles were the most versatile form of visual messaging: displayable, wearable, portable, recyclable, they could carry information from place to place, from person to person. Colour choices declared allegiances and intimate relationships. Stitched political and personal statements were declared within the folds of a skirt or on the drapes pulled around a state bed. It was a rich material world. Its presence and practice signalled wealth, power and lineage.

In palaces all over Europe, embroidered cloths dressed the nobility, cushioned benches, were smoothed over tables, hung on walls and used to screen off commodes. They fluttered in tournaments and processions in autographed billows of banners and pennants and created spectacle at masques and pageants. But they were not there as mere decoration. They were vital proclamations of power, disseminating reminders of longevity, virtue, sovereign strength and divine entitlement through family crests, classical and biblical allusions and in the symbolic potency of specific motifs. Their display was not only intended to impress their immediate audience, but also to have impact vicariously and internationally through the letters and reports in which they were described and the painted portraits for which the sitters wore their costliest garments and sat against backdrops of their most luxuriant textiles. Such portraits advertised prestige and prosperity, communicated by the delicate brushstrokes that depicted hand-crafted lace and the oil-painted shimmer of silk. In Renaissance art, different painters commonly worked on the same portrait, each contributing their own specialist skill. The artists who painted fabric were paid more than the portrait painter himself and were allowed access to the most expensive grades of paint. The portrait miniaturist Nicholas Hilliard (1547–1619) saved the highest and most expensive grade of white pigment for capturing the gleam of white satin. For a painter who could capture a monarch's finery there were rich rewards indeed.

This was an exclusive materiality. Sumptuary laws ensured that only the nobility had access to luxurious imported fabrics like silks, cut velvets and brocades. Only they could afford the smooth, slender needles that slipped through cloth like butter. Others had to make do with home-spun fabrics and rough, hand-hammered needles, still so precious that they were kept in special cases chained to a woman's waist.

An extraordinary example of the time and money invested in material sovereign power was the meeting between the two young royal colts, Henry VIII of England and Francis I of France, in 1520. They met in a field near Calais, ostensibly to sign a treaty of peace. The rendezvous was an excuse for a competitive show of rival kingship. It was christened the Field of the Cloth of Gold because of the amount of gold fabric, thread and trimmings on display. The royal parties were transported in embroidered litters to their brocaded tent cities, which were weighted down with 200 pounds of silk fringing. Thousands of tents were partitioned by richly embellished fabrics to create reception rooms, private apartments, chapels and connecting galleries. One tree was hung with 2,000 satin cherries, another bedecked in gold and damask leaves. And the kings themselves were dressed in the finest tissue of gold spun from the beards of mussels.

The Catholic Church had led the way to such indulgence. It communicated the wonders of faith through its material appeal and invested heavily in its textured power, procuring an excess of seductive textiles to transmit the word of God. For a time, medieval England was the source of the best embroidery that could be had. Its embroiderers had developed techniques to bring a three-dimensional quality to the flat plane of cloth and thread. Silk thread was laboriously split, stitch by stitch, to achieve a subtlety of detail more precise than any fine brushwork could attempt. Gold thread was overlaid at intervals with the lustre of silk by means of a method called *or nue* (shaded gold). The dimpling of the gold cast shadows and caught light, producing a three-dimensional evocation of the suffering of saints, the ecstasy of angels, the mystery of faith itself. The embroiderers amplified the splendour of cloth and thread with precious jewels – rubies, diamonds, pearls, emeralds – and attached sequins so loosely that they would tremble and glitter in cathedral candlelight. Their embroidery, named Opus Anglicanum (English work) was coveted for its brilliance, prized even above manuscript illumination as the most persuasive depiction of the life of Christ and the tenets of Catholicism. This was faith kindled by a mastery of embroidery to emanate spiritual light and illuminate the very darkest shadows of sin. They conjured visual hallclujahs. They were inordinately expensive. The Vatican owned over a hundred pieces.

It wasn't just the professional embroiderers, men and women, who were amply rewarded for their service to the church and their God in lucrative payments, noblewomen could achieve social and spiritual prestige through their ecclesiastical needlework, as could nuns who received a welcome contribution to their religious coffers as well as an increased investment in spiritual grace which they could store up for the hereafter. Their donations of stitched devotion could secure salvation for their souls as well as a public reputation for virtue. St Margaret of Scotland (c.1045–1093) was described as having a workshop 'of celestial art' where 'there were always copes for the cantor, chasubles, stoles, altar-cloths and other priestly vestments and decorations for the church.'

St Edith of Wilton (c.963–c.956) embroidered vestments 'interwoven with gold union pearls . . . set like stars in gold . . . Her whole thought was Christ and the worship of Christ'. Sewing sacred embroidery entitled these needlewomen to have their names inscribed in the church's inventory of the good, the Liber Vitae, as being worthy of special prayers. If their embroideries were interred with a saint, their reputation was increased by association and some were honoured by a sainthood of their own, such as St Margaret, St Edith, St Clare (1194–1253, the patron saint of embroidery) and St Ethelred (c.636–679), who were sainted in part for their stitching in God's name.

But in sixteenth-century Britain, the Reformation stripped churches of their textile wealth. This ended women's access to public status in honour of the church. Women had already been largely excluded from the London Guild of Broderers, the trades guild of embroiderers which had existed since the thirteenth century and officially chartered in 1561, when it faced a reduction in commissions following the Black Death, the plague that decimated Europe and Asia between 1347 and 1351. Now the Reformation put an end to ecclesiastical embroidery work. Monasteries and nunneries were shut down. Many priests and nuns fled to Europe, and some nuns took their sewn masterpieces with them. Nuns from the Bridgettine convent in Syon in Middlesex escaped abroad with a cope on which sentinel angels and seraphs bordered the life stories of the Virgin and Christ. Worked in silver and gold threads on an embroidered ground of red and green, it was an exceptionally fine example of Opus Anglicanum. The cope survived and was brought back to England when the Order was re-established at the start of the nineteenth century. It remains a rare remnant of the golden age of embroidery. But many ecclesiastical embroideries were less fortunate. The most precious were burned to extract their costly gold thread and jewels, their silk thread unpicked. The choicest were recycled for secular use. Most were destroyed.

As the Reformation took hold, secular embroidery gained ground, serving the dynasties now endangered by the threat and cost of war, unstable alliances and religious unrest. The rivalry between monarchs intensified, with an unprecedented number of European female sovereigns competing for a small pool of eligible suitors. In France, Mary, already the established Queen of Scotland, was a prized commodity. Her legitimate claim on the English throne made her politically and economically precious to the ambitions of the French, who were keen to expand their territory. Her value was displayed through the investment made in her clothes, even as a child: dresses in violet velvet, gold damask, Venetian crimson silk, cloth of silver, one in white satin adorned with over a hundred rubies and diamonds. But the death of her young husband and the accession of Elizabeth as England's queen made her less profitable to the French. All that was left to her was Scotland.

Mary returned to Scotland's shores an untested monarch. Having left as a child, she had been nurtured in French culture and its Catholic religion. To many of her Scottish nobles and people, she seemed a foreigner. Moreover, she was a woman. Only three years earlier John Knox, the leader of the Scottish Reformation, had circulated his *First Blast of the Trumpet Against the Monstrous Regiment of Women*, a seditious tract denouncing the right of women to rule. Mary had to counteract not just his misogyny but also the mistrust of her people with a forceful assertion of her right to rule as their legitimate queen, daughter of their king, James V. She needed every device at her disposal to exercise her sovereignty and demonstrate capacity.

For her voyage to Scotland Mary had packed ten cloths of estate (the ceremonial cloths which hung above monarchs' thrones emblazoned with their coat of arms), forty-five bed sets, thirty-six Turkish carpets, twenty-three suits of tapestry, eighty-one cushions, twenty-four tablecloths and a variety of embroidered wall hangings. There was her own wardrobe of fifty-eight dresses, thirty-five farthingales (hooped or padded underskirts), several cloaks and shifts, petticoats, stomachers, drawers and coifs. They encompassed thousands of metres of luxurious fabric: embroidered, appliquéd, braided, beribboned, fringed, tessellated and studded with jewels. But the real worth of Mary's textiles did not lie in their quantity or quality. What Mary brought with her to Scotland was much more precious than these: the presence of her power. Her vast trove of embroideries bore witness. These were autographed proof of her birth right, testimony to an unbroken line of accession, an impressive accumulation of sewn royal ciphers, monograms, coats of arms and emblems. They fixed her dynastic power and divine right on cloth.

As a queen, Mary embodied her nation. She was the personification of Scotland; her visual projection mattered. At nearly six feet tall, her height was an asset but, even then, she amplified her physical presence by an expansive volume of skirts and cloaks and the outward flow of veils. These ensured she inhabited a separate physical space. She exhibited sovereignty as a physical act and a visual show. The weight of her clothes, thick with embroidery, studded with jewels, slowed her to a stately progress on ceremonial occasions. She chose to wear colours that marked her out from those around her. While her courtiers were dressed in coloured finery she would don the dramatic contrast of black and white, a trick she had learned from Diane de Poitiers, the mistress of her French father-in-law. She understood the impact of the flicker of candlelight falling on silk and the glint of gold embroidery in sunlight and used it to good effect. This was not an indulgence in conspicuous wealth; it was a strategic, theatrical performance of the magnificence of her monarchy, a public display of the power and sophistication of her nation.

Female monarchs had greater need of the advocacy of textiles than their male counterparts. The public display of their handcrafted emblems and symbols meant that for women, even when physically absent from court through childbirth, banishment or imprisonment, the textiles they had commissioned or sewn remained on display as their representatives, still messaging their lineage, still acting as a presence of sorts.

Mary brought her armoury of textiles with her as a defence. She also brought her skill of sewing. But while Mary clearly learned embroidery in France, there is little evidence of her use of it there. Even the book with an embroidered cover she gave to the Dauphin as a love token was wrought by professional craftsmen. She seemed to prefer other pursuits: the riding, falconry, hunting in which she excelled; writing poetry, playing the lute, chess. Back in Scotland, however, sewing became a pursuit she zealously embraced.

In Privy Council meetings, Elizabeth's envoy Thomas Randolph reported in 1561 that Mary 'ordinarily sitteth the most part of the time, sowing at some work or another'. Maybe it allowed her to concentrate on deciphering the unfamiliar accents. It certainly offered a pleasing show of female docility. What is indisputable is that with her interiors shabby and the public purse depleted, Mary, with the skills of her professional embroiderers, set about restoring the royal textiles. They were propaganda, and politically expedient. If Scotland was to survive independently of its European vultures, it had to maintain the fiction of wealth, visible evidence of its continuing power. Her sewing represented metaphorically (intentionally or not) her protection and care of her country. As its newly returned queen, it signalled her mission to regenerate her realm so that it could stand on equal ground with other European nations.

At the start of her active reign in Scotland in 1561, Mary wrote to King Philip in Spain lamenting her fate as 'the most afflicted woman under heaven, God having bereft me of all that I loved and held dear on earth and left me no consolation whatsoever.' She became more and more depressed, given to fits of weeping. She is reported to have confessed that she needed 'the fortification of a man': a husband, an heir. Suitors were suggested, considered, rejected, but any choice was dangerous: to choose a Catholic would certainly alienate Protestant England; to choose a Protestant might risk the loss of the support of Catholic France, Italy and Spain. Against the wishes of her council and her cousin she chose Henry Stuart, Lord Darnley, her step-cousin. He was a direct descendant of the Stuart line, English but Catholic, young but dissolute, handsome but vain, bisexual and alcoholic. To Elizabeth I's alarm and the disquiet of Mary's nobles, the Scottish queen became smitten. She pursued Darnley with unquenchable zeal. Feverish textile activity was noted in the margins of her palace inventories. Bed furnishings were taken out of storage: the cloth of gold embroidered with the works of Hercules (a hero with an auspicious connection to childbirth), the gold and silver cloth embellished with ciphers and another embroidered with flowers. She reclaimed a green velvet bed set fringed in green silk and another in crimson, their silver braid redeployed on green and gold curtains, their damask recycled as a bed cover. Three damask curtains were remade as a bed pavilion. Against all advice, she and Darnley married in 1565.

The redeployment of so many bed furnishings and the rein-statement of the gold-grounded Hercules seemed to have been a worthwhile investment. Mary became pregnant with the promise of an heir. But before long the marriage faltered in the face of Darnley's debauchery, his naked ambition and his part in the murder of her favourite courtier, Rizzio. With the immi-nent birth of an heir, Mary seemed prepared to forgive Darnley's involvement in Rizzio's death and bury their differences. Much to Darnley's fury, however, she refused to confer on him the Crown Matrimonial, putting an end to his hope to reign as her equal and be crowned King of Scotland should she die. Darnley grew more querulous, more abusive. Once Prince James was born the marriage fell once more into disarray. Darnley became ill with syphilis and although it appeared that Mary was solic-itous, visiting him on his sickbed, in truth she was desperate to escape the marriage, and she and Darnley separated.

Within the pages of his inventory Mary's *valet de chambre*, Servais de Conde, recorded the break-up and Darnley's move to separate lodgings in Edinburgh's Kirk O' Fields. He noted down the relocation of textiles from the royal store: a splendid set of violet-brown velvet drapes, stitched in gold and silver: 'In August 1566 the Queen gave this bed to the King furnished with all things and in February 1567 the said bed was taken in his lodging.' And to his separate lodging also went a black velvet cloth of estate, a canopy of yellow taffeta, a green velvet tablecloth, two quilts, various velvet cushions and six pieces of tapestry.

On 10 February 1567, Darnley's Kirk O' Fields lodgings exploded. Darnley was found dead in the garden, strangled, assassinated after he escaped in a botched attempt by Scottish nobles to blow up his house with Darnley inside. The canopy of yellow taffeta was 'lost in the King's lodgings when he died in Feb. 1567'; the tapestries were 'lost in the King's gardrop [his wardrobe or dressing room] at his death'.

James Hepburn, the powerful fourth Earl of Bothwell, was accused with others of the king's murder. He was tried and acquitted. But, three months after her husband's murder, Mary bestowed on Bothwell the additional titles of Duke of Orkney and Marquis of Fife and three days later, on 15 May, she married him. A group of Scottish nobles calling themselves the Confederate Lords refused to accept Bothwell's innocence or Mary's marriage to him. They marched into the city of Edinburgh in full armour carrying a printed proclamation announcing their intention to avenge Darnley's murder, to deliver the queen from the clutches and ambitions of Bothwell and to protect their prince, the future King James. Battle lines were drawn. The two armies mustered on Carberry Hill outside of Edinburgh on a hot day in June. Mary, wearing a short, shabby robe she had borrowed from a countrywoman, rode with Bothwell behind the royal standard, a red lion on a yellow ground. The Confederate Lords' banner depicted Darnley's murder, his half naked body stretched out on the grass behind Kirk O' Fields and beside it the kneeling figure of Mary and Darnley's son, the young prince James, from whose mouth floated the words 'Judge and Revenge my Cause, O Lord.'

From eleven in the morning until five that afternoon there was a stand-off with protracted negotiations. The adversaries grew weary and dehydrated in the heat. Mary's troops had no water and some of her men fell away. Eventually, the Confederate Lords agreed to let Bothwell flee if Mary would put herself under their protection. Just a month after their marriage, Mary and Bothwell said goodbye. They would never see each other again. Mary rode back to Edinburgh escorted by her nobles in full expectation of their loyalty. But as she entered the city she was confronted with the taunts of jeering crowds crying 'Burn the witch. Kill the whore', the banner depicting the murder of her husband leading her humiliation. The Scottish nobles had no intention of restoring her to the throne. They imprisoned her for the night in the heart of the city, hanging the banner across from her window for her, and all her people, to see. The next night they led her by the light of a thousand torches through the city streets to Holyrood Castle, the banner still leading her way. From there they rode on to the desolation of Loch Leven Castle, where Mary was imprisoned for almost a year.

On 24 June 1567, Mary miscarried Bothwell's twins and, just three days later, she was forced to abdicate in favour of her infant son, whom she never saw again. The Scottish queen was kept in humiliating impoverishment at Loch Leven and only allowed a paucity of essentials. She wrote letters pleading for clothes, for linen to make underwear, for pins to secure her coifs, for woollen bed hangings to keep out the winter freeze, for an embroiderer, for cloth and thread. It took a month before she received any supplies: a small package with a few articles of clothing, some pieces of linen stitched with outlined flowers and some coloured thread. There was no embroiderer. So it continued for almost eleven months: parsimonious parcels delivered with some garments, fabric, thread. Eventually, in May 1568, Mary escaped with the help of George Douglas, the brother of her gaoler. Under cover of the May Day festivities, dressed as a servant, Mary simply unlocked the gate and walked out. Three days after her escape, the cook and his wife at Loch Leven were commanded to make an inventory of the possessions Mary had left behind. There were just seven gowns, three waistcoats and petticoats, a pair of sheets, a handkerchief, napkins, some hose and two pairs of drawers. The list demonstrates the speed of her downfall: reduced, in less than a year, from glittering queen to a fugitive in her own land.

Less than a fortnight later Mary had raised an army and marched against her captors at Langside in Glasgow. But she was defeated and fled to England for sanctuary. There she was to languish in captivity for nineteen years while the English queen and government debated her fate. In her first year of imprisonment, Nicholas White, Elizabeth's envoy, wrote of his visit to her:

She said that all the day she wrought with her needle, and that the diversity of the colours make the work seem less tedious, and continued so long at it till the very pain did make her give it over.

Bereft of the exercise she loved, Mary became lame with rheumatism. She was in constant pain. Embroidery became her main distraction and to some degree, her uncensored form of writing. For some years, she was held in Tutbury Castle under the guard of the Earl of Shrewsbury and his wife, Bess. Bess was an accomplished needlewoman and together she and Mary began 'devising works.' These were small roundels and octagons, many sewn with meaningful symbols from their lives. Mary sewed small slips (embroideries sewn on linen or canvas, cut out and applied to larger cloth) mourning her past: a crowned dolphin leaping over waves, a nostalgic reminder of her young Dauphin, and a tortoise attempting to climb a tall crowned palm tree, an ironic cartoon encapsulating her marriage to the ineffectual Darnley. She fretted over the present: a scurrying mouse eyed by a ginger cat, an allusion to the red-haired Elizabeth and her quarry, Mary; a droop of marigolds, a symbol of Mary herself turning to snatch the rays of the sun. But there was more to Mary's embroidery than distraction: it was her autobiography.

She created a set of bed furnishings, sadly now lost but described in contemporary accounts, which she bequeathed to her son, James. They contained images of imprisonment: a lion caught in a net, a ship with a broken mast, a caged bird. She also added over thirty devices (the heraldic logos of identity) of the royal houses with which she was associated: Guise, Lorraine, Valois and Stuart amongst others, and metaphors of her conflicted relationship with the English queen: two women on a wheel of fortune, the eclipse of the sun and moon. The bed canopy was embroidered with an image of Mary herself kneeling before a crucifix, the royal armorial of Scotland at her side.

Under the constant surveillance of her gaolers, with her letters censored, embroidery became a way for Mary to preserve her sense of self and continue to exercise her power. Unlike the careful text she crafted in her correspondence, which, she was only too aware, was read by others, or the letters she smuggled out that were in danger of being intercepted by Elizabeth's spymasters, embroidery gave her freedom of expression. Under the guise of innocent motifs, her embroidery became a covert form of communication.

She received Elizabeth's envoy Nicholas White sitting under her cloth of estate, on which there was stitched a phoenix, the symbol of resurrection and the motto: *In my end, is my beginning.* The phoenix was a Catholic symbol and coupled with its motto, the embroidery was a warning: the threat of her elevation to martyrdom, should she be executed.

Mary had other plans. The fourth Duke of Norfolk was one of the richest men in England, who had been the English Earl Marshal and Elizabeth's Lieutenant in the North. In 1569 he and Mary plotted to marry, overthrow Elizabeth and jointly rule over a united Catholic Britain. Mary sewed for him an embroidered cushion cover and sent him her gift. On it she embroidered a lace-cuffed hand descending from the divine of heaven and clutching a pruning fork, with which it was cutting back barren vines to allow younger, more fecund shoots to flourish: a clear reference to the virgin Elizabeth and the fertile Mary. Under the rolling clouds a stitched scroll proclaims VIRECIT VULNERE VIRTUS (virtue flourishes by wounding). There is a sturdy church to signify steadfast Catholicism and its architectural counterpart, a windmill, to represent the shifting religious instability of English Protestantism. There is a stag, the Catholic symbol of victory over non-believers, and two birds winging free. Mary added the Scottish royal arms and her own monogram so that the cushion's authorship could not be in any doubt. The embroidery was discovered and the cushion cited as damning evidence in the trial of the Duke of Norfolk for high treason. He was executed in 1572 and this small embroidered cushion cover played a part in his downfall. Mary's hopes of rescue and reinstatement were dashed and her fate became even more precarious.

In desperation, she began to woo Elizabeth with embroidered gifts. It was a calculated generosity. Such presents in court etiquette represented a bond or inferred an obligation: used publicly, they declared intimacy. In 1574 Mary tasked the French ambassador to procure 'eight ells of crimson satin, the same colour as the enclosed sample, the best that can be found in London' and 'a pound each of single and double silver thread.'

Her request was urgent. She needed a delivery in a fortnight. With the crimson satin – the colour of love and of blood – Mary created a skirt for Elizabeth. With the silver thread, she embroidered on it intertwining silver thistles and roses as symbolic reminders of their separate but inter-related monarchies of Scotland and England, and of their personal ties. It was a deliberately gendered appeal, employing a womanly skill they both exercised and appreciated and evoking the sisterly empathy they had once enjoyed. With it, Mary sent a message insisting that the gift was 'evidence of the honour I bear her and the desire I have to employ myself in anything agreeable to her.'

There is no record of Elizabeth ever having worn the skirt. But she did send word, through her envoy, to say that she found it 'very agreeable, very nice.' Mary's response is not recorded. More gifts to Elizabeth followed: a delicate and intricate piece of lacis work (a form of embroidered fine mesh) and three decorative night caps. None led to Mary's release.

She also sewed gifts for her son, the future James VI of Scotland and James I of England, whom she hadn't seen since he was an infant: a pair of child reins with its breast plate stitched in symbolic flowers that represented protection, love and fertility, its red silk ribbons inscribed with the blessing 'God hath given his angels charge over thee: to keep thee in all thy ways' and between each word, painstakingly, lovingly, she stitched tiny, meaningful motifs: crowns, hearts, lions. She sent him a book of prayers, for which she had embroidered the cover and written out each prayer in her own handwriting.

After nineteen years of imprisonment, in 1586 a plot was discovered to assassinate Elizabeth and put the Catholic Mary on the throne. It was led by a Jesuit priest and a young recusant, Anthony Babington, who hoped to enlist the support of France and Spain. Mary was implicated in the plan when coded correspondence with the plotters, supposedly in her own hand, was intercepted by Elizabeth's spymaster, Francis Walsingham. This was treason. Mary was tried and sentenced to death. Her cloth of estate was torn down, her one remaining embroiderer dismissed. Her material trappings of power were forever silenced.

Except that Mary had one final declaration to make. As she went to her execution, her waiting women divested her of her black outer dress. As Mary, Queen of Scotland faced death she stood resplendent in a petticoat and sleeves of blood red. It was no idle choice. Mary was a woman for whom the subtext mattered. Red was the Catholic colour of martyrdom.

They burnt the clothes she wore that day so that no relics would remain, no scrap of cloth would be left to venerate. An inventory of all her belongings that had been made at Chartley Hall in 1586, before she was moved to Fotheringhay Castle for her execution, is illuminating. Some textiles were bequeathed to those closest to her; she had requested that others be sold to pay her servants 'in their journey homeward.' The inventory listed what remained of her sewing: over 350 small embroideries, evidence of her stitching hands suddenly, unexpectedly, stilled, 'unfinished, not yet enriched, bands painted only, not completed, uncut, prepared for a design.'

Most of her needlework is now lost. Cloth, like power, is fragile. But some of Mary's embroidery survives in England at Oxburgh Hall and Hardwick Hall and in London's V & A Museum collection. There are only two small pieces in Scotland at Holyrood Palace in Edinburgh. A baleful ginger cat regards a scurrying mouse, a lily and a thistle are surmounted by a crown: symbols of her captivity, queenship, Catholicism and fragility. Visual metaphors for the life of Mary, Queen of Scots.

It is thought now that Mary suffered from porphyria, the so-called Royal Disease passed down through the Stuart line, and the cause of the temporary madness of King George III in the late eighteenth century. She certainly displayed many of its physical symptoms: abdominal pain, ulcers, fits, muscle weakness. But within her personality lurked its more sinister shadow of mental illness, manifested in her rashness, depression, poor judgement, and her desperate need for approval.

In recent years, studies into mental health have explored the use of sewing as a panacea for mental distress and proved its efficacy to regulate mood, enhance self-esteem and encourage a rhythm of calmness. While Mary used it to assert her sovereign power and campaign for her reinstatement, perhaps there also lay behind her stitching a more basic human impulse: to maintain self-control, create order and exercise choice among the tumult and humiliation of her life.

3
Frailty

I am working on a textile project in Leverndale Hospital, Glasgow, with a small group of men with severe mental illness. I don't need to know the details of their damage: it's better to know them as I find them, week to week, not as they might be, or have been, or could be again. But I do have to be delicate, for each man is on a brink, absorbed in the fragile poise of himself, vigilant against upset, wary of emotional trespass. They prefer to work silently, hardly conversing. Simple instructions are sufficient, their questions abrupt. Any attempt at conviviality seems to exhaust them.

We are designing and making new curtains for the hospital's refurbished café. The men seem pleased with the practicality of the task. The hope is that the project will loosen their social guard. But it is best, the staff advise, to aim for small progress. In our first two sessions, the men have been designing and sketching a variety of shapes, drawing and cutting around swirls and scrolls, triangles and squares and gluing them together to make a collective pattern: a paper patchwork of undulating geometry which will become the template for the curtains' deep borders. Today we are to agree the colour scheme.

Deciding on colours is a challenge because it requires consensus among a group of people unsettled by opinions. I place an empty basket in the centre of the table. The men eye it cautiously. Then I let tumble a clatter of felt tip pens, filling the basket to the brim with colour. The group gladden a little. In a world of apportioned space, food, staff time and medication, such a plenitude is cheering. I bring out a sheaf of small strips of blank paper, select one and, with a turquoise felt tip, draw a thick line across its top. I return

34

the turquoise to the basket and remove an orange pen and draw its line beneath the turquoise. Then I fold the paper over, leaving only the orange visible, and pass it to David on my right.

He feels it thoughtfully between his thumb and forefinger and considers my orange line. His hand stretches out towards the basket and hovers. No easy decision. His fingers rifle through the pens, searching, thinking, feeling out a good choice. The rest of the group are tense, concentrating hard on David's rummaging fingers, willing him to complete the task. He eventually selects a purple pen and slowly draws a wide violet line below the orange. The group relax. David secretes away the orange stripe and scrapes his fingernail across the fold to sharpen it before passing the paper on.

And so we spend the morning folding colours away, passing strips of paper to each other and marking down our choices. The creation of our rainbows takes time: time to register each other's breath, to catch the wheeze of a cushioned chair as someone shifts his weight, to eavesdrop on the trundle and bing of hospital activity, the muffled sounds of the faraway world outside our room.

After an hour or so we have six concertinas of paper. We unfold them and smooth them out into their disparate palettes. We lay them down beside each other, numbered one to six. I suggest we decide by vote: a hand raised for the strip that each person finds pleasing. The process of elimination is easier than I could have hoped. The favourite is an unusual medley of apricot, mauve, pink, pale turquoise, grey and red – an odd combination that somehow has harmony, yet offers surprise. Here is our collective and creative consensus.

Over the following weeks, the group snip, shape, pin, tack and sew. They become more companionable, if not talkative. When the curtains are finally unveiled to the clapping admiration of staff and visitors, the men allow a group photograph to be taken: a tiny moment of shy success, no great show. The curtains are modest adornments. Yet they express, in their softness and muted tones, the tenderness in the hearts of fragile men.

John Craske was a third-generation fisherman, catching crabs and cod with his brothers in the coastal seas of north Norfolk. When the fishing industry declined, he moved with his parents further inland and worked in the family fishmongers, gutting and dressing the catch of the day and selling fish from a little shop and cart. He married and at the start of the First World War he tried to enlist, but was rejected due to an unnamed illness. In 1917, when the search for recruits became more desperate, he was called to the front. But his war only lasted a month: he caught influenza, which developed into a brain abscess. He was hospitalised, briefly moved to a lunatic asylum and, after a year, sent back home incapacitated to his wife, Laura, prone to bouts of stupor and prey to episodes of amnesia. At first there were some periods of respite. He and Laura rented a cottage, borrowed a boat and explored the waters around their home. He began to paint, and for a while it was peaceable enough: sailing with Laura, painting, making toy boats to sell. He captured the sea he knew so well in thick waves of oil paint and the wash of watercolours – furious, beguiling, tranquil, restless. But his illness weakened him further. He and Laura could no longer go sailing and John could barely leave the house. So he brought the exterior world into their home, painting the seascapes he held in his imagination and kept in his memory on any surface available – doors, chairs, the mantelpiece – until paper and household surfaces ran out.

As John Craske became increasingly bed-ridden and he couldn't paint lying down, Laura offered him a piece of calico she'd got to wrap a Christmas pudding for boiling and taught him some rudimentary embroidery stitches. Through sewing, he found his way back to the sea. He discovered that cloth and thread allowed him to create the texture of the softness of sand dunes and the fray of water even more tangibly than paint. He devised his own way of stitching, digging his needle in and out of the cloth's surface to cluster a tight blue of sky, and letting it loosen along a tangle of waves. Through embroidery, the sea water he loved could run through his fingers.

He stitched the thick of its storms and the bob of its boats, the curve of shoreline and the lace of sea spray. In thread, he could trap the rhythm of lapping waves, evoke the rustle of water at a shore edge and the fading smooth of a distant horizon. His sewing held the comfort of exploration, a reunion with the tactility of a watered land he understood, which could be transported to the confines of his room to soothe his heart and settle his mind. And so he kept it close, running his fingers over the swell of its waves, feeling out the direction of its currents. His biographer, Julia Blackburn, has written movingly of Craske's empathy with the sea, of how its loss was almost unbearable. Her book, *John Craske: Threads of a Delicate Life,* mirrors her own loss when her husband died while she was researching the book, a journey he had shared with her for a while. My understanding of Craske is caught up in the threads of her emotions, in an ache of absence.

Near the end of his life he began work on his most ambitious embroidery: *The Evacuation of Dunkirk.* It is a panorama of war pandemonium: bursting bombs fountaining the sea, burning planes belching dark smoke into the clouds, a ragged armada of boats fringing the water's edge, and in and around them the dead, the wounded, men half-submerged as they reach for rescue, others already clambering onto the safety of a ship, phalanxes of men walled on the shoreline awaiting evacuation. Above and around them lies the sky, the sea, the shore. They are impassive and timeless, dwarfing the human scrabble for survival.

John Craske put all he knew about the world that lay beyond his reach but stayed settled in his mind into his *Evacuation of Dunkirk*: the world of the sea and the men who travelled upon it, fought in its waters, risked its temper and relied on its power to lead them home. It was his war effort. He died with only a tiny patch of blue sky left unfinished.

In the nineteenth century, three different women, confined like John Craske by mental illness, made their voices heard through their embroidery. In the 1830s a seventeen-year-old nursery maid, Elizabeth Parker, sat hunched, day by day, night after night, over a rectangle of cream linen less than three foot in width and length. In red thread, with meticulous care, she stitched her story:

As I cannot write I put this down simply and freely as I might speak to a person whose intimacy and tenderness I can fully entrust myself and who I know will bear with all my weaknesses.

Each letter was sewn in exacting cross-stitch: sixteen stitches for a lower case c, twenty for an m: tedious, punishing, eye-damaging needlework.

She wrote of her childhood, the piety of her parents, of her wilful departure from home when she was only thirteen to take up an independent life in service. She told of the cruelty of her employers, of her attempted suicide and of her rescue by a local doctor who advised her to atone for her wish for death and put her trust in God. It is a litany of sorrow and regret, its vocabulary relentlessly bleak: wickedness, sin, evil, forgiveness, disobedience, vanity, temptation.

Why she chose to testify to her mental and spiritual anguish in laborious stitches is puzzling. Elizabeth Parker was literate, if not literary, and she could have written her life story down in pen. Perhaps she was afraid her writing would be discovered but more confident that sewing would be overlooked; perhaps she thought that her cloth would persist, that through sewing her autobiography would persevere. I transcribed her words, trying to imagine the toil of her stitching each separate letter in such minute precision. As I wrote them down, I realised that Elizabeth Parker's needlework was as an act of contrition, her penance, her chosen route to salvation. Her confession ends abruptly with a final plea to God: 'I returned to thee O God because I have nowhere else to go how can such repentance as mine be sincere what will become of my soul'. Happily, she lived to the ripe old age of seventy-six and became a schoolteacher. Her sewing, it seems, brought her the redemption she sought.

Born in 1844, Agnes Richter came from Dresden in Germany, although she spent part of her life in America. By 1888 she had returned to Germany, where she earned her living as a seamstress. But just five years later, at the age of forty-nine, she was admitted to Dresden's City Lunatic Asylum. She was sectioned by a Dr Hirschberg who reported that, after causing public disturbance that required police intervention, Agnes was found to be mentally unstable, which was manifested by a persecution complex. She believed that people were trying to steal her money and endanger her life. Despite the asylum doctors' assessment of her as clear minded and credible, Agnes remained in the asylum for a further two years, during which time her mental state worsened, although it appears she was rarely aggressive. In 1895 she was transferred to another asylum, the Hubertusberg Psychiatric Institution near Dresden, and a district judge was appointed as her legal guardian.

At Hubertusberg Agnes' behaviour degenerated. She became disruptive, given to rants, until she was no longer intelligible or capable of normal conversation. It was there that she took up a needle and thread and began to embroider text on the grey green linen of her regulation asylum jacket, re-fashioned to her own shape. Using different coloured thread and an antiquated German cursive script, she furiously stitched outrage in over-lapping words, jagged letters, repeated assertions of self, *Ich* (I) sewn over and over again: emphatic avowals of existence. While historians and paleographers have attempted to read Agnes' text, it remains largely indecipherable, mysterious even. It is not set out in neat lines but rather words, phrases and sentences are crowded together at odd angles across the cloth, strewn haphazardly like random snatches of thought. They do not seem to have been written as messages to others, but as a protective second skin for Agnes herself: words as magical agents in a mnemonic code, an incantation of sorts.

While some of her text is stitched on the outer surface of the jacket, more is hidden inside. Over time, this secret script has worn away, letters broken by the fray of thread and obliterated by the rub of her body and her stains of sweat. The jacket itself became even more moulded to her shape through her wear of it and has preserved it, ghost-like, through the centuries following her death, still carrying the multiple perforations of her jabbing, stabbing, furious needle.

In her book *Agnes's Jacket*, the psychiatrist Gail A. Hornstein explores how such manifestations of madness, which appear chaotic, might be a different kind of language, a visual one used to capture the actual experience of mental fragmentation. While the precise meaning of Agnes's text might be lost to us, the articulation of her disturbance is undeniable. There is something else which is curious: the buttonholes of her jacket are neat, their stitches even and the seaming and pattern cutting skills required to fashion such an elegant garment from asylum uniforms is testament to her ability as a seamstress, and yet she chose to sew her text in letters that are crooked, irregular, roughly sewn. Did she ever intend her words to be read, or was she using the distortion of her stitchery as a way of expressing her mental state, to represent it visually?

Agnes died in 1918. The asylum kept her jacket and the anonymous note pinned to it, which read: 'memories of her life in the seams of every piece of washing and clothing.' It is possible that her jacket was just one of many other garments. This one survived to end up in the care of Hans Prinzhorn in the 1920s, an art historian and the director of a psychiatric clinic in Heidelberg who took a special interest in creative forms of expression by those suffering from mental illness. Among his collection of over

Frailty

5,000 artefacts, Agnes's jacket has become one of his most studied acquisitions: the contrast between the fine stitchery of its construction and the wanton waywardness of her sewn text makes it a conundrum, which perhaps was her intention all along.

The same year that Agnes was sectioned in Germany, another older woman, Lorina Bulwer, was locked away in Great Yarmouth's workhouse by her brother when their mother died. At fifty-five years of age, she was destined to play out the rest of her life among another 500 unfortunates. Like Agnes, Lorina felt her fate was unjust. But Lorina's testimony was a comprehensible, if tangled, narrative. Stitched on long stretches of coloured fabric, some as long as fourteen feet, she composed lengthy epistles of accusation in large, emphatic capital letters that documented abuse and injustice:

I HAVE WASTED TEN YEARS IN THS DAMNATION HELL TRAMP DEN OF OLD WOMEN OLD BAGS.

Her thoughts and anecdotes are linked only by the thread that loops them together. Thought to be the ravings of a lunatic mind, it is only recently that curators and genealogists have turned to local history records, medical archives and census reports to see if there is any factual genesis to her complaints, and they discovered that much of what Lorina relates does refer to real people and actual events. What was thought to be the nonsense ravings of an unstable mind has been revealed as an eclectic autobiography. The boldness of her colours and the scale of her lettering, the extreme form of her needlework – in stark contrast to the delicate stitchery of her day – was a desperate attempt to gain attention, a plea for help writ large. This was no random choice but like Agnes's purposeful. Lorina made her sewing aggressively eye-catching to convey her palpable anguish and anger at her abandonment.

These three examples give us an insight into how needlework can be used against itself, how women who understand the sewing conventions of their age can purposefully subvert its

41

form to evoke and exorcise powerful emotions. Their sewing wasn't done as a form of temporary release from frustration, nor did it represent momentary outbursts. Instead, these women spent hours, days, weeks and months on their alternative texts. Elizabeth Parker used a sampler, a form more often used to extol moral virtue, as a medium through which she could confess her moral failings; Agnes Richter deliberately made a muddle of unevenly stitched words to articulate, and perhaps exorcise, her mental illness; Lorina Bulwer created a deliberately bold-coloured backdrop on which to embroider her vehement declarations to ensure they would be noticed and she would be heard. These women were all fragile in their way but, through sewing, they found a way to register their strength of feeling.

Fragility was clearly visible in some of the men who returned home from the carnage of the First World War: a leg amputated, a face distorted, eyes blanked by blindness. In others, the shell-shocked and traumatised, the scars of war were less overt, but nonetheless present. They had been left with an inability to concentrate, a lack of co-ordination, sudden attacks of the tremors. These casualties of war had lost their hold on the life they had left. Now disabled, unable to resume their trade, or even find less demanding work, they were doomed to a life without purpose, without social or economic value. They were isolated, marooned in makeshift hospital wards or imprisoned in their own homes.

Their exposure to new forms of warfare like mustard gas, whizz-bangs and mortar attacks left wounds that could not readily be fixed by a surgeon's knife or an extended period of rest. There had to be a new approach to healing, one that provided psychological support as well as physical repair. Occupational therapy was born.

Handicrafts played a major role in therapeutic post-war rehabilitation. Through a coalition of government, voluntary and medical authorities, artists and craft workers were recruited to organise projects, workshops, exhibitions and commissions to ensure that ex-servicemen not only had access to continued camaraderie but were also reconnected to the world outside of hospital and home. Mastering craft skills boosted self-esteem and confidence in new abilities, but also had other physical benefits: the exercise of wasted muscles, the practice of hand-eye coordination, the steadying of hands and minds. Among the crafts on offer, sewing seemed the least likely candidate for male recuperation, yet it was embroidery that became the absorbing occupation for thousands of ex-servicemen, affording them not just the satisfaction of skilled accomplishment, but also a means to boost self-worth and earn a little income.

Needlework commissions were a way for the wealthy, the titled and the church to play a part in the support of war-wounded veterans. St Paul's Cathedral in London commissioned over 130 ex-servicemen to sew an altar cloth for its 1919 Service of Thanksgiving. Billeted in different hospitals, stitched with guidance from staff and volunteers at the Royal School of Needlework, the project generated a new democracy in disability. Privates, gunmen, fusiliers, lance-corporals, sergeants, riflemen, captains and lieutenants worked collectively on the same commission and embroidered something beautiful.

The altar cloth was thought to have been destroyed in the bombing of the cathedral during the Second World War but, just a few years ago it was rediscovered, restored and put back on display. When I went to see it, I found a gleam of brilliance: the sheen of brocade and silk threads caught in a shaft of light. It seemed worlds away from the rotting, mud-thick ditches of trench warfare. At its centre is a golden chalice, the symbol of sacrifice, framed on either side by intertwining palm fronds to signify martyrdom. The outer panels are embroidered with cascading flowers and leaves in which birds, representing freedom, nestle. To the side, on a lectern, rests a roll call of its sewers. Its preface reads:

This book contains the names of sailors and soldiers of the British Empire wounded in the Great War of 1914–18; who, while lying in hospital, embroidered an altar frontal for St Paul's Cathedral in memory of their fallen comrades.

I wonder what those embroidery sessions between the genteel women of the Royal School of Needlework and the battle-worn men in their hospital wards were like. Did cultures converge in the heartbreak of a shared loss, of comrades, of would-be husbands, of damaged sons, husbands, fathers? And did the men, already grappling with disability, anxious about their future, see sewing as a further emasculation? Or did they enjoy the diversion of the female company of the women who taught them, and find absorption in the intricate skill of embroidery? A similar sewing project was reported at the time in Kensington's St Mary Abbots' church circular:

. . . with what ease the soldiers learn to do the work, and although some are better than others there seem to be no failures, for every man who has the desire to work shows wonderful skill and aptitude; and those who have been employed previously on the roughest work, such as bricklaying and plumbing are amongst the best at the finest silk work. They are all totally disabled men who are unable to leave their home to work, and they are constantly expressing the great pleasure it gives them to have this employment, which can be carried on so easily at home, and which they find absorbs their whole interest and makes the weary hours of sitting still pass so quickly.

What did the minds of these soldiers dwell on as they fingered the slide of their rainbow threads, as they coaxed a silken rose into full bloom under their hands? Did they discover mental and physical salve in the delicate demands of a needle and the pull of thread? During and after the war, embroidery proved to be therapeutic for disabled soldiers on many different levels. Physically relaxing and mentally soothing, it also offered sensory respite in the smooth feel of beautiful cloth as a welcome contrast to the filth of war, the roughness of khaki and the cold steel of guns.

One of the men to return from the horrors of the Great War was the actor Ernest Thesiger, best remembered for his sinister portrayal of the maniacal Dr Septimus Pretorius in James Whale's 1935 classic *Bride of Frankenstein*. In the scene in which the doctor promises the monster a bride, Thesiger's skeletal fingers idly fondle a luxuriant cigar. But his hands were celebrated for more than play-acting, for Ernest Thesiger was an embroiderer of repute.

I first came across him when I was researching the use of sewing in post-war rehabilitation. Key among the many needlework projects devised to keep ex-servicemen occupied was The Disabled Soldiers' Embroidery Industry. Its blue oval trademark bore the legend *Made by the Totally Disabled, 42 Edbury St., London*. In the little I could discover about the organisation, Thesiger's name was mentioned as its Honorary Secretary Cross Stitch. That title alone begged further investigation. With a little foraging, I found out that Thesiger's papers were safeguarded in the British Theatre Archive in Bristol. An email later and I had arranged to see them.

I ascended a flight of steps and entered a light-filled room. The archivist had already searched for my requests and, within minutes, I was leafing through Thesiger's hand-written autobiography, *Practically True*, penned a century ago. It is a tightly worded volume, written in an elegant, flowing hand which is rarely corrected. Here are accounts of his privileged childhood, anecdotes of his time at the Slade School of Art and his early entry into the world of theatre. It spills with the cheer of pre-war carelessness in the social melee of upper-class Britain before its youth were mowed down in the trenches of France.

In Chapter IV there is a brief mention of sewing:

To the surprise of many and the horror of some, I have also found great pleasure in needlework, which, after all, is only another way

45

of making pictures. It started when, in France with William Rankin [the Scottish artist], my brother-in-law, we used to buy for a very few francs pieces of seventeenth and eighteenth [century] petit point and gros point. They were often rather dilapidated and so we set about restoring them.

But, despite avid searching, I could find no reference to The Disabled Soldiers' Embroidery Industry and scant mention of his involvement in soldiers' sewing, beyond a couple of nonchalant sentences tucked in among racier stories of stars of stage and screen:

During the first war I found many hospital cases busy with their needles, but with more skill than taste . . . I took them some of my old bits and encouraged them to reproduce them.

I next turned to his letters, sent from the front from Rifleman 2456, D Company 9th County of London. First, there is bravado: a good crossing, much marching, high spirits. Then discomfort: torrential rain, long marches, mud. And finally, the reality of the front line: burying the dead; five hours marching with a rifle, spade and ammunition; digging trenches for three hours before a five-hour march back in relentless rain, bullets buzzing all around; mud, more mud. By 12 December he is near tears. By 23 December four of his company lie dead outside the trench while another three lie dead inside, stiff with rigor mortis. As they can't be moved the surviving soldiers cover them with earth and sit on them.

In January Thesiger and his company were stationed in a barn when it came under attack. The barn was struck, caved in. His hands take the brunt: fingers broken, distorted, covered in blood. He's surrounded by the sound of his company in agony with broken limbs and blown-off body parts and he can do nothing to help. He cannot lift off the beams that pin them down, tie a tourniquet or wrap wounds. His hands are useless.

He says he was convinced that he would never be able to use

them again. Thesiger was evacuated to a dressing station and returned home to an honourable discharge. He became Honorary Secretary Cross-Stitch, creating sewing kits for soldiers to follow in their own homes, in their own time – a distraction from pain, his and theirs. He designed small embroideries for them to sew, to earn a little money and to salvage self-respect, and negotiated commissions which won them royal support, including an altar frontal for the private chapel at Buckingham Palace. For him it was a reparation for uselessness.

I picked up his autobiography again. Surely there must be something more about his involvement with post-war needle-work? I turned the pages more intently but found nothing there. Just as I was closing the book, resigned to a fruitless search, some loose hand-written notes fluttered out in front of me:

Somehow or other the Ministry of Pensions got to hear that I was teaching the disabled how to do needlework and they sent for me to ask whether I thought there was any future in it, as they had many pensioners to whom it was impossible to teach any trade, as they only had will enough to work in short spells. I insisted that if the men were given good designs that in truth their work might be quite saleable . . . But the officials of the Ministry had a firm conviction that it was too effeminate an occupation for men . . . At that time the Friends of the Poor were visiting hospitals and giving men simple bits of work to do . . . They took up the idea with enthusiasm and from that small beginning was started The Disabled Soldiers' Embroidery Industry

Thesiger's autobiography was published in 1927, and twenty years later he wrote another book, *Adventures in Embroidery*. You can see him turning its pages on YouTube in an old British Pathé film. The background music rises to a crescendo of violins as a cut-glass English accent describes the scene:

All film fans know Ernest Thesiger, the man who plays sinister parts, usually murderers and madmen. Now meet him in a very different light as an expert embroiderer. Needlework has always been his hobby. He's written books on it and we take you to his London home to see examples of his work.

And there is Ernest Thesiger, peering over his spectacles as his long fingers stitch a cluster of grapes on a stretch of canvas. He removes his glasses and looks up, with studied interest, at a row of his own framed floral embroideries. Thesiger, rakish, camp, sardonic, the man who sat with Queen Mary on many an afternoon, both bent over their petit point, as Queen Mary (the actor Simon Callow once told me with relish) tested out her honours list on Ernest, eager for the gossip on sexual predilections: 'Mr Gielgud?' she would inquire. 'As a coot, ma'am, as a coot.' Rifleman 2456; banner bearer for the Men's League in the 1909 suffragette mass rally in London; the Fairy Queen at Ivor Novello's birthday party; Vice Patron of the Embroiderers' Guild. Ernest Thesiger, O.B.E., unsung hero of war-damaged soldiers.

We think of embroidery as a confined art. It is true it requires very little space, and can be easily worked within the frame of the human body. Hands, eyes and a lap are all that are required. But that constricted environment can be expansive, a creative portal to other worlds, a way of staying connected: sewing not only as mental and physical comfort, but also a channel for knowledge, imagination and passion.

I think back to those taciturn, cautious, tender men in Leverndale Hospital, and I know that in the simple act of making those curtains they rediscovered capability and found a release from being incapacitated. They also found a wordless way to communicate through the colours, patterns and shapes they selected. They told of the moments of mist and clarity that formed the weave of their world and its duality. Through the choices they made – angular against round, red against apricot – they expressed, translated, explained their inner and outer selves on café curtains.

4

Captivity

Sewing is unobtrusive. It can be done in company and still allows the stitcher to take part in conversation. It can be done secretly, quickly folded away should the need arise. If necessary, it can be easily hidden. For those in prison – divorced from the people they love, disconnected from their everyday lives – sewing can be a way to maintain a sense of self. And, when writing is censored, sewing can be a covert form of expression, of communication, of independence. Some of the most poignant needlework has been sewn in captivity.

In Glasgow's Burrell Collection (the hoard of historical artefacts collected by Scottish shipping merchant William Burrell during the late nineteenth and early twentieth centuries and donated to the city in 1944), there is a small sampler dating from around 1830 and embroidered in blue, red and yellow threads. In its bottom left-hand corner is the solitary figure of a woman, dressed in a sprigged dress and matching bonnet. She is in a prison cell, its barred windows, iron bedstead and wall chains all detailed in tiny cross stitches. To her right is a thistle, which indicates a Scottish provenance, and beside it a peacock, the symbol of love. These motifs and the little self-portrait are dwarfed by a verse sewn in black, which runs across the linen cloth:

> I ENVY NOT VICTORIAS CROWN
> ALL HER GOLD IS VANITY
> I AM HAPPIER IN MY LONELY CELL
> THAN ANY QUEEN ON EARTH CAN BE

FOR GOLD NOR TREASURE HAVE I NONE
NO ONE ON EARTH TO CONVERSE WE [WITH]
BUT I HAVE WHAT IS NOBLER STILL
THE KING OF QUEENS FOR COMPANY.

And below it is written: DONE IN EXILE BY I McK.

No one knows I McK's story or who she was. All we know of her is this small sampler, which she sewed to leave us evidence of her spirit.

It is the humanitarian Elizabeth Fry who is credited with first introducing needlework into prisons. When she visited Newgate prison in London in 1813 she was appalled at what she found there. Women and children were crammed together, irrespective of the severity of their crimes. They were imprisoned in degrading conditions with little sunlight or fresh air, dreadful hygiene, a starvation diet and little to occupy them. She founded the British Ladies' Society for Promoting the Reformation of Female Prisoners to campaign not just for improvements in sanitation and overcrowding, but also for the provision of educational opportunities as a foundation for rehabilitation. She introduced what she deemed to be the absorbing, mind-settling activity of sewing. Patchwork was Fry's chosen technique. It required little space, being worked in small pieces; it was repetitive, which calmed frustrated spirits; and it was also cumulative, allowing the satisfaction of growth, a sensation rarely experienced by prisoners diminished by poverty. Moreover, it allowed women to gain skills in sewing, skills that could lead to respectable employment on release. Her initiative was surprisingly successful and was soon adopted by other women's prisons elsewhere in the country.

A century later, women prisoners of war in Singapore also turned to sewing during the Second World War. At the fall of the island to the Japanese in 1942, 130,000 allied troops were forced to surrender. Homes, hospitals, clubs, hotels were appropriated for Japanese use. Tokyo time replaced local time and Singapore itself was renamed Syonan-to. Allied civilians were rounded up and marched through the streets, paraded in front of their former Singaporean employees, the servants who had mixed the cocktails, cooked the meals, nursed the children, tended the gardens. Of the POWs, 500 were women, most of whom had led cushioned, luxurious lives as colonial wives, with tea and croquet on the lawn and aperitifs at sundown: a privileged existence. Now they had lost their palatial homes, their place in society and their husbands, who were being taken to separate POW camps. Under a blazing sun, the women were marched on a nine-mile trek to Changi prison on the city's outskirts, carrying their babies and holding tight to the hands of their children. The women clutched the contents of their lives in just one small suitcase, all the Japanese would allow them to bring, that and the clothes on their backs.

Changi prison had been built to house 600 prisoners in peace time. Now, in war, it had to accommodate thousands: by 1944 there were 4,000 POWs. The conditions were dire and dehumanising. Malnutrition, brutality, disease and death became everyday nightmares. The cramped conditions, the lack of privacy and the scarcity of food bred resentment and frustration. But worse than this was living with the uncertainty: not knowing how long their incarceration would last, whether they would survive, when and if they might be reunited with their families. They were separated from their fathers, sons, brothers and husbands, who had been imprisoned in the adjoining camp – so near, yet out of reach.

One of the women, Ethel Mulvaney, proposed using sewing as a subterfuge to stay in contact with their menfolk. The women would make quilts – one British, one Australian and one Japanese – the last as a decoy to convince the guards that their motives were innocent. The quilts, they would say, were humanitarian gifts to comfort patients in the prison hospital, an act of womanly care for the suffering. Their captors were so convinced that they allowed Ethel Mulvaney to leave the camp under guard once a month to purchase thread from the local market. Not all the women were pleased with the privilege. Some felt that it was squandering sparse resources to buy embroidery threads when food and medicine were so badly needed. But the materials were bought, and the women sewed their quilts.

Ethel Mulvaney exhorted the women to 'sew something of themselves' into their allotted six-inch square. And this they did: on each quilt of sixty-six small squares, each square bore a sewn autograph and a personal image.

An old friend, John Cumming, told me that his mother was one of these women. In fact, he said, both of his parents were imprisoned in Changi, although they didn't marry until after the war. They, like many British young people in the inter-war climate of the 1930s, were desperate to escape the doom of unemployment and broaden their horizons away from Britain. John's father, a doctor, and his mother, a nurse, both from large families, were lured to the Far East by the promise of a good life, worthwhile work, the camaraderie of ex-pats. They found all they had hoped for in Singapore. But the invasion by the Imperial Army of Japan in 1942 brought their life of comfort and plenty to an abrupt end.

John's mother was only twenty-nine at the time. With a Japanese invasion looming, the British Government had instructed its civilians to leave and she had secured a place on an evacuation ship. She could have gone home. But at the very last moment, his mother decided to stay, feeling she was of greater use to those left behind. The ship she had been assigned to was torpedoed and all aboard drowned. John's mother escaped one tragedy only to find herself as part of another, as a prisoner of war in Changi for the next three years.

I discovered that the quilt she worked on is archived at the headquarters of the British Red Cross in London. I contacted John to tell him and we agreed to go and see it together. I made the arrangements and we met the archive's curator at reception and followed her down to the basement. There, behind glass, fixed to a wall and preserving a remnant of John's family history, was the British Changi quilt.

John and I stood and absorbed the grid of the sixty-six embroidered and autographed squares. For me, there was something disconcerting, almost disappointing, in its prettiness: the pale cream backcloth, the pastel threads, the abundance of stitched flowers. I had not expected such a frivolity of femininity; I had anticipated something darker. But when I looked more closely at the individual squares I realised that the delicacy of the stitches masked an almost unbearable poignancy. Trapped in the squalor on the camp, surrounded by the uncertainty of survival, these women embroidered motifs that symbolised what most sustained them. They stitched patriotism, hope, defiance and love.

There is a map of Scotland with a ship sailing to its shores; there is a butterfly, the symbol of freedom, and a drawing room tastefully furnished with a blue three-piece suite and matching standard lamp. There are forget-me-nots for remembrance and pansies for thoughts and an idyllic English landscape dotted with grazing sheep and spring-budding trees captioned: 'It's a Long Way to Tipperary,' reassurances to loved ones, of spirits unbroken, missives of remembrance and reminders of home.

But John was searching for an angel. He knew that his mother had embroidered an angel. I searched too, scanning anxiously along the rows for his mother's presence. Just when John became uncertain, momentarily and sadly doubtful that this was the quilt his mother sewed on, he found it: a bluebell-frocked angel with a flutter of wings, clutching a posy of flowers.

It is girlish, almost whimsical, in pink, baby blue and cream, a confetti concoction of colours chosen in the grimmest of times. At her angel's feet, stitched in the prettiest of pinks, is his mother's signature with her maiden name: Marion Williams. There is an immediacy in the freshness of its colours, the crispness of her stitches. It is as if his mother has just that minute put down her needle. It conjures her up at that time, in that place, John's mother's girlhood fixed in a six-inch square: innocent, romantic, the girl she was before liberation, before marriage and the birth of a son. It was, for both of us, a revelation, but for John it was also an insight.

We read aloud the roll call of stitched autographs: 'Dorothy Tadgell, J. Davidson, E.M. Murphy, M. Love.' Some names snagged at John's memory, but faintly; it was too long ago to be certain of any connection. But as we left and said goodbye, his memories stirred to remember reunions, the 'old crowd' from Singapore getting together over jolly evenings, much laughter and large whiskies. There was a couple who were particularly close to his parents, Jack and Elizabeth Ennis, and he wondered what happened to them. Elizabeth's signature wasn't on the quilt. For whatever reason, she hadn't chosen to embroider a square.

The next day I visited the Imperial War Museum. I had arranged to meet Alan Jeffreys, the museum's Senior Curator of Social History, who had other examples of POW needlework from Changi to show me. Alan led me to a basement store room where, on another wall, behind another glass, there was another Changi patchwork quilt, this one made by a group of girls aged eight to sixteen. It had been created before the women decided to make their hospital quilts. The girls' quilt had been their inspiration. Alan told me the story.

The girls were quartered in Hut 16, designed for thirty-four prisoners but housing a hundred. They took turns to sleep in a bed. They witnessed the fear and hopelessness of adults, the injustice of guards and desperate acts of survival. Their staple diet was rice. One of the women in the camp organised them into a Girl Guide troupe to bring some activity and a little normality into their lives. The girls were grateful. When they learned of her birthday they decided to make her, in secret, a surprise gift as a thank you. They decided on a patchwork quilt, but it was no easy task. They had none of the privileges later afforded to Ethel Mulvaney, so fabric and thread had to be scavenged from scarce belongings, from precious clothing that was already threadbare.

The girls unpicked thread from clothes that had rotted in the sun. Their patient unstitching took time. They hid purloined rice and flour sacks in the folds of their dresses. They sharpened blunt needles on stone floors with frustratingly little success. And, small piece by small piece, they made the birthday quilt.

It is worked in plain and patterned hexagons clustered into rosettes. The girls' stitching is unsmoothed by time; you can see difficulty in the clumsy stitches, the fiddle of joining the quilt's pieces. This is not neat needlework, but the evidence of inexperienced, halting hands gives the quilt an authenticity. It emphasises their determination, generosity and courage. For the making of the quilt was fraught with fear: some girls were too frightened to take part. Discovery of their recycled threads, the cotton sacks or the making of the quilt itself, might have led to reprisals. Despite the dangers and difficulties, seventy-two hexagonal rosettes were cut out and stitched together and, despite the paucity of materials, each girl signed her name in a cobweb-thin stretch of thread.

The quilt, Alan Jeffreys told me, came home with Elizabeth and Jack Ennis. I was momentarily distracted. The friends of John's parents? Time and worlds conflated. I had come to the museum to explore an experience annexed in history on a far horizon from my own, but its reality was within touching distance: John's mother stitching her angel and signing her name, Elizabeth Ennis receiving her birthday quilt – people just a friendship away from my own life.

We left the basement and Alan led me to a small study room where he had looked out other textiles made in the Changi POW camp. We put on white gloves and unfolded them gently, tenderly even, one by one. The first was a tray cloth: an embroidered illustration of the arrival of women civilians at Changi. The cloth captures its maker's first awful view of what was to become home for the next three years: a looming watch tower, armed patrols by the gates, a length of austere cell blocks, a high fence, a stone yard. Curving to the right of the cloth is a straggle of women reaching the camp, some shaded by sun hats, others pushing prams, carrying babies, grasping children's hands.

It is possibly the only first-hand POW depiction of the women's arrival at Changi. The woman who sewed it obviously felt that this moment should be documented, to record women's courage in the face of humiliation, to capture the spirit of those marching women; for it to be remembered, perhaps to remember it herself. Above the prison tower she sewed a speech balloon in which she stitched a snatch from a patriotic song, 'There'll always be an England,' the song the women reputedly sang as they stumbled towards their years of incarceration.

No one knows who sewed it, Alan said. It has no provenance, no signature. It turned up in a jumble sale in Bristol a few years ago, discarded by its maker or her family after her death with little awareness of its historical value. It was only an embroidered tray cloth. It was only women's work. On its border is registered the place and time of that exodus: 'Katong – Changi, 9 miles, Singapore 1942, 8th March'. And what tripped me up is the irony of that date: these women were marching to uncertainty on what has now become International Women's Day. The day, 8 March, was chosen in 1975 to honour the March marches of American and British suffragettes who, in the early years of the twentieth century, campaigned for equality and for enfranchisement.

Alan also showed me cloths threaded in signatures. Sewn autographed cloths, often tablecloths, had been a popular way to raise funds and support for social causes since the nineteenth century. Supporters penned their names, which were later over-sewn in thread, and the cloth auctioned off. But the POWs in Changi had a different motivation. They had no causes to support. Instead they shared a fear of elimination, of the gradual fade of self in a camp where death had become unremarkable, where they were cut off from the outside world. In Changi, there was every possibility that they had been forgotten; that they themselves might forget.

A POW named Mary Thomas collected 126 signatures on a blue cloth. The fourteen-year-old Vilma Stubbs recorded forty-nine in her patriotic rectangle of red, white, and blue. Hilda Lacey gathered 216 and stitched a dangerous and defiant border to document the conditions of camp life: a rice bucket to show the scarcity of food; *kiri* (the deep bowing required of prisoners to their guards) to illustrate a daily humiliation; a prison cell sewn to arithmetic scale; an emaciated man in a loin cloth digging for nutrition that he would have no right to claim. Most subversive of all was the Japanese flag fluttering from the prison tower, which she entitled The Flag of Tyranny. Discovery of such a cloth would have meant severe punishment and possible execution, but she still stitched out her truth. I noticed on Mary Thomas's cloth a familiar signature: Marion Williams. It is there again on Hilda Lacey's sheet and on Vilma Stubbs' autographed fabric: John's mother registering her existence again and again, fearful of obliteration, asserting her presence, keeping her sense of self alive.

Alan and I talked about the fate of these textiles: The British Red Cross quilt found in a drawer at the Red Cross headquarters decades after the war because no one had realised its significance; the little tray cloth destined for a jumble sale; Hilda Lacey's sheet, which came to the Imperial War Museum with no information. If it wasn't for her signature at its centre, no one would have known who had made it. Memories safeguarded but unvisited, unknown except to those who made them and the women who signed them. Many more have been lost, either disappeared or left behind after liberation, secreted away as new lives were built.

In the written memoirs and diaries of the Changi POWs, none of the women talked about their sewing. Why did they keep it so private? Was it because these remnants of incarceration were too tangible, kindled memories of humiliation and despair too keen? Or was it that, among terrible tales of male hardship, of sickened soldiers trudging hundreds of miles through the jungle to face death-threatening hard labour, that the women thought their stories of sewing would seem frivolous, disrespectful even? Those who later claimed a part in the needlework never explained why they omitted it from their memoirs. It can't have been forgotten. But in the aftermath of war perhaps it seemed a small, selfish act among such death and disease to stitch flowers, a three-piece suite, your own name on a scrap of cloth.

When I got home I searched the internet for the Australian and Japanese quilts made in Changi, the companions to the British quilt. They are now part of the collection of war embroideries at the Australian War Memorial. I scrolled down and across their squares, and on the Australian quilt I found what I was looking for: Marion Williams, her name stitched along with two others beneath a cluster of pansies. On another square I found Elizabeth Ennis. She had sewn a passenger liner sailing the high seas across the Atlantic Ocean, and beside it she had embroidered her hope: Homeward Bound. There are other Changi embroideries: an astonishing white linen skirt, part-pencilled, part-embroidered, encrusted in sewn text. Its central panel lists the programme of a concert party held on 2 May, 1942: The Changi Stroll, Hilda Barbour and her Hummingbirds, Prison Song. Clustered around it are 400 signatures. There is another signed cloth made by a Mrs Cuthbe and among its signatures I find a familiar autograph: Marion Williams.

The women in Changi prison stitched alone and privately. Their embroidery was not done during a jolly, spirit-reviving sewing bee. In the crush and claustrophobia of the camp, there was little privacy. Sewing allowed a moment of respite, of retreat, some moments in which to revisit individuality.

I told John about his mother's signatures, copied the photographs I had taken and sent him links to the Australian War

Memorial site. Her autographs are strange echoes of a past, known about but unknown: a mother tracked in an unusual way through her youthful embroidery and through the persistent stitching of her name.

Men sewed in the Second World War POW camps too. Patchwork was included in the occupational parcels provided by the War Office to POWs along with food and cigarettes and sports equipment, the parcels they and the Red Cross tried to get through to POWs on a regular basis. Every soldier was already issued with a sewing kit known as a 'housewife.' Major Alexis Casdagli ran sewing classes for fellow prisoners in his Dossel-Warburg camp in Germany and unravelled wool from old jumpers to cross-stitch defiance. To his young son, Tony, he sent an embroidered letter enveloped in cotton fabric. On one corner is a butterfly:

Oflag 1X/AH Germany, January 1944

Dear Tony,
I am so glad you are doing so well at school. I hope you will continue to try your hardest at work and play. It is 1581 days since I saw you last but it will not be long now. Do you remember when I fell down the well? Look after Mummy till I get home again. God bless you, Love from Daddy.

In another of those strange coincidences that life sometimes offers, it turns out that Tony is a neighbour of John's and on my next visit to London, John arranged for me to meet him. The door opened to a stairwell lined with embroideries, just some of his father's sewing, Tony explained. Images and patterns partner cross-stitched text. One of the smallest is a bookmark that lists his years of imprisonment: 1939, 1940, 1941, 1942, 1943, and at the bottom the optimistic: 'Any day now.' It was made as a gift for his wife, but it would be another two years before they were reunited.

Gifts of love, markers of time, acts of defiance, poems of yearning, records of daily life: they are all there in Alex Casdagli's embroideries. He sent them home via Portugal, a neutral country. But according to Tony, his father never talked about the war or the sewing he had done in his POW camp once he was home. Later, Tony took up embroidery himself and would sit with his elderly father, both stitching and not saying much to each other but comfortable with their companionship of needlework.

The Australian corporal Clifford Gatenby wasn't daunted when his army-issued darning needle became too blunt to use. Instead, he improvised others from old toothbrushes and spectacle frames. Searching for something to do in the long months of captivity in German POW camps, he turned to embroidery. An army blanket became the canvas on which he stitched a sewn medley of his war: regimental badges and embroidered snapshots of Hohenfels, Marburg and Spittal, the prison camps in which he had been held, Spittal with its snow-capped Alps glimpsed beyond a stitched prison wall. He traced his journey of war in thread – Egypt, Bombay, Giza, Palestine and Crete – framed in tight stitches against a background crowded in pattern. In each corner, he embroidered symbols of home: a kangaroo, koala, emu and kookaburra. Among the jostle of his needlework, he sewed a tiny map of Australia. At the top, it was signed with his prison and service numbers and the name of his camp:

1562 OFLAG IIIC C A GATENBY CPL. NX17797

When it was finished, every inch of the blanket had been encrusted with his war record and his thoughts of home. It is now on permanent display in the Australian War Memorial, a unique autobiography of one man's war.

For prisoners of war with few resources, the ability to craft something beautiful from so little demanded not just ingenuity but courage. No wonder these textiles carry such potency. They are triumphs of improvised tools, scavenged materials, achingly slow progress. Yet overcoming obstacles, being resourceful and creative, was life affirming. It held the satisfaction of stubbornness, of a refusal to accept limitations. It brought the small thrill of victory.

One of the most poignant needlework relics of POW stitching is also the simplest: a small white handkerchief embroidered with the signatures of seven girls. It belongs to Jan Ruff-O'Herne, a Dutch Australian who, during the Second World War, was taken from her comfortable home in Java along with her mother and sisters and forced into the privations of hard labour in a POW camp in Indonesia. Despite the hand-to-mouth existence meted out by the Japanese, the family survived for the next two years. But there was worse to come. In February 1944, an inspection was ordered and single girls over the age of seventeen were ordered to step out of the line. They were herded towards a waiting truck. As Jan stumbled forward, a woman thrust into her hands a white handkerchief. Jan and six other girls were transported to an old Dutch colonial house in Semarang. There they were photographed, given Japanese names and brutally raped. Their photographs were exhibited outside, along the veranda. The house was renamed The House of the Seven Seas. It became a brothel, and the girls were forced into sexual slavery as the comfort women for Japanese officers.

The night they arrived, Jan got each of the girls to sign the handkerchief. With needle and thread, she retraced their autographs in different colours and, at the handkerchief's centre, she sewed the date and the place of their hell: *Semarang, Java, 26.2.44*. Her captivity in the brothel was the stuff of nightmares. She was repeatedly raped and beaten. When she became pregnant, she was forced to abort the baby. She cut off all her hair in a desperate attempt to repel the sexual abuse, but it only marked her out as a novelty.

After four months, the horror came to an end and Jan was reunited with her family at a camp in Bogen in West Java, with the warning that if she talked of her experiences her family would be killed. She did, however, tell her mother about her ordeal the night she came back. After that, she and her mother never mentioned it again; Jan learned to keep silent. She was liberated in 1945 and, shortly afterwards, met and married a British soldier, returning with him to England before emigrating to Australia.

She held on to the handkerchief. It alone bore witness to her terror. In her book, *Fifty Years of Silence,* Jan talks about what that handkerchief meant to her:

It has been one of my dearest, most intimate and precious possessions, but also my most hidden: the secret evidence of the crimes done to us. Later in life the handkerchief became almost sacred to me. There were times when I would take it out from wherever I had hidden it, and I would hold it close against my cheek and cry for what it stood for.

In the 1970s Korean women began to campaign for restitution, an apology and compensation from the Japanese government for the suffering they had undergone as comfort women during the Second World War. Of the estimated 200,000 thought to have been abducted, terrorised and forced by the Imperial Japanese Army into sexual slavery, over fifty percent were Korean. Many died from the injuries inflicted on their bodies; others became permanently infertile; more committed suicide and some were executed by Japanese soldiers to ensure their silence. Jan Ruff-O'Herne was asked to give evidence at the International Public Hearing in Tokyo in support of them. For Jan, it meant that her story would become public, that her past would be revealed to her daughters, her family, friends and neighbours. But she went to Tokyo and spoke out. She laid a wreath at the Memorial to the Unknown Soldier as an act of forgiveness. Then she came home to Australia, donated her handkerchief to the Imperial War Museum in Canberra and began a tireless campaign against the sexual violation of women in war, a campaign she continues to this day.

For those held in captivity, the lack of space and privacy, the constant surveillance and a scarcity of resources, curtails not just independence but the means to express an individual self. It is this that is most threatened. For some, sewing, the act of making one's own mark, stitching a signature or embroidering images of a personal world, is a way of holding onto an elusive individuality and tethering an identity. Its very physicality – the joining of cloth, the creation of texture, the making of something substantial from discarded remnants – is a comforting metaphor for personal growth in the face of an enforced reduction. Elizabeth Fry chose needlework as a redemptive task for female prisoners, not just because of its economic implications, but because in its very nature it was an antidote to powerlessness. It offered creative self-expression. Her motives in selecting needlework as a salve especially suited to a prison environment are still pertinent today.

The social enterprise Fine Cell Work has been organising needlework classes in predominantly men's prisons since the 1980s, with support from the Royal School of Needlework and volunteers. An online shop, pop-up-shops, exhibitions and charity auctions generate sales, interest and support. Fine Cell Work has been commissioned by major cultural institutions including the Tate Modern, the National Gallery, English Heritage and the V&A; the writer Tracy Chevalier commissioned a quilt; artist Ai Weiwei invited the prisoners to contribute to his exhibition at the Royal Academy; and on a brilliantly conceived replica of the Magna Carta designed by the artist Cornelia Parker, prisoners helped to embroider text stitched by diverse hands: politicians and poets on the same page as the prisoners.

Like the women in Changi, these men sew privately, stitching in their cells and discovering an antidote to boredom, a retreat from the boom and bluster of prison life. Collaborating with artists, curators and other embroiderers brings them into different kinds of conversations and provides social and creative stimulus. Unlike the prisoners and convicts of Fry's day, the men get paid, which brings not just monetary recompense, but also an acknowledgement of the value of their skill, an appreciation of their artistry. They do not sew the decorous, decorative patchwork of

Elizabeth Fry's reforming textiles, but rather wry and intimate expressions of their reality. A bag has the word 'SWAG' writ large across its surface; the V&A commission explores prison life and features embroideries of a caged bird, the interior of a prison cell and the words 'I will go home'. Through sewing, these men can forge a different identity from that of prisoner, criminal, no-hoper. Fine Cell Work now operates in over thirty-two prisons in England, Scotland and Wales. Hundreds of prisoners take part.

5

Identity

I have come to the Women's Library in Glasgow, an oasis of women's experiences and camaraderie in the East End of the city. It is snuggled in a splendid old library and, within its panelled walls and whitewashed galleries, women explore their history and their connections with other women, past and present, through discussions, exhibitions, events and projects.

I am here to see an exhibition called Palestinian Embroidery: Empowering Women, Strengthening Communities, the culmination of a 2016 needlework project organised by the textile designer Claire Anderson that involved women replicating traditional embroidery patterns of Palestine in Fair Isle knitting. It initially seemed to me a strained concoction that somewhat stretched the idea of cultural connection but, up on the wall, the marriage is surprisingly successful. Unless you look closely you could mistake one for the other, but for the texture of the wool, which yields a mistier rendition of the Palestinian original. Today, as part of the project, there is to be a talk by Olivia Mason, a young human geography researcher based at the University of Durham, who is investigating a new kind of travel: experiential tourism.

Olivia is no rabble rouser. She does not harangue us with her outrage at the statelessness of Palestine, the injustices heaped upon it. She is not here to talk about the conflict. What she is here to do is to tell us about a people, like too many others in the world, who have been displaced from where they belong and annexed from elsewhere. In Palestine, they have been separated more emphatically than most by the physical reality of the wall. But, as she explains, refugees all around the world are

65

separated, not just physically but emotionally: by exhaustion, fear, their own powerlessness. And it is women who become most isolated from everyone but family. War has immobilised them, but for the sake of their family they must create a still point of safety. They are the steady, unmoving, unchanging core for men and children to return to.

The idea of experiential tourism is simple: home stays. But the purpose is more complex and compelling. Visitors don't just stay with a refugee family; they sign up for an activity run by their host, such as cookery or traditional embroidery. The activity is a crucial part of the experience. It is an alternative to the sometimes detached voyeurism of cultural or political tourism, focused not on the history and effects of conflict or the tragic stories of displacement, not even on telling or showing the ordinary life of war-torn victims. Instead, through home stays, visitors share in the everyday activity of a household, they live the difficult reality of family life. They are there when there's a power cut or a water shortage; there when a mother frets over the late return of a child from school; there to hear first-hand tales of harassment at the border controls, the nightmare of travel. As the visitor and her hostess knead dough or sit close over stitching, an empathy develops. The visitor becomes involved and her understanding grows. It is this she will take back home with her, not snapshots of a place and its heritage, but intimate images of family life. This form of tourism offers a different kind of journey of human discovery and personal connection. It is journey on which you learn to care.

For refugee women in Palestine and elsewhere who feel forgotten and unheard, this kind of experiential tourism gives them access to people in the wider world, beyond the socially curtailed home they inhabit. It offers a sense of mattering. Through home stays, refugee women can exercise their social skills, offer the dignity of hospitality and have the boon of financial reward. They are no longer passive as victims, but are active as hosts whose traditions and experiences matter. It is a small release from anonymity and a way to replenish worth.

At the end of her talk, Olivia introduces a live feed to Palestine, where a young designer, Noora Husseini from Ramallah, talks enthusiastically about the forthcoming launch of her new collection from the social enterprise Taita Leila, which references traditional Palestinian embroidery through modern designs and will be promoted and sold online to a worldwide market. As she talks, the signal fades and goes; we hear her apologies but can no longer see her. Then she re-connects. It seems like a metaphor for her life in Palestine: erratic, dislocated, uncertain. But through such technology, however sporadic the signal, lies the possibility of connection, of being able to participate in a creative consumer world that lies beyond the political and emotional divide.

Traditionally, Palestinian embroidery and dress provided an intricate code of social signalling, each village marking difference in distinctive stitches and patterns, the construction of a garment or sleeve design, the kind of threads used and sewing techniques, colours and motifs. Needlework was a form of detailed genealogy – each motif and stitch had a specific name, each detail an ascribed locality. It encapsulated human diversity in an internal system of personal and intercommunity communication.

In 1948, when the State of Israel was established, Palestinian villages were destroyed, abandoned or occupied. Survivors were resettled in refugee camps in the West Bank or the Gaza strip, in Jordan and Lebanon. Their traditional way of life was eradicated. Communities, no longer separated geographically, were jumbled together in overcrowded camps, their identities displaced, their distinctive embroideries no longer relevant. This human fragmentation resulted in a scattering of meaning, and the age-old significance of sewing as a form of embroidered mapping lost purchase.

At first, Palestinian women continued to sew as they had

always done, safeguarding their village stitches, holding on to their diverse material identities, honouring their unique stitched heritage, filling the absence of their past identities with their patterns. Over time, however, such markings mattered less. In the camps, they were all refugees. A new homogeneity emerged; a shared memory of loss. What was more important was solidarity and the collective forging of a united national identity.

During the 1980s and 90s, Palestinian needlework began to change. Patterns became conflated, colours mixed, a mixed repertoire of stitches became fused. A younger generation began to include patriotic symbols within regional variations: the Dome of the Rock in Jerusalem, the Palestinian flag, the word *Palestinian* stitched out in letters. It indicated a changing sensibility, a strengthening of a national consciousness. Village variations became subsumed into a more cohesive and radical symbolism which reinforced national pride. This was embroidery shaped by resistance, and is what is now being stitched in camps and settlements in Palestine in needlework cooperatives and small design studios: embroidery that, while respecting the past, articulates the present and traces out a future.

Embroidery is often the last remnant of identity to be salvaged by the dispossessed. Emerging from the fray of war, women often take up a needle and thread as a practical occupation. It is accessible, cheap, requires limited space and basic tools. Through it they can create saleable goods to market in the camps themselves and, with the help of aid charities, sell to wider markets. But their motive is not solely financial. Sewing has a deeper resonance. It re-threads a sense of identity, reclaims a culture, anchors communities adrift from their social history and generates a community spirit, at the same time keeping future generations in touch with their heritage.

Throughout the world, in the culture of textile, it is clothing that carries the most clearly articulated political and social values of a community. Its sewing is imbued with culture, beliefs, history and landscape. For most refugees, as for Palestinians, the loss of place is the saddest loss of all because place is not just a physical location, but also the wellspring of a community culture through which identity is collectively shaped and individually represented. And what we wear is its most intimate expression. Our clothes, worn next to our skin, are mediators between ourselves and the external world. They tell others who we are and where we belong. They protect us and declare us. They carry our social stamp.

The kilt is the material mark of Scotland. Since I am Scottish, it would seem natural for me to claim tartan as my defining fabric. But coming from Glasgow, a city of sharp urban style, I had limited exposure to kilts, which were a costume, in my experience, to be donned only when Scotland was in sentimental mode: on television at Hogmanay, at Burns suppers or for a big rugby game. But when I first met my husband and went to his father's birthday party, I discovered a world comfortable in a ceilidh of kilts not worn with self-consciousness or a tokenistic nod to national identity, but simply because it was the natural dress for the occasion. When we married and set up home in a small glen, I grew to delight in the flare of kilts tossing up and down among a burl of dancers in the village hall. In time, I found myself altering the kilt my husband had worn as a boy to fit our son, pieced, as was the tradition, from his grandfather's kilt. A tactility of generations, material rites of passage handed on from man to boy: a quiet, precious heritage.

The kilt is more than a national dress. It carries the triumph of victory, of Scottish identity and independence reclaimed. Kilts were banned after the defeat of Bonnie Prince Charlie at Culloden in 1746 in the Dress Act of that same year, amended with more censorious measures in the Proscription Act of 1747. The failed attempt to restore a Stuart dynasty to Scotland so incited the rage of the English King George II that he was determined to destroy Highland culture and its clan system forever. Speaking Gaelic was forbidden, the playing of the bagpipes was made a criminal offence and the most visible representation of Highland identity, of rebellion and male virility, the plaid (or kilt, as it is now more commonly called), was proscribed. The people of Scotland were forbidden to wear:

the plaid, philibeg, or little kilt, trouse, shoulder belts, or any part whatsoever of what peculiarly belongs to the highland garb and that no TARTAN or partly-coloured plaid or stuff shall be used for great coats, or for upper coats.

The penalty was imprisonment for six months; a second offence risked transportation to a plantation for seven years. (Ironically, the order book of one of the major suppliers of tartan, Wilson's of Bannockburn, records the export of tartan cloth to plantations, where slaves were made to wear it to ensure their high visibility should they try to escape.)

The Proscription Act remained in place for nearly forty years before finally being repealed in 1782. At the start of the nineteenth century, Sir Walter Scott, the Scottish nation's most celebrated novelist of the time, took it upon himself to enhance Scotland's appeal with typical romantic and nationalistic fervour. He fictionalised the concept of a Scottish, rather than Highland, entitlement and even enticed the English King George IV northwards in 1822 to participate in a theatricalised spectacle of Scottish pageantry. The King's Jaunt, as its sceptics nicknamed the royal visit to Edinburgh, owed little to Highland tradition and much to the imagination and showmanship of Sir Walter himself. Here were the Scottish gentry festooned in a kaleidoscope of kilted splendour, and George himself swathed in a fat-camouflaging insult of Stuart tartan, his legs decorously clad in pink tights.

The upsurge in material clan identity was a boon to Scotland's burgeoning weaving industry. In the early nineteenth century, Scotland, still bruised by its cultural reduction by English command

and longing for an identity emphatically its own, embraced the ambitions of the Sobieski brothers, christened Allen, who claimed direct descent from Bonnie Prince Charlie himself, and became the feted if bogus claimants to the royal Stuart line. In 1842 they produced a beautifully illustrated inventory of 'ancient' tartans, the *Vestiarium Scoticum*. Some people questioned its authenticity and when it was shown to be largely fictional, with many of the tartan designs exposed as figments of the brothers' imagination, their duplicity was revealed. The brothers retreated to London, but many of the tartans they had invented were adopted despite their spurious heritage. They can be seen in tourist gift shops throughout Scotland, at Highland Games, village ceilidhs: the tartans of the Sobieski brothers, an inauthenticity embraced, more splendid and more diverse than its original.

If traditional dress is not erased by the breaking apart of community traditions, its use can be disbanded through fear and force. Oppressors' assertion of power has frequently been enforced through the suppression of traditional dress. Their intention is not only to sever a community from its past, but also to rob it of its spiritual protection and its cultural and ceremonial values; to silence its ability to communicate identity, beliefs, relationships and mutual significance. To rob a community of what nourishes its sacred and secular meaning is to render it mute. It makes assimilation more easily managed.

Missionaries, those proselytisers of Christianity who, since the sixteenth century had travelled to un-Christian regions of the world with conversion in mind, were, despite their preaching of goodwill to all men, equally guilty of wiping out the ancient spiritual and social significance of tribal clothing. Scandalised by 'pagan' symbolism, alarmed by riotous patterning and horrified by magical connotations, they mounted zealous campaigns to re-clothe tribes in more suitable apparel, the adoption of which signalled compliance and conversion. Missionary wives were keen to make their own contribution to the Christian cause and set up needlework schools to introduce what they considered to be more demure forms of sewing and dressmaking.

Emma Hahn, the wife of the Lutheran missionary Hugo Hahn who established the first Rhenish mission station in Gross Barmen in the desert plain of Namibia, began organising sewing classes there in 1846. She introduced the women of local tribes – the Herero, Oorlam and Nama – to the fashions of Europe: stiff bodices, full gathered voluminous skirts and layered petticoats accessorised with bonnets and shawls. The women adopted the cumbersome weight of these clothes and their cloying warmth with surprising zeal. To them, there was much more to such attire than a borrowed modernity. It represented the capacity of a powerful and economically strong nation. It embodied authority. By 1850, Emma Hahn had a class of forty women, and by 1867 she needed to import a sewing machine to cope with the demands of production. European clothing and cloth became valued as tradeable goods, worth stealing if necessary. They represented status. Local tribesmen began to adopt trousers and suits; some even took to wearing dresses and bonnets. Towards the end of the nineteenth century, German colonial rule took hold in Namibia. Already weakened by inter-tribal wars, in 1904 the Herero rebelled against German domination. Their resistance was met with violent acts of enforced subordination: they were hunted down and shot. Many of those who escaped the genocide fled to the Omaheke Desert and died there of starvation or exhaustion. Those who survived became enslaved and were imprisoned in concentration camps.

When German rule ended in 1915 there were few vestiges left of traditional Herero life. The Herero had lost their lands, their cattle, their customs and their rituals, and their social cohesion and identity was all but erased. To rebuild a community, re-organise a society and reclaim tribal dignity, they turned to the social structures and ceremonial displays of their oppressors.

Herero men organised themselves into regiments called Otreppe, which, although non-military, stratified social groupings, their differences indicated through hybrid versions of military dress: some in bowlers and trilby hats, others in ostrich-feathered helmets or colour-coded epaulettes and belts. They customised the uniforms left behind by their colonialists, concocted their own motley adaptations, and paraded in colours that symbolised key moments of their history. This was military and capitalist power transformed into a public expression of reclaimed independence.

The women too retained the fashions they had been introduced to by Emma Hahn over fifty years earlier but, freed from German rule, they now caricatured them with skirts made from over ten metres of fabric, exaggerated in bold, brash patchwork, to amplify their presence and emphasise their appropriation of Western needlework traditions. Through such clothes, the Herero wore not just a heritage, but their specific history. And they still wear them today as an everyday mark of who they are, even in the fifty-degree heat, to record a community identity altered by cultural contact, persecution and survival. The photographer Jim Naughton has photographed the Herero tribe in his book *Conflict and Costume*. It is a vivid portrayal of a community told through portraits that leaves us in no doubt as to the Herero tribe's reclamation of self-respect. Such a repossession is dearly bought; it requires a major investment of time in a country where many sewers are still reliant on hand-worked sewing machines, where water for washing must be fetched and carried and irons heated on hot coals. For the Herero, though, what they wear is a self-proclamation, a mark of pride and also a protection of sorts, ensuring that their story will endure.

We can find the legacy of Western colonialisation in many parts of the world and in the unlikeliest of places. In 1991, when I visited Rarotonga, the largest of the Cook Islands in the Pacific Ocean, I was surprised to find women quilting under the shade of palm trees. It was a cultural remnant of the proselytising European Christian missionaries who had come to the island in 1821 as part of the London Missionary Society. The missionaries brought with them calico cloth and, having persuaded the islanders to forgo their animist culture and their worship of tribal gods and idols and adopt a Christian God instead, they instructed the local women in Western techniques of needlework to make clothes and home furnishings. This is why an anomaly of needlework survives, in their quilts, a form of sewing designed for cold countries, but now transported to a climate where, even in cool periods, the temperature rarely drops below twenty-five degrees. The Cook islanders have, over time, reintroduced into their quilts some elements of their indigenous culture, such as a love of bright colour and symbols that held meaning in older traditions, but in the tidy arrangement of their quilted blocks, they retain a constraining Western influence: stitched squares corralled within a tight framework, a sewn archive of their religious conversion.

In some instances, oppression or the prudery of missionaries did not mean the complete abandonment of traditional dress, but rather its customisation. Invasion often led to a deliberate neutering of the spiritual and symbolic language of a vanquished nation, leading to a country diminished not by ethnic cleansing but by cultural erosion, by the re-fashioning of its visual language and folk costumes into a more sterile form and the reinvention of them as innocuous and charming remnants of rural peasant life.

When the Soviet Union was created there was no place for the diversity of languages and cultures of what had been, until then, independent nations. Any lurking expression of national identity could fan unrest and encourage uprisings. In Ukraine the wearing of national costume was forbidden, denounced as a provocation of anti-Soviet feeling. Its wearers could be, and were, imprisoned. Museums were instructed to destroy their traditional costume collections. The Soviet Government did not banish national costume entirely, however; that might have led to it becoming a dangerous clandestine symbol of defiance, of it gaining rather than losing power. Instead, they designed a different secularised and theatricalised version, which Ukrainians were instructed to wear for public dance performances and festivals. By maintaining a Soviet-wrought neutered version, the authorities reduced its potency and stayed in control of its meaning.

Ukrainian stitched heritage was destroyed. By enforcing a break with tradition, the Soviet authorities engineered a natural loss of embroidery practice and knowledge. Traditional Ukrainian embroidery of red-and-black stitched designs on a white background conveyed goddess worship and family connections though symbols, codes and talismanic motifs. It was ritualistic, honouring the divine genesis of man and nature translated through a geometric abstraction of circles, stylised branches and spirals. It harboured family chronicles of ethnicity and belief. The new Soviet patterns, reduced to simplified, pleasing arrangements of shapes and motifs, were no longer organised in meaningful relationship to each other. The making and displaying of traditional textiles no longer amplified the rites-of-passage ceremonies they had originally been designed to accompany.

After the Soviet Union was disbanded in 1991, states had to grope their way back to a lost sense of nationality and try to revive their dormant cultural identities. Ukrainians took to wearing traditional dress to celebrate their independence. But the cultural dislocation during the decades of Soviet rule had led to an interruption of the visual literacy of traditional needlework; the lines between authentic and Soviet-invented designs became blurred.

Like the kilt, contemporary Ukrainian embroidery has become a fusion of reality and romance. Ancient symbols are still apparent but lack their traditional context, robbed of the rituals that endowed them with spiritual significance. Soviet-bred folk art has been subsumed into a more general design pool. But does that matter? It still references Ukraine, and that is what its young people want to celebrate: the culture of their country and its independent spirit of survival. What if its contemporary embroidery harbours traces of political upheaval or tells of domination? That, too, is part of the fabric of its nation.

More recent upheavals in Ukraine have brought a new world-wide political and emotional significance to the wearing of its embroidery. It is as if its presence, not its particularities, have become important. Vyshyvanka Day, which began in 2007 and takes place annually on 21 May, is a demonstration and affirmation of Ukrainian national identity. All over the world the Ukrainian diaspora join the people in Ukraine to don embroidered *vyshyvanka* shirts. This is a partriotic act of solidarity by a freed people, supported by celebrities and international fashion designers, restoring the social fabric of Ukrainian heritage and stamping their claim to a distinct identity.

Many revolutions, in their overthrow of a ruling class, have led to a crisis of identity in which the emergent democracy is a new equality that demands a visible sign of a newly forged homogeneity. A different form of dress is an obvious strategy. During the French Revolution, the exquisite, extravagant dress of the nobility became a passport to the guillotine. People of all classes quickly donned survival clothing in the form of simpler garb. The more zealous revolutionaries even adopted a Republican assemblage of red, white and blue.

The tricolore cockade, a rosette attached to hats, became a ubiquitous symbol of the demise of the old regime and the triumph of the people, but it became contentious when a law was passed imposing its display. Thousands of women took to the streets in protest and the laws on dress were changed again. Women would be free to wear what they liked and did not need to sport a tricolore cockade. But their fashion liberty came at a cost: women's political organisations were disbanded to avoid any further demonstrations. Men fared little better. Their revolutionary leaders devised a strict code of male attire based on occupation and political office. A new material hierarchy came into force, manifested by what men wore.

During the Russian Revolution there were various attempts to invent a suitable dress as a visible signal of the arrival of a new socialist dawn. But ideas among the revolutionaries were conflicted. Some wanted to adopt peasant dress as a symbol of egalitarianism and to promote the new elevated status of agricultural workers. Others advocated the invention of a modern, utilitarian fashion and, responding to the challenge, constructivist artists designed versions of functional dress. They imagined clothing for workers that was safe and efficient, with pockets for those whose needed ready access to tools; streamlined workwear for assembly-line workers endangered by heavy machinery; bold geometric shapes for sportsmen and women that emphasised their flow of movement at a distance. But however visionary, such clothing proved too expensive to manufacture.

Finally, with more serious issues to contend with, the Russian revolutionary leaders settled for a laissez-faire approach of eccentric nonchalance. A lack of care about what you wore became a political act: crumpled clothes, mismatching accessories and patched shoes all announced revolutionary loyalty.

China was more decisive. Its Cultural Revolution banned what was termed the Four Old Things: old customs, old culture, old ideas and old habits. Western dress was confiscated and people were instructed to destroy their traditional *cheongsam* dresses. An obligatory uniformity was imposed, known as 'cadre clothes.' This consisted of a suit or unisex jacket and trousers in dull colours of blue or grey. Chairman Mao's heroic posters show him dressed in it, clutching his little red book in his outstretched hand. It can still be seen in China today, worn by an older generation still in thrall to Maoist fear and revolutionary hope.

National upheaval, whether through colonialisation or revolution, often leads to an alteration in the visible identity of its people. Traditional costume has been outlawed, redesigned or reinvented to create a different version of a tribe or nation. But in post-war Holland, a new form of dress was invented as a rallying call to women to more clearly demonstrate their changing identity. It was their new idea of themselves that was to become the trigger for the creation of a garment which could represent an altered female consciousness.

During the German occupation of Holland, women had played an equally courageous role as men through civilian resistance. They had suffered the same personal, social and political damage. Despite Holland's declaration of neutrality at the start of the Second World War, Germany invaded. In just five days, in May 1940, 10,000 Dutch soldiers were killed, injured or reported missing. Rotterdam was blitzed and 25,000 homes were destroyed. The royal family and government fled to Britain for safety and Holland came under German control. Its population became divided between passive collaborators and active resistance. It was to lose the highest percentage of its Jewish citizens per capita than any other European nation with seventy-five percent killed, over 100,000 of them in concentration camps.

The organisation of society in Holland, termed 'pillarisation', encouraged social, religious and political groupings to live independently of each other with separate facilities, schools and organisations. This social structure meant it was more complex for Dutch citizens to develop networks of mutual support during the war years. But non-Jewish citizens did provide support to Jewish civilians through Dutch resistance fighters. Mies Boissevain-van Lennep was one. She became involved in the reception of Jewish refugees fleeing from Nazi Germany, by hiding fugitives and providing them with false papers to aid their escape. Her house was a base for Dutch resistance and two of her sons were members of the resistance cell known as CS-6.

In 1943 her home was raided by the Nazis. They found the falsified papers for secreted Jews and a cache of ammunition in the cellar. Her eldest daughter was imprisoned in Holland, her husband and one of her sons were taken to Dachau concentration camp, where they died. Her two other sons and her nephew were executed by firing squad, but not before they had scrawled on the wall of their cell in their own blood '*No regret for things past, no fear for the future*', the family's motto. Mies was incarcerated in a holding camp, before being moved to the notorious Ravensbruck camp where she shared a cell with seventy-three other women. Some of her cell mates died, other became deranged, all were traumatised. By the time she was liberated in 1945 over 90,000 women and children had died in the camp.

After the war, Mies, like many other Dutch women, was determined to play an active part in the reconstruction of her war-damaged country. The war had changed women's view of themselves and they were not prepared to return to their pre-war gendered roles as politically passive wives and mothers. They had been transformed by their war experiences, when they had worked alongside their male counterparts, shared their acts of resistance and paid the same price of personal loss, deprivation and, for many, imprisonment. Dutch women campaigned for their right to participate in the economic and social reconstruction of their country.

In 1946 they formed new organisations: the Dutch Women's Movement, the Dutch Women's Committee and the Union of Women Volunteers. Mies herself set up a women's political party called Practical Politics and, while it never won a seat in government, it was influential in raising the profile of women's demands. But lobbying, being on committees and campaigning still did not prevent the old male order regaining ground and political authority. Mies decided on a different tactic to promote the altered ambition and political awareness of post-war Dutch women by creating a visible marker of their war contribution as a symbol of their potential and strength.

She took as her inspiration a small hand-made patchwork-scarf she had found hidden beneath her laundry when she was in a prison camp. The scarf had been fashioned by friends from tiny, bright fabric remnants from her own life: her children's clothes, her dance gowns, scraps from friends' and fellow resistance fighters' clothes. It had been smuggled in as a touchstone of support, to remind her of who she was. That scarf had become her talisman of survival. Now, she decided, there was need of something similar to publicly demonstrate the courage, resolve and solidarity of Dutch women, to remind others of women's place in Holland's history and their right to play a part in forging its future.

She called on women to make what she called the 'skirt of life' and others named the 'liberation skirt,' the 'national celebration skirt' or the 'magic skirt of reconstruction:' a patchwork skirt with its separate pieces made meaningful by a personal connection to a past event or person. Each skirt border would be hemmed in fabric triangles on which were to be embroidered significant dates of family or political life. The first triangle was to mark Holland's first Liberation Day: 5 May 1945. All the skirts were to be registered and receive an official stamp, and women were to wear them at public events, family weddings and on the annual Liberation Day women's processions.

One that survives was sewn by Mrs J. de Jong-Brouwer. Its hem is bordered in orange triangles, the Dutch colour of defiance during occupation and the colour of Holland's royal family. The skirt has sixty patches on which are embossed vignettes of a war-torn Holland: a candle to record electricity shortages; a fingerprint to represent the enforced carrying of identity cards during German occupation; a chocolate bar, one of the small luxuries that appeared after liberation. The Jewish yellow star sits alongside the Nazis' own emblem, the swastika. Kidnappings, arrests, executions are all documented. Mrs J. de Jong-Brouwer's skirt was just one of 4,000 made in total, skirts pieced in cloth fragments that held memory: the remnants of a hidden child's coat, a dead son's shirt, fabric from a refugee's coat, parachute silk, cloth that might have been stitched, washed and ironed over and over again, felt in a hug, folded into a drawer, packed in a case.

Mies intended these skirts to be therapeutic as well as symbolic, a way to heal past pain and record present effort and future joys. She suggested that they were made in the company of other women so that stories could be shared, solidarity found and confidence strengthened. Their making would be as much a political and patriotic act as the wearing of the skirts themselves. And women wore them as declarations of their readiness and capacity to share in the reconstruction of their country, as reminders of the sacrifices they too had made and overcome. The skirts were metaphors for women's ability to unify, from diverse and damaged parts, a swirl of promise and progress. As the women processed past the houses of parliament in 1948 wearing their skirts they sang 'The Hymn of the National Celebration Skirt':

> Shape by your skirt a together-connectedness,
> Unite multiple forms, colours and lines;
> In the stream of historic events
> Embroider the design with your heart and your hand.

> Stamp your skirt with the mark of your days,
> Colour your flag with what Was and Will Be;
> The Present, the Past – merrily borne,
> Let them adorn your costume, your family, your life.

The refugees in Palestine, the revolutionaries across Europe, the Ukrainian diaspora, the Herero tribes, the women of Holland all found diverse ways to assert an identity through what they stitched and wore. They harnessed the skill and connotations of needlework to reclaim, restore and register the value of the societies that shaped them, and create visible reminders of their nations' past heritage and future possibilities.

6

Connection

My husband's aunt has decided to clear out her house. She enlists the help of my husband to trawl through its contents. With a small allowance for sentiment they separate the worthless from the valuable: the worthless destined for the skip; the potentially valuable kept for an auctioneer to survey and take what might sell. She leaves the attic for Charlie and me to take care of. We can take, she says, anything we like.

It's strange to go into a home that's on the cusp of becoming just a house. Everything that made it a home is still present but misplaced, huddled in piles of dislocation. Books that were once in order on the shelves are now pillared on the floor, toppling towers of crockery cluster on table tops, a drawer of old kitchen utensils is cushioned on the drawing room sofa and a long-silent dinner gong sulks on a high shelf.

There are traces of past gentility, of soirees, servants and supper parties, all now gently erased. Bone china cups lack saucers, engraved and fluted wine glasses are clouded in dust, elaborate dinner services are incomplete, the gleam of silver cutlery dimmed. It is all too grand for our little house. I pick out an enamel bread bin and a plain pale-green jug that will do justice to a posy of garden flowers. These we will keep.

We go up to the attic. There seems to be little here: a few cardboard boxes of books, an old trunk tucked under the cobwebbed eaves, the acrid smell of mouse pee. I open the trunk. Neatly folded, each one obscuring the next, is a tightly packed trove of textiles. I bring them out into the light. There are damask napkins, their woven sheen revealing floats of flowers;

a deeply fringed cream silk shawl embroidered in cascades of roses; an entire gypsy outfit, its black velvet bodice jingling with a trim of gold coins; a fur-trimmed tribal coat of rich brocade; a set of place mats in delicate turquoise voile embroidered with pagodas and men on camels. There are half a dozen Victorian baby dresses, ghost white, their broderie anglaise ruffles still sharp with starch. They look unworn. I unfold a long, stiff apron with a red cross stitched to its bib: part of the regulation uniform of a First World War nurse, which Charlie thinks must have belonged to his great aunt. Another apron of hers, its bib inserted with lace. Later, we find a photograph of Great Aunt Maime wearing this very apron. She is young, dreamy, her eyes fixed on faraway possibilities, her hair swept up in fastidious curls and her hands demurely fastened in her lap.

At the bottom of the trunk, folded below lace-edged table-cloths, hand-stitched linen folders filled with skeins of silk thread and tea cosies in a seasonal shift of embroidered flowers, at the very bottom, lying drowsy in its own warmth, is a vast patchwork quilt.

We lift it out. It is perfectly worked in a wonder of tiny figured cotton hexagons in pale browns and apricots, faded pinks and fragile blues. I do a rough count. There are over 6,000 pieces. That means over 6,000 hexagons drawn and cut out of paper, another 6,000, slightly larger, drawn and cut out of assorted fabric. Each and every fabric hexagon folded over its companion piece of paper and stitched to it, each of its eight corners tucked neatly in, a fiddly and laborious task. Only when each piece has been individually stitched can assembly begin: each side of each hexagon attached edge to edge to another with meticulous care, in tiny stitches on the reverse, to ensure strength in density. Such an intensity of stitches is vital if the quilt is not to break apart in the endless lifting and shifting of its weight as it does its duty over the many years ahead.

Only once all the hexagons are stitched together, these ones in a repeating pattern called Grandmother's Garden, can the stitches that held the paper in place be unpicked and the paper removed. Only then can the quilt be backed and pressed and bordered in binding, ready to smooth over the large, high bed, where it will cover the love-making, conceiving, sleeping, recuperating, dying of my husband's family, generation upon generation.

Along with the jug and the enamel bread bin, we take the quilt and the other trunk-trapped textiles back to our own home. I simmer the age-stained cottons in large pans from which vapour wafts in a nostalgic scent of starch. I lay the more delicate fabrics in baths of tepid water and watch them relax, rehydrate and reclaim their softness. For hours I stand at the ironing board and press each piece into the best version of itself that can be mustered. It is a ritual of respect, a kind of honouring of its makers, of women long gone. While I have no connection to them, they play a part in my husband's and our children's history. Once every piece is pressed and folded, each tangled strip of lace unravelled, smoothed out and rewound, I invite my in-laws to come and take their pick of the fabric bounty. What they leave I keep, not as commodities, but as keepsakes of past lives, the remnants of women's labours of love.

Two years after we had discovered the quilt in her attic, Charlie's aunt came to visit. I showed her the quilt and asked about its memories. She was dismissive; she thought it might have once belonged to her mother's neighbour, who had been a housekeeper in some grand house. Perhaps the housekeeper gave it to her mother, having no use for it herself, but she could not be certain. Whatever its story, she was adamant it had nothing to do with the family.

The romance of hope: how easily we fashion a history for ourselves. I was disappointed, of course, but still in awe of the skill, time and patience that went into the quilt's creation. I could still stroke the minute patterns of its sprigs and stripes, and feel, when we lay beneath it, the weighty warmth of other peoples' lives.

Many of us have textile keepsakes in our homes, rarely used but treasured for their sense of connection to a person, a place, a moment in time. They are sensory and emotional triggers, too precious to throw away. We keep hold of these tactile tokens, these tangible family links, passing them on to the next generation as material evidence of where and who we have come from. I have hoarded a small velvet cuff, braided in cream, which was sewn by my father's mother as part of a costume she made for him when he was a boy. My parents had always told me that I had inherited her sewing skills. When my father died and we left the house I grew up in I salvaged it, and when I trace my fingers over the rise of its braid I feel connected to my grandmother and to my father. It is a memento of family. More than that, it is a touchstone of belonging.

But are the textiles we keep just sentimental scraps of the past or does their tactility allow us to retrieve something more than anecdote? In her book *A History of the Senses*, Diane Ackerman says that touch is our very first sense, the first tool we use to register and remember difference, to record heritage. The textiles we keep demand to be lifted, stroked, handled. They literally keep us in touch with our past. Cloth softens with handling. It absorbs human touch and the drift of odours that surround it during its making: sweat, spices, perfume, wood smoke. Bury your face in a textile and you can nose up the scents of lives far away and long ago. If it is an heirloom, it can transport you to a forgotten blend of family fragrance.

In 2016 I organised a project called Material Matters. The idea was simple. Ten women from different parts of Scotland were to make a small wall hanging that told the story of a textile that mattered to them. In Dundee, Ishrat replicated the tiny cotton dress her mother had made for her when she was born, then kept safe. She gave it to Ishrat when she left Pakistan to marry in Scotland. Even now, with four grown sons, Ishrat says that if she is upset she will go in search of that little frock and hug it close, to comfort her in the aroma of home, the lingering scent of her mother.

When the exhibition of the wall hangings was launched in Glasgow and Edinburgh the public were invited to bring along a textile they cherished and tell its story. The stories people told were surprisingly emotive: a young girl held up dress pattern pieces, still pinned to fabric, cut out by a mother who never survived to sew them together, kept by her as proof of her mother's care. There was a Christmas tablecloth signed each year by family members until, decades on, it had become a family diary of sorts, chronicling festive get-togethers and fallings out. An older woman produced an apron she had stitched as a little girl at school, which she had discovered among her mother's effects after her death, treasured for years. The daughter of a Second World War refugee showed us the small lace mat her mother had carried with her from Poland to Scotland on the long and hazardous journey to safety in Scotland, brought as a tiny remnant of a lost land and community. These stories encapsulated the emotional and tactile agency of needlework. Each person, as they held in their hands their chosen textile, was holding a conduit to someone they loved. But much of the needlework people brought with them was newly discovered, pieces that had been folded away, only to be re-discovered after death. Why was it that these past lives, the attachment of mothers to daughters, had been so secreted away? The answer surely lies in the belief that needlework, pieces made at a particular time by a specific person in a place long ago, is a freeze frame of the time when it was made. It is part of a personal memoir.

Cloth holds on to its material memory. Cotton will stubbornly retain the mark of its folds in the faintest of lines that no amount of ironing can fully erase. Velvet, pressed against its pile, will flatten to a sullen sheen and resist resuscitation. If you scrunch a piece of linen in your hand it will emerge peaked and dimpled like a small mountain range, waiting for the wind or a hot iron to restore it to plateau. In many cultures, the persistence of old cloth, stitched by others, endows it with greater value. Conserved within it is the passage of time, harbouring the spirit of those who created, wore and handled it.

In the eighteenth century, the desperate mothers who left their infants in the care of London's Foundling Hospital were encouraged to leave tokens, both as a memento and as proof of parentage should they be able at some future point to reclaim their child. Many chose to leave a small fragment of cloth, and these now represent the most extensive archive of eighteenth-century fabric in the world, safeguarded at the London Metropolitan Archive and the London Foundling Museum in what are called 'billet books'. Intrigued to see them I visited the archives, filled out a request form and waited for a delivery of history.

The billet books, when they arrived, were filed in grey cardboard boxes, each volume covered in dark green marbled paper. They seemed more like the ledgers of a bank clerk than the poignant scrapbooks of impoverished mothers and abandoned babies. I laid one down on the bookrest and opened it at its first page: 23 February 1760.

The writing is beautiful, elegant in delicate copperplate, registering each child's date of arrival, its gender and age, and allocating it a number. Below is a printed list of children's clothes, such as cap, gown, petticoat, bib, waistcoat, shirt, shoes, familiar terms alongside others no longer in use, like biggin, clout, roller, pilch, long-stay, words ticked off to account for what each child was wearing when it was left, a scrupulous record of material possession. The relevant items are ticked off on the left, but on the right is an unexpected and illuminating hand-written description of the exact nature of some of the garments: 'blue and white flowered lining', 'figured ribbon', 'purple and white sprigs, scalloped, round with pink and brown rosettes', 'red leather shoes', 'Irish rag'. Most babies arrived only with basic necessities, but a few were clad from head to toe in bonnets, robes and stockings, tucked into blankets and wrapped in coverlets.

But the tokens themselves were the most telling, each one skewered with a hand-hammered pin to each child's inventory. The tokens are tiny, just an inch or two of cloth, snipped from a shawl, a skirt, a blouse, a bonnet ribbon, cut off from the mother's clothes at the point of separation. Many are grimed in dirt, some thinned with wear, most dulled by poverty. The majority are plain weaves such as checks and stripes, but there are occasional glimpses of prettiness: a floral print, a gather of pastel ribbon. One child was left a pale blue satin-soft rosette. In the company of the other, more austere tokens, it appeared as luxuriant as a full-blown rose.

I thought about that moment of choosing, of mothers deciding what remnant of themselves to leave, how best to communicate love, regret, hope, a small explanation to the child they will never see again, while the registrar hovered with his scissors. Many tried to leave something of their hearts, choosing to snip off a motif that could be symbolic, like a heart, flower bud or butterfly. Some cut their piece of fabric purposefully in two and, hopeful of reunion, kept one half as evidence of parenthood. One woman, Sarah Bender, came back eight years later clutching her half of an embroidered heart and was reunited with her son.

A few of the tokens are pinned to other papers, such as a confirmation of baptism signed by a curate, a scrawled record of a baby's name, its date and place of birth, or a mother's message to the hospital governors:

While my father is abroad, fighting for his king, receive into your Protection this helpless infant, who through your generous goodness may likewise be enabled hereafter to offer that life you now Preserve for the Service of his country in which he will so greatly owe it.

and:

The Mother of This child was willen to part from It For She was not Abel to ceap it. This child was crisend by Mr Huberd of Suren. And its name is Mary.

As I turned each page I felt I was turning back time itself: the pages were so pristine, the handwriting still clear, the pins un-rusted, the fabric undimmed. The urge to offer a benediction was irresistible. I pressed a finger lightly on a rough inch of wool, turned a page and gently lifted back the fold of the next token. It revealed an acorn printed on coarse linen, still colour-sharp. I felt a slip to sadness. Here I was, 250 years later, a stranger able to revisit these shreds of care, these tokens of love, with a level of access denied to the women who left them, and their children. The tiny tatters of fabric spoke as regretfully as they were meant to do when a mother chose them. They moved me not just because I knew their stories, but because they had the palpable, inextinguishable, imprint of loss.

There are a hundred pages in the billet book. I checked the date for the final entry: 29 February 1760. This large tome represented one week's intake of children: 100 babies left in just seven days. I closed the book with no appetite for another. It felt intrusive enough to have glimpsed the desperation of 100 women's lives, 100 women who had no means to raise their child. In an age when pregnancy, if unmarried, brought shame, censure, unemployment and sometimes exile from family and community, when women had little say over their bodies and few economic rights, destitution and abandonment were common fates. I was replete with the pity of it all. Between 1741 and 1760, 5,000 scraps of fabric were deposited. Of the

16,000 children left in the care of the foundling hospital during that time, only 152 were ever called for again.

Rags have long been believed to hold special powers. The agents of mythical, magical and mischievous worlds – Harlequins, Mummers, the Lord and Lady of Tatters, shamans, dervishes – all wear costumes pieced from cloth patches. The Japanese *sashiko* cloth, layered and patchworked with pieces of fabric, was known as 'the robe of rags'. Pilgrims to sacred wells and ancient trees often bring and leave pieces of cloth, some cut from the clothing of the sick, some from their own clothes. These are appeals imbued with a human essence. As their colour fades and the fabric disintegrates, so, it is thought, an illness will ebb, a dilemma will be resolved. Travellers to the Clootie Well in the north of Scotland still tie fabric strips to the surrounding hedgerows to make a blossoming of hope.

Sewing pieces of fabric together was believed to endow the pieced cloth with spiritual power, the needle's magical strength permeating every join, the more joins, the greater the potency. This is the traditional source of the allure of patchwork and of quilting: sewn acts of resurrection, reconstitution, re-connection. In many cultures it is believed that patchwork and pieced quilts made from peoples' clothes transferred energy between generations, the dead and the living, mother and child, creating a collective human power, each salvaged piece transmitting its own force of identity.

The belief in the collective strength of cloth continues today. In Syracuse, New York State, in 2008, the World Reclamation Arts Project covered an entire abandoned gas station, complete with pumps, offices, garages, with 3,400 cloth panels embroidered with messages about the environmental damage caused by our global dependence on oil. Its impact lay both in the unexpected splendour of the visual transformation of an industrial site into an exuberance of colour and texture, and in the scale of its collective action. Fabric panels had been donated from twenty-nine states in America and from fifteen countries. This project by WRAP, the first event of its International Fiber Collaborative, had physical and accumulative force.

It is not only joined patches of cloth that can bind human spirits together to create a denser energy; layers of cloth stitched together are also thought to strengthen connection. *Kanthas*, the quilted and embroidered cloths of Bangladesh, are tradi- tionally crafted from uncut cloth. Seamless, they prevent the entry of evil spirits, layered, they trap greater psychic force. From used materials such as the unpicked fabric and unravelled thread of old saris and *dhotis* (men's garments), each reclaimed cloth was traditionally laid one on top of another, ensuring a combined connected force. The layers were sewn through with clusters of tiny running stitches to form talismanic symbols. This was an act of restorative restitution, of harnessing the energy of the dead to the spirit of the living and linking gener- ations in a combined amplified strength. *Kanthas* are still made today, but not with the same purpose. They are made for the tourist market, simplified and impersonal. They are still pretty but lack emotional investment; even when older patterns are reproduced, their effect is diminished. But why should that be apparent if the stitches, motifs and techniques are the same? Why do they not look or feel the same as older traditional *kanthas*? The answer must surely lie in our sanitized age in which we demand cloth untouched by others, in which the idea of recycling the clothes of dead people to make something for ourselves seems disrespectful. Of course we recycle, but we rarely know the provenance of the clothes we buy from charity shops. We have lost the concept of directly connecting to our ancestors by using their garments to endow us with the residue of their spirit. The pristine cotton of modern factory-made kanthas has none of the quality, meaning or emotional value of the originals.

A similar fate has befallen the *molas,* the embroidered bodices of Kuna Indian women, most of whom live in the San Blas Archipelago along the Atlantic coast of Panama and Colombia. These appliquéd and embroidered blouse panels traditionally have eight layers of cloth that represent each universe a soul must travel through on its journey to the afterlife. The designs originated as tattoos, but Spanish colonialists in the sixteenth century introduced cloth into the Kuna culture and, advocating modesty, encouraged women to cover their breasts. The women began to wear blouses onto which they transferred their tattoo designs. They adopted a technique called reverse appliqué in which, rather than stitching cloth on top of cloth, layers of differently coloured cloth are placed together and each layer is then cut through to reveal the colour below in an increasingly intricate and detailed design. Traditionally, *molas* were spiritual objects that carried tribal myths and beliefs passed on through generations. Now, like *kanthas*, they are made for tourists, but not as blouses. Instead they are sewn as small panels, generally just on two layers of cloth sewn with contemporary motifs. But in private, Kuna women conserve their traditions even today, sewing detailed embroidered *molas* for ritual ceremonies to preserve a complex and ancient culture retained through stitched patterns, symbols and sewn myths.

Layers of cloth and patches of fabric were what Ann West used in 1820 to reconstruct the world around her. Her remarkable quilt is a fabric memoir that contains local personalities and familiar scenes from her everyday life, sewn down for posterity on an array of fabric off-cuts, scraps of coats and uniforms and pieces of wool. No one knows who Ann West was or where she lived. There is strong evidence to suggest she came from Warminster in Wiltshire, and an Ann West appears on its 1841 census. If it is her, she was a seamstress, married to a tailor, which might explain her access to so many kinds of scraps of cloth and because she signed and dated her quilt, we are sure of her as its maker. What she did with her scraps was to animate scenes from her life. Here a milkmaid is milking her cow; chimney sweeps are wending their weary way home; a sailor with a wooden leg begs for alms; a rich man goes about his business as his black servant follows on; someone receives a letter; actors put on a play; a gardener trundles his wheelbarrow back home along the road; a fiddler plays out a melody; a man sits under a tree enjoying a leisurely cigarette and a pint of ale. Over seventy tiny figures are represented, real people immortalized, personified, by Ann's attention to detail: the jaunty angle of a hat, the stoop of a beggar woman, the vanity of a man's combed whiskers and, amongst it all, maybe Ann herself on her wedding day.

Ann West's quilt is more than an illustration of what lay around her. In it, she has sewn her curiosity, her lust for life, her empathy, stitching down her social world as it crowded around her. It is an act of connection to, and a commemoration of, a place and a community. With her scraps of fabric she has literally textured the world of early nineteenth-century England.

Amongst her many portraits Ann West embroidered forget-me-nots and hearts and stitched a final message 'Remember Me, Forget me Not'. Ann West wanted to stay forever connected to a world she had preserved in fabric in a future she would be unable to share.

It is 2011 and Harriet's eighteenth birthday. Her mother wants to give her something special to take away with her on what is to be a new adventure: leaving the farm in Perthshire where she grew up, in a remote rural glen, for the urban excitement of Glasgow. Harriet's mother enlists the help of family, friends and neighbours to secretly sew a patchwork quilt which, through small, individually designed squares, will be an intimate and personal capturing of the different strands of Harriet's life.

There is a stitched version of the Pythagoras theory made by her maths teacher; hearts in the clan tartans of both sides of her family; the embroidered house number of her new flat in

Glasgow and the cross-stitched street view of where she sometimes stays with friends in Edinburgh; her dad has appliquéd his red tractor; her mum a reproduction of a much-loved family photo of Harriet, bare-bottomed at the age of two, trying to round up sheep. Among all these are other references and mementoes of her life so far: horses and thistles, fabric-printed selfies. Her interests, hopes and friendships are all gathered together in a personal biography of family and friendship made by those who wish her well.

On her birthday, Harriet receives her quilt. Its makers gather at the house for a celebration and to see, for the first time, what others have made, how their piece fits into Harriet's story. For Harriet, the quilt is an unexpected gift of farewell and fortune, made by those who have helped shape her life. It is an album of connection to places and people, redolent with personal bonds and special memories.

Sewing not only traps memory; it can also help to rekindle it. Some years ago, I ran sewing workshops in a psychiatric unit of an Edinburgh hospital where I was working with a small group of elderly people whose lives had shrunk to the limits of the hospital's footprint. Each week those in the group suffering from dementia would be unsure of who I was and what I had to do with them. I would be greeted with scathing remarks like 'I suppose you've come for that nonsense,' or 'What mess are you here for?' as they grumbled their way to their chairs.

I would bring out their work in progress and, as I handed them round, each person would examine their creation forensically, turning the fabric this way and that, smoothing skeleton fingers over the imprint of its stitchery, taking time to wonder at it being there at all. One by one, I would bring them back to whatever they had begun and, once fixed to their task, they would reconnect to a past skill, an able self: the feel of the cloth and the rhythm of sewing triggering a physical memory. Once reconnected with their needlework, they held their sewing tightly in their hands, as if it were a precious harbinger of an elusive now.

Quilts are increasingly used as a way to help people with dementia relocate themselves and their families through the tactile rekindling of shared memories. Vintage fabrics, familiar buttons, evocative textile textures all serve to make personal links, to rediscover a thread of self. The charity Alzheimer Scotland has its own quilter-in-residence, Ann Hill. Her quilts stimulate not just sensory recall, but also family conversations, a way for a carer to get to know more about the individual in her charge, personality and autobiography revealed through touch that re-awakens personal meaning.

In 2013, Ann masterminded what she called the Hampden Park Quilt Challenge: a call to quilters to create enough quilts to cover a huge football pitch in Glasgow as a fund-raising event for Alzheimer Scotland. In all, 5,000 quits were donated. Some were memory quilts, designed in reminiscence sessions with people suffering from dementia, stories retold through a quilter's needle and thread. The quilts went back to those who had inspired them, the re-gathered strands of a forgotten sense of self helping them reconnect the past with the present.

Each winter, Aunt Jean's quilt covers our bed. Torn in parts, faded in others, it acts as a link between now and then, folding where others have folded, mending where others have mended. Lying beneath it, we lie where others have lain. It is our keepsake and our protection. Suffused with past spirits, it is both a celebration and a commemoration of the story of other peoples' lives.

7
Protect

One frosty March morning in 1996, my neighbour phoned me in a state of dread. Her husband, a local minister, had received an urgent call to go to Stirling Royal Infirmary, where he was chaplain. There had been a serious incident at Dunblane Primary School. She knew nothing more. Later that morning we learned that a gunman had walked into the school, gone to the hall where the Primary Ones were having their gym lesson and shot dead sixteen five-year-olds and their teacher in little over three minutes. More children and staff were injured before he turned the gun on himself.

Televised news reports showed terrified parents, keeping vigil by the school gates, waiting for news of their children. Eventually they showed scenes of some parents being reunited with their children while others were led into the school. There, it was reported later, they were told of their children's death or injury. The traumatised families and community of Dunblane could barely comprehend the nightmare that had been unleashed on their small Scottish town that Spring morning.

I had recently been commissioned by Strathclyde Regional Council to make a series of banners with and for communities as part of Glasgow May Day parade. Now one of these would be for Dunblane. I sewed an angel with ivory wings nestling a child in her arms. The child is stretching up to try to touch the stars in the sky. Sixteen silver stars symbolised Dunblane's dead children: Emma, Joanne, Megan, Hannah, Victoria, Kevin, Melissa, David, Brett, John, Sophia, Charlotte, Ross, Mhairi, Abigail and Emily. A single gold star honoured their teacher,

Gwen Major, who had died in their defence. I encrusted the angel's cream silk robe with blood-red embroidered poppies and below the starry sky and beneath the angel and child, I stitched a quotation from Laurence Binyon's First World War poem, *For the Fallen:* 'At the going down of the sun and in the morning, we will remember them.' This was chosen by my neighbour the minister, who'd had to find comfort for the families of the dying and the injured that morning and in the days that followed, as well as words for the bereft parents sitting next to the bodies of their children in Stirling Royal Infirmary.

It was to this very hospital, just a year earlier, that my husband and I had gone when I twice became pregnant, when I twice miscarried. The great gentleness and concern we had found there helped to salve our grief at the time. And I stitched those poppies and appliquéd those stars with our own lost babies in my heart. The banner mourned the promise of children that were no more and the loss of a family that might have been. It was carried through the streets of Glasgow that May Day, then donated to the infirmary, where it was installed in its tiny chapel, hanging above the book of remembrance in which people could write something of those they had lost. I wrote about our children there.

Protecting our family is one of the most primal of human urges. It is not just illness or accidents that must be guarded against; protection in many cultures must reach beyond the threats of the physical world to the darker realms of the supernatural. There, some believe, dwell malevolent spirits who can blight a harvest, maim a child, blind a father or make a woman infertile in a nonchalant nanosecond. Such beliefs are not rooted in naive superstition. They are based on the evidence of ancestors and a lived experience of the fickleness of nature. Even today, many societies fear and respect worlds beyond their human understanding, worlds they believe can alter destiny. The evil eye, capricious gods or malign spirits are all in constant need of thwarting, distracting or appeasing.

Traditionally in many cultures throughout the world, embroidered textiles were thought to be as efficacious as a shield for protecting human beings in this world and the next. Imbued with the force of nature – the plants from which dyes have been extracted, from which thread has been spun – textiles provided a natural armoury to ward off attack. Through needlework, however, greater defences could be assembled to ensure human safety.

Evil could slip and slide into any opening. Clothes, therefore, were cunningly constructed to withstand danger especially in areas most vulnerable to entry. The hems, cuffs and necklines of many traditional garments were densely patterned in an array of different colours. This was no idle fancy for ornamentation, but purposeful safe-guarding. The reproductive zones, such as breasts, pubic triangle and genitalia, were protected with intricate embroidery and embellishments on the cloth that covered them. Some traditions persist. The mirrored bodices of the Rabaris tribe in India, the floral twists and turns of folk costume aprons in Eastern Europe, the repetitive cock's comb symbol stitched into shaman's regalia in southwest China are all designed as guards against trespass.

An uncut cloth, such as a sari, offered the most effective sanctuary. It had no seams to penetrate; its wholeness was defence enough. The skirts of the Batak tribes of Sumatra were woven as circles so there would be no beginning and no end, and the pleated men's skirts in Greek folk costume were unbroken spheres with no obvious point of entry. Neither seams nor gussets could be ignored or left unguarded. They had to be camouflaged, over-sewn with braid or bands of stitchery.

And complexity is still sewn into traditional cloths. The *bawan bagh* (wedding shawl) of the Punjab in India can have as many as fifty-two stitch patterns in one cloth. Kuba cloth from the Democratic Republic of the Congo has a repertoire of over 200 stitch patterns. The folk art embroidery of Karnataka in India can include more than 60 motifs in a variety of colours. The simple chain stitch is commonly used in India because each stitch is linked to the next, allowing no gap for evil to penetrate. Its deployment, along with that of other intricate stitches, is designed to create unassailable barriers.

But in the way in which they sewed, embroiderers who followed tradition, ensured extra safeguards. They cunningly created intentional diversions in order to disconcert harmful spirits, such as deliberately interrupting the flow of a pattern to abruptly change direction, altering the type of stitch used, introducing a sudden change of colour, piecing strips of cloth in conscious irregularity, intermingling different needlework techniques and using appliqué and patchwork on the same cloth.

Embroidered safety was not limited to clothes. Wells, springs, crossroads, wash basins, mirrors, windows and hearts were all thought to be susceptible to the encroachment of malign forces. But the proximity of textiles sewn with defensive strategies deflected harm. The space, that layer of so-called thin air, that separates earth from heaven, the temporal from the spiritual, was protected by sewn canopies. Women's headdresses and men's caps served a similar purpose: in part a protection against the encroachment of evil but also signalling humility to the Gods above.

The threshold was the most significant place in the home, as it represented the crossing from one life to another, from public to private and from community to family. It required special protection. Textile hangings draped over, around or above doorways, often fringed and tasselled, presented a barrier of moving energy to discourage evil trespass and, through embroidered symbolic motifs, they bestowed blessings on those who entered and the promise of safe-keeping. Hindu curtains made in the Punjab called 'torans' usually still feature an irregular number of flaps along their bottom edge, a device originally adopted to confuse evil spirits by their lack of symmetry. Even today churches, temples, mosques and synagogues make use of curtains to demarcate an outer secular space from an inner sanctum. The Kaaba, the house of Allah at the centre of The Sacred Grand Mosque in Mecca, has interior and exterior hangings. Its sitara (curtain) is hung up on the ninth day of the Islamic month of Dhu'l-Qi'dah, one of the four sacred months in the Islamic calendar. Stitched with invocations, supplications and Quranic verses in gold and silver thread the presence of the sitara amplifies the spiritual and devotional significance of the Kaaba itself. Even in a modern secular world fabric is used to divide the worlds of the known and the unknown, witnessed nightly in the raising and lowering of the curtain in theatres around the world.

While patterns and symbols were the conductors of protective warnings, colour added another defence, a preventative sub-text. It underscored cultural signals with additional safeguards. Red was thought to be the most efficacious. As a transmitter of positive energy, it represented the passion and strength of the blood of life and had the power to guard against harm and promote fertility. It became the dominant colour for celebration and campaign. Blue represented the power of water, an essential element of survival, and being the colour of the sky it symbolized the heavens and spirituality. Green signified youth and new life; black, the earth, ever-present and everlasting. In many cultures, it became the colour of mourning.

Embedded deep and still within all these various forms of protection are talismanic symbols. Ciphers in needlework have complex meanings. The exact implications of many ancient symbols are lost to us today, their significance has blurred over time even to those who still sew them. And generation upon generation have extended or changed their meaning until they no longer can be 'read' with any certainty. A few, however, have endured with clarity: the heart of love, the tree of life, the butterfly of liberation. Most widely used is the triangle, one of the most ancient of protective symbols, which represents the pubic site of women's fertility, the peaks of a defensive mountain range, or the teeth of a saw or of a dragon. It persists as an agent of defence still apparent in the bunting we use to decorate our local fêtes and children's parties.

Even when all this was done – seams hidden, the complicated patterns embroidered, the symbols stitched – traditions dictated that extra defences be added by attaching light-reflective or mobile adornments like sequins, small mirrors, beads, tassels, shells, bells, coins and fringes to gleam, flutter and clink if evil spirits venture too close to humans. For the stitching to be effective there had to be plenitude, a cumulative force. Additionality was all.

It was not only a matter of preventing the ingress of evil, however: benign gods must also be courted and appeased. This required different strategies. In some cultures, leaving a tiny part unfinished or including an intentional mistake was thought to placate the gods and not invite their jealousy or anger at the sight of humans aping divine perfection. Palestinians introduce a different colour or a blue bead to deliberately mar their needlework so as not to risk the envy of the gods. The Amish in America insert small errors into their quilts so that God will not think them prideful. In Japan monks sew a small rough patch on to their robes to signal their humility to the Buddha, and in the Ukraine, they embroider a different colour of thread on a small section of just one sleeve of a bridal shirt to attract spiritual approval.

It is not just *what* is stitched, but *how* it is sewn that has meaning. Tibetans sew with the needle pointing towards the body, pulling in the needle's strength to combine with their own to create more power in the stitch; whereas the women of India and Pakistan make *phulkaris* (the flower-embroidered shawls and head scarves from the Punjab) by pointing the needle away from themselves so that it comes from the heart and goes out to others. In some cultures, a marriage quilt is begun with a cross stitch, left to right signifying a woman, right to left signifying a man, their union marked as an anchor for what might follow. Embroiderers often embed secret stitches as private talismans. In Ukraine, they embroider from the bottom to the top to follow the path of life, and the needle that starts the works must be the same one that finishes it, so the flow of its energy will not be broken. Any mistakes are left as they are, in the belief that the past cannot be undone.

In all cultures, it is babies and children who are the main focus of safeguarding. In some it is believed that a baby is born adrift from the human world and, unless its family proves its human identity, the spirits will claim it for themselves. Most cultures, conscious of a baby's vulnerability, have traditionally protected their new-borns with sewn coverings to keep them safe.

The Rabaris tribe of India stitched cradle covers with wide borders made from numerous narrow strips of embroidered patterns in a dazzle of different colours and patterns to confuse and overwhelm malign spirits. In the centre of their cradle covers they appliquéd auspicious symbols as appeals to benign gods to keep watch. The Turkmen in Central Asia swaddled their infants in specially decorated appliquéd bands, embroidered with warnings to would-be intruders from the spirit world. They sewed *doga*, tiny triangular amulets, which were worn by a child or hung above its bed, sometimes filled with additional talismans such as a verse from the Koran, salt or coal crystals, a rag from a powerful person or protective herbs.

In Japanese tradition, a mother's spirit, identity and strength were transferred to her new-born by the re-fashioning of her own clothes into her infant's swaddling cloth, ensuring an adult defence. Similarly, an Indian grandmother provided her own embroidered *phulkari* as a baby's first protective shawl, and in parts of China they dressed the baby in clothes made from fabric cut from cast-off family clothing. Georgian Jews went further in the deception: they sometimes clothed their babies in old garments from family members but turned them inside out or dressed boys as girls, and vice versa, in a desperate effort to confuse the spirits.

It is not only the nature of the cloth that could safeguard babies, but also the act of stitching itself through which the protective hand of a mother or grandmother was evident. A Hawaiian mother believed that the sewing of a quilt for her baby imbued the quilt with her own aura to keep her child safe. In West Punjab, the grandmother puts in the first stitch of a new-born's cradle cover. In Tajikistan, a marriage coverlet is begun by the mother of many children. The garment made for a Jewish boy's circumcision was traditionally sewn by a mother who had never lost a child. In parts of China the protection of children used to be a community affair. A new mother would be brought strips of cloth by neighbours to be joined and made into a baby's coat, a communal cloak of combined cherishing. Alternatively, families would bring the mother small pieces of embroidered silk to be pieced into what was known as the Hundred Families Coat, so that the strength of many – the many pieces, stitches, blessings, families – would ensure a child's safety. The same concept existed in Japan, although not for children but for soldiers going into battle. The *senninbari* (the 'one-thousand stitch belt') was a protective talisman made by female relatives who went to a busy location, such as a railway station or street corner, and collected stitches from passers-by, which they were asked to sew on a stretch of cotton. Once 1,000 stitches had been gathered, the belt was given to the soldier as a form of protection, the accumulation of many diverse energies acting as a human shield against his injury or death. Some of these customs prevail, others have been replaced by the making or purchasing of more modern talismans.

When my twins were eight, in 2006, they came home from school with pompoms. They told me how they'd made two discs of cardboard with a hole in the middle and pulled wool round and round until the discs were very fat and the hole had disappeared. Then they had cut the outer edges and tied a ribbon around the middle. Once the cardboard was torn away, to their astonishment they had a big fluffy ball, a transformation of their own making from flat to round, hard to soft, still to dancing. I told them they had also made magic: that from just a bit of cardboard and a length of wool they had created a talisman to keep them safe. Because that is what a pompom is: a protective charm that sees off evil with the bounce of its bobbing sphere. Its origins are uncertain but its use has been widespread through time and place: on the headdress of the Viking God Freyr in Norse mythology, the traditional Balmoral caps of Scottish Highlanders, the national costume of Greece, the hats of Hungarian Hussars and as ornamentation on Peruvian dress. We still knit or buy baby hats with pompoms, unaware that we are carrying on an ancient tradition of protecting our children by making wearable adornments to deflect evil spirits.

Protective hats for small children are evident in many different cultures: hats with tassels, triangular ear flaps, adorned with glinting shells, beads and mirrors. Some have long protective cloth shields that hang down from the nape, heavy with stitched decoration. Others have padded flowers over the fontanelle. In China they disguise their children as animals so they will be overlooked by natural and supernatural predators. Their children's hats ape ferocious creatures like dragons, lions and bats. Tigers are a popular choice. Brightly stitched with popping eyes, flapping ears and wide snarls of appliquéd teeth, the sewn tiger headdress is often accompanied by other protective symbols to offer double immunity from harm: Double Tiger, Lotus Petal Tiger, Flower Tiger.

Chinese children's shoes are similarly animal inspired: little feet are disguised as pigs with bright pink snouts, or cats with threaded whiskers and pricked-up ears that tremble when children start to walk. In Chinese embroidery, symbolic sewn duality can be visual and aural. The peacock, representing love, and the cockerel, representing strength, also carry auditory alarms because of their loud cries. Homonyms are stitched to ward off evil and bring good fortune to the wearer: an embroidered tiger, *lu*, acts as a warning but is also the homonym for wealth; a bat, *fu*, is the homonym for good fortune.

The tradition among German Ashkenazi Jews is to sew wimpels, or binders, made from the swaddling cloth a baby boy is wrapped in when he is circumcised. Washed and torn into four strips, the strips are sewn together to make a long ribbon of cotton and on this a mother or grandmother embroiders protection for the newborn. It starts with symbols – a lion for the tribe of Judah, a tree of life perhaps, a bird, a harp – which are followed by a blessing stitched in Hebrew: *May God bless this young man* (name of child), *son of* (name of father), *born under a good constellation* (zodiac sign), *on the day of* (date of birth). *May God raise him to a life of Torah* (Jewish faith), *Chuppah* (a good marriage), *and good deeds. Amen.*

Wimpels are not showpieces of fine stitchery or public boasts of wealth and status for display in the synagogue, but family registers used at significant events in a boy's life. They are tangible personal records of provenance and identity, sewn in images and text that document genealogy and community belonging. They provide a connection between generations, representing the bond between fathers and sons, sons and mothers and families and communities. Wimpels bind not just the heart of a child to his people, but also represent the offering of his soul to God as a covenant with the Almighty that promises lasting allegiance to a faith and a people. In some Ashkenazi communities, a wimpel follows a boy through life. Redolent with images pertinent to his hoped-for future, for example his zodiacal sign, a wedding canopy, the tree of life and knowledge, or a bridal couple, the wimple is presented to the synagogue on a boy's first visit there when he is three years old, where it is used to bind the Torah scrolls, a ritualistic act of faith that ties the child symbolically to the service of and devotion to his God. It is unfurled again at his bar mitzvah and again on the Sabbath preceding his wedding when it is wound again around the Torah to confirm his faith. On his wedding day, the wimple is wrapped around his and his wife's hands as a physical manifestation of their ties to each other, their community and Judaism.

The process of making a wimpel is as important as the cloth itself. The rituals of purification, of piecing and re-joining, the embroidering of the litany of familial and religious lineage, transforms a simple cotton cloth into a sacred scroll. As sacred objects, wimples were often stored in a hidden place in the synagogue along with prayer books and other artefacts that bore the name of God. These stitched avowals of religious adherence were conserved as individual and collective vows of loyalty to the Jewish faith, community and culture. More than 500 wimpels dating back to the sixteenth century used to be stored in the synagogue in the city of Worms on the Upper Rhine in Germany. But at the start of the Holocaust, they were destroyed in just one night.

On 9 November 1938, the Night of Broken Glass, or *Kristallnacht*, began. German Nazi troops and their supporters unleashed their hatred of the Jews. Among the smashing of windows of Jewish shops, the burning of books by Jewish authors and the rounding up of Jewish civilians, 191 synagogues throughout Germany were set alight and 76 were left in ruins. One of those reduced to rubble was the synagogue in Worms, one of the most significant sites of the Jewish religion in central Europe, a place of Jewish pilgrimage for over 900 years.

The Worms synagogue had been a symbol of survival in the narrative of persecution and exile that had haunted European Jews since the first crusade in 1096. It was built in 1034, when the city was home to the third largest Jewish population in the Holy Roman Empire. In Worms the Jewish merchants proved to be an asset to an empire set on not just commercial but also cultural progress, and their contribution to the city's prosperity had been rewarded by royal protection. Jews were granted the right to trade, own property and have judicial independence. But such privileges were short-lived. The First Crusade brought prejudice and siege, and 800 Jews died as martyrs in Worms, a tragedy lamented in the Memorabuch, the Jewish Book of Memories. In 1348 the Black Plague, an epidemic that decimated populations across Europe and Asia, took hold. In Worms the Jews were blamed. They were driven out and their royal protection revoked. Rather than leave, 400 of them resisted exile and set themselves alight, burning themselves to death. The Memorabuch recorded their martyrdom, their names read aloud in the synagogue to those who returned once the crisis had passed. Worms' Jewish cemetery, the oldest in Europe, became a place not just of burial but also of heritage.

The synagogue was destroyed again during the Nine Years' War (the 1688–99 war between France and a European coalition that included the Holy Roman Empire) but was restored, rebuilt from old stone, and continued to be a place of worship. The cycle of growth and reduction, exile and return of the Jewish community in Worms was repeated throughout the following centuries. Religious artefacts often had to be removed to safety and then re-installed, but they were always safeguarded. No matter that the martyrs' tombs in the cemetery were recycled into new paving stones for city pathways, nor that the synagogue's pulpit became a patchwork of stones from centuries of assault. The Jewish community in Worms prevailed.

By the eighteenth century, Worms had become a place of

Jewish pilgrimage. Travel writing promoted its worth as a harbinger of scholarly tracts, historical artefacts, architectural sites and ancient customs. With its continuum of Jewish tradition and identity, it gained iconographic status. Then, in 1938, came Kristallnacht, and with it the destruction of Worms' synagogue and its 900 years of settled faith.

There are black and white photographs of its torching: the roof caving into the synagogue's interior, billows of smoke rising to a winter sky while its congregation watch as the flames lick around the architecture of their faith. And there are photographs of the synagogue the following day: interior shots showing its shell of ruination, a building crumpled in on itself, its floor littered with the debris of devotion – shards of smashed statues, ripped-up paintings, trampled cloth, the burnt remains of prayer books. Left smouldering among the wreckage were the wimpels, the 500 embroidered cloths that traced the ancestry of the Worms community family by family, birth by birth. This archive of human heritage, with its embroidered names and sewn blessings, was obliterated.

There is no one left from the original Jewish population of Worms. Those who lived there in 1938 were exterminated in concentration camps or escaped elsewhere. The synagogue has been restored, despite a proposal that it should remain as a ruin as a symbol of a lost history and a destroyed community. While a new Jewish community has begun to emerge in Worms, the synagogue has become a heritage site with only the occasional service. It houses historical objects and sacred artefacts, many of which have been donated from elsewhere. Among them are the charred remains of a Jewish wimpel: the relics of family bonds with no one left to claim them. Worms synagogue has become a place of remembrance.

In 2016 I went to visit the Jewish Museum in London. There, displayed among the grand trappings of Judaism, the giant, shining torahs with their velvet caskets, the silver-gleaming Hanukah lamps and Passover plates, was an embroidered wimpel made in Germany in 1794. Its narrow stretch of cotton was embroidered with motifs and Hebrew text: 'Joseph – son of Joshua – may he live under a lucky star.' Around and between the words was a medley of symbols: birds, snakes, a man and a woman, foliage and the sun. It seemed sewn by a hesitant hand, in rudimentary stitches: a labour of love more than expertise, but it spoke of maternal care: a desire to protect, a blessing of hope. As I left, I noticed another embroidery, a small sampler hanging on the gallery wall. Its maker had stitched her name, its dedication and a date: 'In memory of Hyam Moses, who died March 4th, Mary Myams, July 1825.' Its stitched text seemed prophetic:

Time itself shall shortly cease, the sun look dim with age and nature sink in years, but thy soul shall still remain unhurt amidst the war of elements the wreck of matter and the crush of worlds.

8

Journey

It is Christmas Eve in China, 1995. I am staying in the Hotel for Foreigners in Kaili, southwest China, a dismal place of dark corridors and dangling electrical flexes. I have strung up an arm-length of tinsel and hung a golden star at the window, much to the glee of passing children. Now all is quiet. In my small room, the naked lightbulb casts shadows over a pile of faded quilts folded high on two iron beds. Just as I am starting to feel homesick, the door opens to a sliver of light from the hall and in slides a woman, blurred in the low light, the hump of a bundle on her back. She is rounded in layers of indigo cloth, her hair tied up in a circle of woven red cloth, the traditional headdress of the Miao, one of China's minority ethnic groups. Pressing her fingers to her lips, she lightly closes the door behind her. She looks around, points in silent delight at the tinsel and fingers the star. Then she swings her bundle onto an empty bed, sits down beside it and considers me with interest. I am sitting on the other bed, and look back at her with similar interest. We just sit for a while, studying each other.

She leans over and touches my skirt. I have appliquéd Glasgow-style roses around the hem especially for this trip and she smooths her hand over the satin flowers and their wool background. She sits back and gives me a thumbs-up sign. I point towards her embroidered jacket and return her approval with my own thumbs up. The woman gets up and reaches for her bundle. I think she is about to leave, but instead she unties its knot and lets it spill out textiles, which she then lays out one by one onto the bed: a red woven sash, a bronzed jacket cradled for a second before being laid down, two baby carriers, their tying ribbons embroidered with tiny symbols, an apron thick in black stitchery. There is more. The bed becomes canopied in encrusted cloth. She beckons me over and we examine the textiles together, her touching and stroking, lifting up this corner and that, willing me to see an intricacy here, wanting me to notice a technique there. She picks up the jacket and tugs it over my shoulders, then raises her arms and starts to dance in slow motion, turning heavily. She pulls at my arm to join her and we twirl together in the low light of the room. I put my arm around her waist and dance her through a Gay Gordons, a popular Scottish country dance, in steps suppressed of sound. It is obviously illicit, this visitation, and she is my Santa Claus. I have become a child again. She criss-crosses a baby carrier across her chest, ties it at the back of her waist and mouths tiny baby cries. I laugh.

Grinning, we sit down on the bed together. I pull out my folder of photographs of Scotland, of hills and lochs, ceilidhs and Highland shows and we sit close, turning the pages. She likes the men in kilts but puzzles over the landscapes. I realise that these scenes of Scotland are not so dissimilar to where we are now, in rural China: familiar misty hills fringed with pine trees. But in my photographs the hills are unterraced, the land empty of people, and these differences suggest an elsewhere which mystifies her. I show her photographs of the community banners I have helped to make: appliquéd collages of everyday life in Scotland, featuring dancing couples, fish and chips, grand sandstone buildings, children in play parks. She pores over these, her fingers tracing their contours in deep concentration, sighing and nodding, trying to read their meaning, searching for clues to the world I live in. I mime hand stitching, machine sewing, threading a needle. She mirrors each mime with one of her own. We both do these things. We both sew. We are like each other.

Then she mimes putting something in her mouth. I offer her some chocolate, which she refuses. An orange is also declined.

There is a moment of confusion, of disconnection, as I try to work out what she needs. She gives a tiny nod in the direction of the textiles on the bed and repeats the mime of eating. I pull out my wallet and offer her a note. She doesn't take it, but gestures instead towards the bed. She wants me to choose something. With a play of impossible decision, I take up a small embroidered bag, nothing too flashy, not too expensive. I proffer the note again and this time she does take it. I start to take off the bronzed jacket but she pulls it back around me with a thumbs-up sign. I offer another note, which she waves away. I dig out a tea towel emblazoned with an entire Scottish pipe band resplendent in kilts and bearskin hats and give it to her. She is astonished. She scoops up a long red woven sash and wraps it around my waist, tying it carefully and smoothing down its fringes over my woollen skirt. She steps back and claps her hands, then gathers the embroideries back into their cloth and ties up her bundle. We smile at each other; we embrace in a hug that lasts long enough to tell of the frustration of friendship without words. I mime writing, and she shakes her head regretfully. We clasp hands, holding on tight. Then, with final smiles to each other, thumbs-up signs and jig-jig-ging with our arms raised, we separate, and she is gone, slipping away in the shaft of the hall light, leaving me alone.

Some years earlier I had visited a textile exhibition in Glasgow and become transfixed by a rectangle of embroidered cloth no bigger than a placemat. On it was sewn a scene from a summer's day, villagers out and about, relaxing by the river, some carrying babies on their backs and others laden with bundles. They were making their way to the cool grey drift of water, where more villagers were already swimming and floating in the heat of a sewn sun. But, when I moved in closer to examine its detail, I found soldiers crouching behind fronds of silk-sheened grass, their embroidered guns trained on the swimmers. This was no idyll of summertime frolics. This was a war documentary. It was a sewn snapshot of carnage: terrified villagers trying to escape, their possessions on their backs, children being hurried along, people plunging into waters already clogged with the floating dead.

Among the splendour of the other larger textiles in the exhibition – the mosaic quilts crazed with pattern and the weavings of intense colour – this tiny stitched picture held its own power. It had the intensity of actual tragedy. Its label read: 'The Crossing of the Mekong River. Hmong. Story Cloth'. A simple title for a complexity of the community dispersal which took place from 1975.

The Hmong are an Asian ethnic group of undisputed cultural antiquity. They trace their ancestry back to the Miao (also known as the *Meo* or the *Maew*) said to be the first settlers of present day China. Centuries of ethnic division, warfare and enforced migration pushed them south and south again, until they inhabited the remote and barren uplands of South West China. Through time, the main group splintered and different clans were formed. One of these was the Hmong. They eventually settled in Laos, Thailand and Vietnam. Those in Laos found themselves caught in what became an increasingly complex cycle of political upheaval: Laos' colonial French rule was lost, regained and lost again during and immediately after the Second World War. The Lao royal family, and the nationalists who allied themselves with the royal cause, sought democratic independence in the face of a communist threat. In 1955 America entered the Vietnam War to fight against a communist take-over of Indochina. It recruited Hmong men as its secret guerrilla force. By 1975, when the war ended, the Hmong faced reprisals for their collaboration with America. Although statistics vary, it is reckoned that over 100,000 Hmong lost their lives during the Laotian Vietnam Wars, 30 percent fled the country and 120,000 became homeless. Many hundreds of thousands of them, displaced or under attack, fled their villages, hacking and marching through treacherous jungle to attempt the dangerous crossing of the

Mekong River and reach safety. Many died on the way. Those who survived became refugees in Thailand before being re-settled there or in America, Australia, Canada, France and South America. The Hmong were fragmented across borders: a culture uprooted and a people dispossessed.

The two decades of war destroyed family and community life. Those who escaped the terrors, now regrouped in Thailand's refugee camps, had little in the way of resources to find an alternative way to survive. Hmong women, many of them widowed and in desperate need of income, were encouraged by aid workers to use their traditional craft of embroidery to make products that might find a market. This was not uncommon in refugee camps. Aid associations were linked to networks of international charities through which sales outlets for ethnic needlework made by refugees could be arranged. But the Hmong women did not replicate the traditional colourful patterns that adorned their own clothes. Instead they devised small sewn narratives in appliqué and embroidery, story cloths which told of their recent experiences: of stable rural life, village bombardment, jungle marches, the treacherous crossing of the Mekong River and their meagre existence in refugee camps. In time, they would also tell of exodus, repatriation, of finding their way in a different culture. What the women stitched were their stories of trauma and survival.

The Hmong story cloths became a way of retaining a threatened identity. While the stitching of the panels had an economic trigger, they were also emotionally significant, documenting shared terror and loss. These weren't personal tales, but collective laments. While they undoubtedly had creative and therapeutic value for the women who made them, they effected more than an individual salve. They provided a clan, the Hmong diaspora of refugees still in Thailand, with a cultural archive. Exported to or made in host countries, they became symbolic of a re-formed Hmong identity, one that included its recent history. Their bright colours and tragic tales had a public appeal which was important to refugees trying to negotiate acceptance in a country whose language they didn't share. The Hmong's appliquéd and embroidered stories were exhibited in galleries and community centres. They were sold in charity and gift shops; books and articles were written about them. The publicity and proceeds helped to sustain a new enterprise for displaced families, but more important was what they brought to the dispersed Hmong people. They salvaged a sense of belonging, of still being connected to a culture and a community.

The origin of their story cloths is unknown. Were they an invention of the post-war generation of Hmong or the suggestion of an aid worker, or did they emerge from their more ancient parent culture of the Miao? Intrigued by the possibility of the latter, I applied to the Winston Churchill Memorial Trust for a travel fellowship to go on a quest to see if story cloths existed in the Miao heartland of southwest China. I wanted to discover whether the Hmong sewn narratives had roots in their ancient heritage, reclaimed, like a mother tongue, as a lost language of tribal identity. An interview in London had me grilled on my ability to survive the rigours of an area of rural China that had only been opened-up to foreigners eight years earlier. Something of the determined thrill I showed for the chase must have appealed to the judges because in December 1995 I found myself on a dark and empty country lane that stretched away from Guiyang's airport.

I have spent the day in Kaili sketching Miao designs in the city's museum. The curator was impressed enough with my drawings to switch on the lights and bring me a stool. Although there were wonderful displays of embroidered skirts and shaman's robes inscribed with mystic secrets. There were no story cloths. When I left the museum, bright barrage balloons floated above the main street, marking the opening of a new department store. On the second floor, inside a locked glass cabinet, I saw an exquisitely tooled leather toilet case alongside a plastic bottle of Duck disinfectant. There was no incongruity there. In pre-millennium China, both were luxury items.

The market had glowing hillocks of oranges and teetering piles of hand-made baskets, but the yards of unbleached cotton and the bundled skeins of silk thread that I had hoped for were nowhere to be seen. Instead there were waterfalls of lurid nylon in acid colours and stretches of acrylic wool: China on its new road to consumerism.

I visit the Sichuan University Museum in Chengdu, which is said to house over 40,000 cultural artefacts including a trove of Miao textiles. The museum, once I find it, seems lost in time, as if a sleeping princess might lie within a thicket of briar roses. I am its only visitor. I find Miao costumes stilled behind glass, their colours dimmed by a curtain of dust. Their presence is eerie, as if their wearers had momentarily evaporated, leaving their clothes poised mid-dance. In the quiet of the gallery I take out my sketchbook and begin to draw. Suddenly, a young woman appears at my side in a chatter of chiding. She holds out her hand for my sketchbook, which I dutifully hand over. She thumbs through it quickly. As she peruses my drawings of baby hats and marriage purses, of Buddhist banners and silken collars, of women washing clothes by the river and a family crowded together on a single bicycle, she begins to smile. She closes the book and, crooking her finger conspiratorially, beckons me to follow.

She stops by a small door, which she unlocks. It opens onto a bare room lined with wooden cabinets. A long empty table runs down its length. She opens one of the cabinets. A glory of Miao textiles spills into her arms. With gleeful exclamations, she heaps them on the table. She opens another and frees more embroideries, making a soft hill of decorative cloth. They are all old textiles, their colours muted through time. Where have they all come from? How has so much been lost to the villagers who created them? Have they been given up willingly or taken as plunder, or in some desperate exchange for other necessities? It is a collection way beyond what would pass for cultural conservation.

I pick up a baby carrier and notice a small scrap of paper stuck to its back. It is a price tag. How do you price talismanic textiles? This piece was made by a mother to ensure the exact alignment of her and her baby's hearts, her protective blessings stitched into its ribbons. I turn over another textile and find another price. I have been led to the shop. I am expected to buy.

Preservation of culture and its commercial potential are the dual demands of modern-day China; they are not necessarily incompatible, but require compromise and care. The Cultural Revolution saw the enforced destruction of much of the Han's traditional crafts. But now that the economic lure of tourism has taken hold, the surviving folk art of the country's minorities has much to offer. It appeals to visitors and is a profitable resource, but it makes minority groups vulnerable to cultural loss.

In that small room in the museum in Chengdu there was poignancy in the dislocation of the textiles before me, severed from their communities and their spiritual purpose. Crammed into a dark of neglect they had been denied the meaning they should have had. I bought a jacket. The museum attendant was pleased but I felt unaccountably guilty.

It was on Christmas Day in the village of Shidong that I finally found the story cloths of the Miao.

I arrive at a river misted in winter. A cormorant is straining at its chain to claim a fish as the boat to which it is anchored skims along the water. At the river's curve I can hear the small strangled sound of *lusheng* pipes, the bamboo reed pipes Chinese musicians play at festivals and rituals. They herald another boat which, when it rounds into view, boasts a bride in lustred finery gazing forlornly towards her new home and a different community. With my guides, I climb up from the patch-work of paddy fields, scattering chickens and pigs, to reach the house of a woman reputed to be the best embroiderer in the village.

She is expecting me. She has laid out her embroideries and those of her mother and grandmother on the floor of her newspaper-lined home. She is a rounded, plump woman, dressed for warmth, the final cardigan straining at her chest, her glasses slipping down her nose, her hair knotted up in the style of all the women here, pinned with decorative skewers. Her welcome is warm. She is more than ready for a show. The neighbours cluster outside the open door, peeking in like onions strung on a rope, one head above another.

First, she announces, she will demonstrate. She squats on a low stool by the light of the doorway, drags another stool close to it and gestures for me to sit. With large, calloused hands, she picks up a tiny sliver of a needle and snips off a length of thread whose end she licks with a slick of saliva. Holding the needle aloft in pantomimic style, she slips the thread into the almost non-existent eye of the needle and nods. I nod. We both nod. The neighbours give a collective wheeze of pleasure. She is my teacher and I am her pupil. This is how it should be between East and West.

She shows me how the Miao edge their embroidery with tiny triangles. She demonstrates how to cord glistening threads by twisting them tightly on two sticks, weighted by stones, and how to lay down a thin strip of gold foil and sew across it at intervals to break its sheen and make it glint even more. She sews and I learn. After a while she invites me to take over her stitching. The neighbours inch in, keen on the entertainment. Realising she has thrown me a challenge, I take up the tiny needle cautiously and begin to sew. When I reach a curve where the lie of the thread must change, I look to her for guidance. The neighbours sigh in satisfaction. My teacher jabs an earth-grimed finger on the place where the needle must go next and watches closely while I diligently follow the direction she has indicated. When I have finished she claps her hands approvingly and the neighbours sigh again, this time in disappointment. We take turns, comfortable like this on our low stools in the keen light of winter, sewing together.

Lesson over, she takes me to her display of embroideries, carpeted on the floor for me to see. In among the hats, bags, aprons, jackets, skirts, collars and baby carriers, I spy a small embroidered rectangle crammed with sewn illustration, similar in size to a Hmong textile. I hold it up. 'What is this?' I ask through Li, my guide interpreter. To my surprise and delight, the small indigo rectangle is indeed a Miao story cloth, its tale narrated in embroidery.

We gather around the woman who smooths out the small rectangle and reads its tale as you would read a picture book to a child, pointing to characters as she names them, tracing the circle of their embroidered world with an emphatic finger as she tells their story, her dramatic monologue a lullaby told through Li's laconic echo. He is bored now by sewing and the company of women. The neighbours join in with interjections, corrections and exclamations like a chorus in a Greek tragedy.

'It is,' the woman tells me, 'one of the oldest of the Miao myths.' There is a circle for the earth, I am told. Inside the circle are two bodiless grinning heads with fearsome stitched eyebrows: the gods. Outside the circle are two more gods together with a young woman, her hair knotted high, carrying a basket: the mother when young. A whiskered woman in navy trousers flecked with white: the mother when old. What about the girl in the brightly coloured skirt riding an indigo dragon and the young man on the horse? Her daughter and her son; sister and brother.

In the ancient days, near but not at the beginning of humanity, there was a mother and her son and her daughter and, after the great flood that fell upon the earth, they were the only three people left alive in the world. And the son realised that the human race would end with them unless he could bear sons, but the only women alive were his mother and his sister. His sister, frightened by his intent, bridled up a dragon and rode fast away to the other side of the world to make her escape. But her brother jumped on his horse and rode after her. Around the world they rode, but no matter how much the brother kicked his heels into his horse's flanks, his sister's dragon was faster and she stayed out of reach. Exhausted and frustrated, the brother implored the gods to help him save the human race from extinction. One spoke quietly but wisely: 'Ride around the world the other way and you are sure to meet your sister.' He did what he was told and turned his horse around and rode in the opposite direction, encountering his sister and forcing her to his will. And so mankind was fostered and this tale is told.

All this on a small rectangle of cloth: the story of the procreation of humanity in such a density of stitches you could feel its rise and fall as you stroked its surface. It is an incest myth that would not be thought suitable today as bedtime reading for our children, but it is one of many found in ancient folklore throughout the world in Greek mythology, Nordic legends, Icelandic folk tales and Irish sagas. This Miao tale would have been told over and over again, and sometimes sung about at festivals. It would have been told while a woman embroidered it – a mother to her daughter, grandmother to granddaughter – as her thread looped the characters into shape: the girl on her dragon, the mother with her whiskers, the son on his horse. It would have been told at night as a child sleepily rested in its mother's lap and fingered the mane of the embroidered horse.

The woman pulls an apron out from her textile display. Its central panel is thick with black woollen stitches, its side panels ablaze with narrative. 'This', she tells me through Li, 'is our story of man's harmony with nature.' Her hand guides mine through its maze, tracing out the contours of a serpent snaking centre stage, surrounded by monkeys, birds and frogs secreted in a dense blackness. They are lit only by the pink of the serpent's eye and the gleam of claws. It is the story of evolution, darkly told. The apron's panelled sides animate human history, how man made his accommodation with the creatures of the earth. An Adam figure travels through his universe of cockerels, butter-flies, crested birds, flying fish, centipedes, tigers, horses, dragonflies, owls and rats. The creatures crowd together, sewn in every imaginable shade of red, hues of pink, crimson, scarlet, rose, burgundy and cerise. It is a riot of redness that captures a series of encounters between man and beast, man and insect, man threading his way and trying to find his place on earth.

It's hard to believe you can take a blank piece of cloth and, without drawing a mark, stitch such an intense medley of human history. But yet, this is what Li told me is the way of much of Miao embroidery. Sometimes a paper stencil is made first, pasted on to the cloth to act as a guide, but often the embroiderer just holds the images of a story in her head and sews them free-hand. And here in this apron is the extraordinary truth of that. It is an embroidery that reveals the human capacity for visual memory and the depth of creative intimacy it is possible to achieve between man and nature: a symbiotic collaboration, a communion so practised they can call it into being, into feeling, through the skill of a stitcher's touch.

The Miao are animists, and believe that everyone and everything has a spirit. They manifest the spirit of their sewn cloth softly and slowly through embroidery, coaxing into being something they believe already exists but is waiting for trans-portation from the spiritual to the temporal world. They are responsible for its wellbeing and are the guardians of its soul.

There is no written Miao language. Oral history relates that they lost their original writing system when it was proscribed by an early Chinese dynasty. Any infringement was punishable by death. So Miao women began to conserve the Miao alphabet by embroidering mnemonics on their clothes, although no one can now read its code. It is believed that Miao embroidery is lingual and that their sewn story cloths are libraries that house myths, histories, tales of community experiences and sacred tracts of beliefs. Miao embroiderers replicate complex images and patterns from memory, like oral storytellers do, retaining sewn rhythms and choruses of patterns in their heads.

The wellspring of beauty in Miao embroideries lies not just in the objects themselves, but also in the process of their creation. The Miao sow, nurture and harvest plants in the most reluctant of terrains, coaxing yields of the fibres they need for spinning thread and weaving cloth with community care. They steep the cloth for days in vast vats of dyes, walling their villages in drying drapes of indigo. They pound the dyed cloth for hours, the sound of its hammering rising from each house like an echoing drum roll calling spirits to attention. This mashing ensures durability and adds lustre to trap what little light glimmers in a mist-bound landscape.

The Miao work through the seasons towards the communal begetting of beauty. To each season belongs another process, a shared yearly rhythm of seeding, spinning and sewing. It can take months to produce a small baby carrier, years to create one jacket. Sometimes it can take a whole day to stitch just one centimetre of cloth. But this is their gift to their gods. The difficulties they overcome, the patience they practise, their labour and time, are all gifts. The greater the challenge, the more time spent, the greater the gift they bestow.

I ask my hostess what she would like to sell. She holds out the apron. I am uncertain; it seems too great a treasure. Aware of my hesitation, she shows me another identical apron showing the same story. I ask the price. She names it. I do not haggle; I do not feign astonishment; I do not demur. This is a work of art, a work of undisputed beauty. It is treasure.

9

Protest

In the New Living Translation of the Book of Isaiah in the Old Testament, Isaiah is commanded to 'raise a banner on a barren hilltop: shout to them, beckon them to enter the gates of the nobles' (13:2). The legions in ancient Rome led their armies into battle with banners at their helm. Banners also adorned Roman city streets, where, emblazoned with coats of arms, they marked out who lived where. Throughout medieval Europe, banners were used as a chivalric visual code, to carry the colours and emblems of a king or knight and signal his allegiance to a cause or the woman he loved. The legacy of this 'carrying of colours' still persists in Italy where, for 500 years, the Palio di Siena, a spectacular pageant and horse race, is held twice a year in the Piazza del Campo. Each participating neighbourhood, or *contrada,* is identified by the design of its painted or embroidered banners, which sway from balconies throughout the city and are thrown and caught in billowing bravado by flag wavers in costumed parades. The race itself lasts for just ninety seconds. The winning *contrada* is awarded the coveted *palio* (the word is derived from the Latin *pallium*, meaning 'a precious piece of cloth'), which honours the Virgin Mary and is ceremoniously presented to the victorious *contrada* in the city's grand cathedral.

Banners are public proclamations that tell of the who, the what and the why of social and political fealty. They message solidarity and collective strength. Banners are declarations of identity. They have been adopted by trade unions, friendly societies, fraternity groups, bands of hope, masonic lodges, women's institutes, churches and campaigning charities to create bold, often beautiful, visual statements that encapsulate both a message and a purpose.

In 1984 the Mansfield Trades Council in Nottinghamshire contacted me. It wanted to boost local participation in its May Day parade by encouraging greater community involvement. We agreed on a project of community banner-making with the theme: Mansfield Past, Present and Future. Local groups were invited to make a banner representing their own organisation and join in with the May Day procession. The parade would end with a phalanx of young people wearing headdresses of white question marks. For this was a community uncertain about its future, a mining area where generation upon generation had depended on the pits, not just for their livelihood, but for their way of life. This was the year the miners' strike took hold.

In 1981 the Conservative government had announced plans to close twenty-three pits it deemed inefficient. The new head of National Coal Board, the industrialist Ian McGregor, appointed in 1983, began a further programme of pit closures. By March 1984, 21,000 jobs had been lost and a further twenty pits faced closure. The miners in Yorkshire and Scotland took strike action. The leader of the National Union of Mineworkers, Arthur Scargill, called for a national strike, but stopped short of calling for a national ballot. Instead it was left to each area to arrange its own ballot. In Nottinghamshire, the majority of miners deemed the strike unconstitutional and undemocratic and, confident that their modernised pits would be reprieved, 73 percent of them voted against a strike. Their decision was met with fury and derision by striking miners nationwide who began, with flying pickets and anti-Nottinghamshire propaganda, to shame the non-striking workforce into joining their ranks. But those Nottinghamshire miners who continued to work were averse to bullying and remained undaunted. They set up their own union, the Union of Democratic Mineworkers, and held their ground. For the striking Nottinghamshire miners, now existing without wages and reliant on charity, the decision by their fellow workers was distressing. Mansfield became a divided community.

On Mrs Thatcher's watch, Mansfield became a testing ground for new tactics to curb civil disobedience. Overnight, small villages were invaded by hundreds of police from all over the country. Their large white vans fringed country lanes. At the still-working collieries, small knots of picketers were penned in by walls of arm-linked officers; peoples' homes were invaded after dark by the sweep of search lights; strikers were taken away in the night for questioning.

Through the banner project I got to know women involved in the local Miners' Wives Support Groups. They invited me to their meetings and to village halls where food and clothes were being dispensed to those in need. They enlisted me to drive them to picket lines, negotiating the bends of single-track and back-field roads to avoid being stopped by the police. The Nottinghamshire strikers had no banners of their own, so I began to make them some. The first banner was inspired by a photograph in the local paper of police pushing back a group of protestors: it had a cream silk background with police appliquéd in black satin and a scrolled slogan on a red background that read: It's Your Future. Stand Your Ground'. One for the Silverhill Strikers had a silver-stitched mineshaft silhouetted against an ominous black silk sky. I became, by default or opportunity, a banner maker.

That May Day march was the biggest rally Mansfield had ever seen. Striking miners came in support of their comrades from other parts of Nottinghamshire. They came from Kent and Yorkshire, from Durham and Wales to make a persuasive show. Arthur Scargill, the national miners' union leader, was there his fist raised high to the sky, and all around, swirling among the protestors, were the majestic gilded banners of the National Union of Mineworkers. This was an emblazoned show of pageantry and power, the decades-old red silk banners, fringed and tessellated, threading their colour through the crowds. It was a sumptuous display of strength, a reminder of past struggles and of hard-won victories.

The strike failed to save the pits. The striking miners returned to work, walking with heavy hearts behind their swaying banners, many in tears. They walked in the dark light of an early spring morning with their wives and children. Across Britain, long-term poverty descended on mining communities as, over the following three decades, collieries were closed throughout the country. All of the thirty-six pits still operating in Nottinghamshire in 1984 had closed down by 2015. After 750 years of coal mining tradition in Britain, today there is not a single pit left. Cabinet papers, newly released by the National Archive, reveal that in 1983 the National Coal Board did plan to close seventy-five pits over the next three years. The papers stated that no record of the meeting was to be circulated and that none of its papers were to be photocopied.

The glorious miners' banners have become relics of a condemned industry: their call to 'defend, unite, support' is now eternally silenced. Most have gone to museums to be wrapped in tissue and folded into cardboard boxes: curated but uncelebrated. A few banners hang in museum galleries, stilled and sullen: silent ghosts of human hope.

The only British political banners that survive in any quantity were manufactured by the entrepreneur George Tutill, who began his banner-making enterprise in 1837. Drawing on his background in fairground entertainment, Tutill transposed the gaudy paint-work of amusement booths and the advertisement banners he used to attract customers, which were adorned with gilded scrolls and ornate lettering, to furnish trade unions with the means to parade their strength with triumphant showmanship. His commercial acumen coalesced with the growing ambitions of trade unions. During the nineteenth century, his firm undertook the lion's share of banner-making in Britain, providing 75 percent of trade unions with banners. The banners that Tutill manufactured were not just magnificent in style, but also in scale. He invented and patented a method of coating fabric in rubber, then inking designs into it, which allowed for a single sheet of silk to be illustrated on both sides. It made his banners lightweight and pliable. And when, in the 1880s, he installed the largest Jacquard loom in the world, he could produce banners so big they had to be wheeled down the streets in specially designed carriages. By the latter half of the century, no self-respecting working men's union was without a Tutill banner.

It was no longer a sign-writer's or apprentice's job to pen simple slogans of protest onto a union banner. Tutill employed and commissioned artists of note to craft the painterly detail of socialist heroes, union benefactors, starving children and coal-grimed miners. A litany of virtuous ideals and aspirations could be framed in intricate golden scrolls accompanied by any number of images and symbols to represent unity, strength, industry and justice. With such banner innovation, the Associated Society of Locomotive Engineers and Firemen Union no longer needed to be short of words or economical with imagery. Their two-sided banner invested heavily in aspiration: 'Brothers in Unity for Mutual Help, Industry and Reward, Knowledge and Peace'. It included a miscellany of persuasive motifs and lauded heroes, including James Watt, George Stephenson, Hercules, Vulcan, the figure of Justice, two railway men shaking hands, a union benefactor giving alms to a starving mother, a rocket, a train in a station, birds sitting on a book, a beehive, a laurel wreath, weighing scales and a steam engine.

Although they were large and imposing, however, Tutill's banners and those that emulated his approach, had a uniform style. They bred a corporate brand. Tutill offered a choice of stock images that were distributed among unions, temperance and friendly societies with barely an attempt to indicate a difference of purpose. Banners began to lose the authenticity of the personal appeal of the hand-made, the comrade-crafted protest. Instead, on their twelve-foot poles, they unfurled a blanket authority over protestors.

In the first decade of the twentieth century it was the suffragettes who reclaimed the crafted banner as an emotive tool of campaign. Made by and held in women's hands, their embroidered banners claimed needlework as a way to purposely gender their female presence in their political campaign to win for women the right to vote.

The campaign began in 1832, when Mary Smith petitioned the British Parliament to give women the vote. It came to naught. The National Union of Suffrage Societies was set up by Lydia Becker in 1867 with twenty affiliated groups and Millicent Garrett Fawcett as President but, despite an intensive programme of lobbying, public speaking and peaceful persuasion, women's franchise remained elusive. Impatient and furious, a group of campaigners led by Emmeline Pankhurst launched in 1903 a more intemperate agenda. They formed the Women's Social and Political Union, a breakaway group with' Deeds not Words' as its motto. The WSPU was designed from the outset as a force to be reckoned with. There would no longer be tentative steps towards progress through quietly gathered petitions and respectful letters. Their campaign would be marked by bold and aggressive action. Bastions of male domination were targeted: churches were torched, department-store windows smashed, the homes of politicians bombed. But public sympathy faltered. Politicians and press deemed the violence unfeminine and unrepresentative. The suffragettes began to be ridiculed. Posters appeared featuring hapless husbands attempting to cook and care for children who had been abandoned by their protesting mothers. There were numerous cartoons of women attacking police with umbrellas or rolling pins. Among the merchandise were satirical toys, including a jack-in-the-box with a suffragette caricatured as a harridan springing free from her prison cell clutching a Rights for Women banner in her hand.

The suffragettes urgently needed to find a more effective and engaging means of protest to regain respect and win popular support. They decided on a series of meticulously staged mass rallies, held between 1907 and 1913, with representatives of women from every walk of life, including international supporters. The rallies were designed as showcases of women's capacity and as spectacles of feminine solidarity. Their aim was to counter the accusation that the suffrage campaign was a mere diversion for the idle upper and middle classes, perpetrated by women with intellectual pretensions. The Mud March of 1907 (so called because of the terrible weather) attracted 3,000 women to take to the streets, but had neither the scale nor the impact of suffragette ambition. A year later, the movement marshalled ten times that number, with 30,000 taking to the streets of London in support of women's franchise. This was an unexpected victory at a time when only prostitutes paraded themselves in public.

It wasn't just the numbers that impressed themselves on the media and the political and public consciousness. Women had not only answered the call in their thousands, but they also represented a plethora of backgrounds. Artists, surgeons, clay-pipe makers, homemakers, sanitary inspectors, bookbinders, shop assistants, writers, barmaids, char women, pottery workers, flower gardeners, shorthand writers, fishwives, actresses, pit-brow women, musicians, academics and gymnasts all walked side by side in a democratic swell of determined political independence. The women in the 1908 rally were accompanied by marching bands, pipe bands and mass choirs: women's voices rising to a crescendo of protest, singing Ethel Smyth's suffrage anthem:

Shout, shout, up with your song!
Cry with the wind for the dawn is breaking.
March, march, swing you along,
Wide blows our banner and hope is waking.

Swirling among them were their banners, hundreds of them, billowing above the protestors. The 1908 rally was a glorious visual spectacle that surpassed any trade union show of strength. This was theatrical pageantry on an unprecedented scale, elaborately ornamented in a pronounced show of deliberate femininity. Other rallies followed year on year: A Pageant of Great Women in 1909, the Hyde Park Rally of 1910, From Prison to Citizenship in 1911, in 1913, the Pilgrimage for Women's Suffrage and, that same year, the grand funeral procession for the suffragettes' first martyr, Emily Wilding Davison, who had been killed as she tried to pin a suffragette sash onto King George V's horse at the Epsom Derby.

The artist Mary Lowndes was the architect of the visual impact of these rallies. Trained at the Slade School of Art, she was one of the new breed of art-school trained professional women artists. She had exhibited at the Royal Society of British Artists and was the co-founder of the Glass House in London, a much-commissioned stained-glass studio. In 1907 she set up the Artists' Suffrage League to supply the suffragette cause with bold, eye-catching campaigning artwork including posters, cards and banners, and she became the suffragettes' artistic champion, dedicated to ensuring that suffragette rallies were platforms for the display of women's distinctive creativity. For the rallies, she penned in 1910 a guide for participants, *Banners & Banner-Making*. In it she decried the debasement of banner art in the hands of commercial manufacturers like Tutill and exhorted women to make something extraordinary that harnessed their own heritage of needlework:

A banner is a thing to float in the wind, to flicker in the breeze, to flirt its colours for your pleasure, to half show and half conceal a device you long to unravel: you do not want to read it, you want to worship it. Choose purple and gold for ambition, red for courage, green for long-cherished hopes . . . It is a declaration.

Not just a 'declaration' in Mary Lowndes' eyes, the suffragette and suffragist banners carried the argument itself. Each silk-embroidered motif, hand-wrought, tasselled, appliquéd motif, was a visible refutation of the criticism that suffragettes were de-sexed and unfeminine. Their banners were designed to be defiant, emphatic evidence of women's sensibilities and sensuality: 'the diverse colours of needlework, hand-wrought, are coming into play again, and now for the first time in history illuminating women's own adventure.'

And adventurous it was. This was no borrowed glory from the masculinity of union banners; Mary Lowndes saw to that. The banners paraded at these rallies were sewn in ravishing needlework, employing the most beautiful of fabrics – brocades, silks, damasks and velvets – and using materials deliberately displaced from the privacy of the drawing room to the public arena of demonstration. They were emblematic rather than pictorial, displaying explicit female imagery: flowers, lit lamps, shells, sun rays, winged hearts. They celebrated female heroines such as Boadicea, Elizabeth Fry, Florence Nightingale, Marie Curie, Josephine Butler, Jane Austen, Mary Wollstonecraft and Charlotte Brontë, among others, and, most audaciously of all, claimed 'Victoria, Queen and Mother' as one of their own.

This collective display was the triumph of the suffragettes. There was mile upon mile of women in drifts of colour: the red, white and green of Women's Suffrage Societies; the blue and silver of the Artists' Suffrage League; the orange and black of paper designers and printers; the pink and greens of the Actresses Franchise League – and many participants dressed in their occupational diversity, in academic gowns, nurses' uniforms, servants' aprons and workers' overalls. The procession of thousands of women with its swell of music, scent of flowers, its horizontal rainbow of colour and canopy of embroidered banners was a sensory demonstration unlike anything ever encountered before. Over 250,000 spectators came to watch it pass and its subsequent demonstration in Hyde Park attracted the largest number of people ever gathered there for a political purpose.

More rallies were held throughout the country. In 1909 the suffragettes marched in Edinburgh with their leader Flora Drummond, nicknamed 'Bluebell', heading the procession on horseback, bedecked in a chieftain's sash of tartan. Of the hundreds of banners carried that day, none survive. When I asked Elspeth King, the tireless champion of Scottish women's social history, why it was that so little remained, her answer was curt: 'misogyny'. The suffragette banners that were offered to Scotland's museums were, she told me, rejected by male curators at the time who saw no value in their history. The National Museum of Scotland has only one stitched suffrage banner on display. It is for the Federation of Male Suffrage.

It wasn't only banners that the suffragettes sewed. For the women campaigners incarcerated and force-fed in Holloway Prison, handkerchiefs offered the perfect vehicles for miniature petitions. Embroidered with their signatures and smuggled out, they reassured followers of an undiminished resolve, stitched in the WSPU colours: green for hope, white for purity and violet for dignity.

In America, the suffragettes chose white, purple and gold as their colours. Their fight for the right to vote took on a different tenor. In 1917 Alice Paul, the leader of the National Woman's Party, organised a picket at the White House with what became known as the Silent Sentinels. From 1917 to 1919, women dressed in white stood in silence for six days a week outside the gates of the White House, holding banners on which they had inscribed direct questions and appeals to the then president, Woodrow Wilson:

Mr President How Long Must Women Wait for Their Liberty?
Mr President What Will You Do for Women's Suffrage?
Mr President You Say Liberty Is the Fundamental Demand of
The Human Spirit.

In total, 2,000 women took their turn to be Silent Sentinels during two years of campaigning. Their banners were torn down, the women were arrested for obstructing traffic, some were jailed. Others went on hunger strike and were force-fed just like their British counterparts, and they too had to withstand the taunts of male critics, derided as 'bewildered, deluded creatures with short skirts and short hair'. Their nemesis came on 14 November 1917, when the superintendent of the Occoquan Workhouse, where many of the suffragettes were detained, ordered forty guards to brutalise them. A key campaigner, Lucy Burns, was badly beaten and chained with her hands above her head to the cell bars and left overnight. Dora Lewis was thrown into a dark cell, her head smashed against the iron bed. As she collapsed, her cellmate, Alice Cosu, believing Dora had been killed, suffered a heart attack but was denied medical treatment until the following morning. Others were kicked, clubbed, beaten up and choked. Less than two months later, Woodrow Wilson announced the presentation of the first bill in support of women's suffrage.

These American suffragettes did not use elaborate needlework to further their cause. While these women would have been skilled in sewing perhaps they had less need to publicly present a sewn femininity. Instead, their banners focussed on the suffragette colours and bold messages: slogans, questions, quotations writ large. More socially liberated and lacking the legacy of Tutill's commercial bannered show of masculine political power, there was maybe a lesser need to devise a gendered alternative, to harness the trope of women's domesticity to emphasise women's dissent. But they did use an armoury of textiles as visible declarations of their suffrage campaign. The National Women's Party Collection is guardian to the sashes, capes, ribbons, aprons, bonnets and costumes donned by American suffragettes.

It was the colours of the WPSU – green, white and violet – that dominated the banners at Greenham Common during the 1980s. Women had set up a peace camp there in 1981 to campaign against the deployment of nuclear weapons at its RAF base. While male visitors were welcomed during the day, the camp itself and its activities were exclusively and determinedly female to give a greater emphasis to the political engagement of women in the peace process. Coinciding with the rise of feminism, the women-only dictum was a conscious strategy to ensure that public and media attention was on women's action, undiluted by male interference or limelight. I went there in 1983, responding to a call for women throughout the country to come and link arms to encircle the four-mile perimeter fence. Thousands were needed.

I stepped onto the bus going to Greenham in the early morning and fell into the warmth of women, loud in companionship. Songs and slogans rolled out until the air was thick with the sound of us:

> Carry Greenham home, yes, nearer home and far away,
> Carry Greenham home.
> Singing voices rising higher, weave a dove into the wire
> In our hearts a blazing fire, bring the message home.

When the bus arrived at the camp we fell silent. Tiny tents flapped with a fray of rainbow pennants. Despite their flutter and colour, the women's encampment was grim: stoical, wind-blown protest tethered to a barren wasteland, frontiered in barbed wire. We clambered off the bus and I wandered disorientated, dazed by the throng of women, unsure of what to do or how to join in.

Some women were sitting on the ground tearing up old clothes, knotting the rags of them onto the fence in the shape of birds, trees of life, rainbows, the woman's symbol, woven as high as the wire reached. Others were attaching baby clothes, dresses, jeans. This was a personal world transported to a public stage: home furnishings and clothes appropriated as political protest. The women at Greenham repurposed textiles to high-light the domestic world they had responsibility for, the homes they had left. It strengthened the emotional pull of their protest. In the same way that the suffragettes had used embroidery to signal their femininity, these women deployed the clothes of their children, the sheets from their beds, the tea-towels and dusters of housework to exploit their stereotyped images as wives, mothers and homemakers and redeploy them as the raw materials for protest. They transformed the base with a different materiality, masking the solid concrete with the fluidity of banners, punctuating the bleak landscape with small fabric tents, weaving tufts of cloth into the cold wire of the steel fence.

This generation of women had been taught to sew at school. They were familiar with using materials to create something of their own. They also understood the power of the media and the potency of an arresting image, of the impact of the large scale. They created vast sewn statements, camouflaging the perimeter wire in a continuous length of cloth and parading around it, weaving a giant web to float above the base on helium balloons, decorating the four-mile fence in a fabric petition of individual banners. They used textiles as pages of dissent on which they wrote their messages: Women for Life on Earth, Freedom for Today, Women Say No to War Preparations, Send Maggie on a Cruise.

Thalia Campbell made the first banner to be carried to Greenham Common. She was one of the women who marched from Wales to set up its women's camp. On the eight-day trek she made a banner with young people to map out their route, using basic materials: an old sheet, felt tip pens, pea sticks for poles. Thalia's banner now hangs in the Peace Museum in Bradford, an iconic reminder of a brave campaign, material evidence of a landmark event in women's political history.

I first met Thalia in the 1980s when she and her husband, Ian, were touring the country with their exhibition: 100 *Years of Women1s Banners*. I remembered her as spirited woman, fizzling with energy and ideas, a chatter of political zeal. I arranged to go and see her again in 2016 at her home in Wales to talk about her banners and the role they played in peoples' politics through the last three decades. But the Thalia who came to meet me from the train was frazzled, tired, overwrought. Ian, her husband, had been ill. There had been a series of set-backs and recoveries. Both were frustrated by a tiresome lessening of vigour, both were in mourning for the diminution of the life they had loved as political activists. They were the front liners, the ever-present thorns in politicians' flesh, the sitter-downers at peaceful protests, the rabble-rousing marchers at demonstrations. Now their campaigns were more home-bound.

Thalia settled me in the sun lounge. It was stuffed with books, piled high with newspapers, forested in trailing plants and comfy with mismatching furniture: a radical's den. In the first half hour, we seem to have covered the political canvas of the last fifty years but we had scarcely mentioned banners. Eventually we turned to sewing. I asked Thalia why she chose banners as her form of political attack: 'Because you can fold them up, roll them up in a kit bag, take them wherever you want, send them across the world if you like. They are portable.' And she sews them because she likes the creative mix of embroidery and appliqué: 'With appliqué you can shout in big bold words but with embroidery you can whisper, make small suggestions in chain stitch.'

Her banners are a vivid concoction of emphatic lettering, striking images and small, ironic twists referenced through the fabric she chooses, or lurking in small, sardonic motifs. She wants people not just to see her banners, but to scan them, to catch their double meanings and enjoy the fun. She believes that beauty and humour, side by side, are powerful weapons. They have become her trademark.

Thalia provides a bridge between the suffragettes and us. She uses the tactility of fabric, her skill in sewing, her understanding of women's iconography, to bring the suffragettes with her into what she stitches, to bring us back to them. A banner commemorating Hilda Murrell, the anti-nuclear campaigner found dead in suspicious circumstances in 1984, mirrors the structure of the early suffrage heroine banners. By honouring her in a suffragette style Thalia has, through association, added her to the roll call of the heroines in history who the suffragettes carried aloft.

Another banner offers a more explicit link. Its slogan, WOMEN'S STRUGGLE WON THE VOTE, USE IT FOR DISARMAMENT, is writ large in gold across its surface. It features an apron and a tea towel both inscribed with landmark dates in women's struggle for equality. In her banners Thalia strives to draw women into campaigns, encouraging them to remember their history, to lure them into action through gendered visual appeals that are familiar, that bear their name.

Thalia tells a good tale. She attempted to get a section of the Ribbon (the 1985 frieze for peace made in America to wrap around the Pentagon) displayed in the House of Commons. It was a venture fraught with establishment distress. 'Get this women's rubbish out of here now', was heard booming through the corridors as she pinned the panels to the walls. She likes to think her own self-deprecating humour and the intervention of the M.P. Joan Ruddock, helped to charm people. The Ribbon stayed.

The Ribbon had been an event to mark the 40th anniversary of the nuclear bombing of Hiroshima and Nagasaki by America in August 1945. It was a US-wide demonstration advocating peace and an end to the arms race and nuclear testing that used fabric panels as political and personal statements. Justine Merritt, a retired school teacher and mother of five, was behind the project. Once her children were grown, she had become involved in organisations concerned with social change and justice. In 1975 she converted to Catholicism and took up

needlework, running 'embroidery memory classes' where participants sewed small panels depicting what they cherished in life.
One night, in her sleep, she dreamed of an angel tied by ribbon
to the barrel of a gun. The image stayed with her, and from it
evolved the idea 'to take our fear, our rage, our guilt and thread
feeling into our needle and draw the needle through the fabric
into an affirmation of life, while praying for peace.'

She talked with friends and family about her idea of involving
people in sewing peace panels that could be stitched together
and wrapped around the Pentagon as a silent act of remembrance for the victims of Hiroshima and Nagasaki, and as an
anti-war public protest. She spoke about it at church gatherings
and, without any formal organisation or network, the idea
began to spread and people started to make panels to a template
size of 91cms by 45.5cm.

Interest grew. A mailing list was set up, and in summer 1982 the
first *The Ribbon* newsletter was distributed to 600 people. People
held meetings in their homes and in church halls and displayed
completed panels in local museums, and Justine Merritt travelled
around America giving talks and generating support. For Justine,
her proselytising of the need to create a mass statement against
nuclear deployment was a devotional practice. She called herself
an 'itinerant preacher' and while her message was not overtly
religious, she did feel that her faith guided her in her mission. With
its strapline 'Honour the diversity, celebrate the unity', support for
the Ribbon gathered momentum. By 1985, there was a mailing list
of 10,000 names and 25,000 panels had been made.

But why did so many people respond to the invitation to
become involved? Why were so many thousands willing to participate, not just as makers but also as volunteer co-ordinators,
administrators, event organisers, fund-raisers, workshop hosts
and promoters? The Ribbon was the idea of a single woman
who lacked any of the resources to see her plan through. But
such was its appeal that support came in many different guises.

As she made her way across America canvassing support, people provided Justine with accommodation, a train fare, an evening meal or a house or hall in which to hold a meeting. Administrative costs were met through donations, many very small, sent by participants or raised through fund-raising events and sales of Ribbon merchandise.

Participation expanded through the interest, will and energies of people, most of whom were not involved in anti-nuclear activities, but who wanted nevertheless to express their concerns about the threat of nuclear war and the pollution of nuclear waste. While involvement was never designed to be gender specific, a survey undertaken in 1985 discovered that 95 percent of those who responded were women who would not describe themselves as political activists. But they found that the invitation to use their sewing skills for an issue they cared about struck a chord. Sewing was a medium they felt comfortable with. It was non-confrontational, personal, something they could do in the privacy of their own home and it required little expense. For some it seemed a natural extension of America's needlework tradition of women making quilts for causes, auctioned as fund-raisers for the anti-slavery and temperance movements, sewn as comfort blankets for soldiers during the civil war, signed in stitches as part of political canvassing or gifts of friendship.

So many people responded that the Washington authorities became alarmed. They said that so many panels joined together could cause a dangerous traffic obstruction and insisted that the panels be carried separately by people walking in single file. But they conceded to two minutes of unity, during which the panels could be tied one to another: just two minutes for all those present to exercise their collective desire for peace.

On 4 August 1985, 20,000 people arrived in Washington D.C. to take part in the Ribbon. Panels were distributed to people as they arrived. People didn't necessarily carry their own panel but were given one that someone else had made. This added to the sense of a shared action. The Ribbon didn't just wrap around the Pentagon. It spread across the Arlington Memorial Bridge, around the Lincoln Memorial, down the Mall, around the Capitol, back up the Mall, back to the Lincoln Memorial and the Pentagon. It was fifteen miles long. When the signal came – the release of hundreds of balloons – people tied their panels together. There were no speeches, no celebrity appearances, no razzmatazz. Instead, the culmination of the Ribbon, as envisaged in Justine Merritt's dream, was realised in that permitted two minutes as the Pentagon and its surrounding area – the sites of governmental and military power – were enveloped in an alternative unification of human hope, a mass evocation of the preciousness of people, family and the earth.

In interviews during the lead-up to the Washington event, and in subsequent publications, women told of how they found the process of making a Ribbon panel reflective, how it allowed time to think about the consequences of an escalation in nuclear power. Moreover, they said, working from home meant that their sewing of a panel triggered family discussions on the nuclear question or, if part of a community group, debate on the issue. And some said that making a panel had absorbed some of the anxiety they felt about the nuclear threat. By sewing images of their family and children, of local flora and fauna, they felt they had marked them down and, by doing so, had protected them. One couple made a T-shirt for their small daughter to wear on the day. It read: I'm my parent's ribbon.'

The use of fabrics left over from making clothes for family members heightened the emotional investment in the Ribbon's panels. But there was something else. Many of the sewn panels made use of techniques and patterns that had a deeper resonance for women. Quilters could recognise the meaning behind a specific block pattern. Embroiderers could identify styles of needlework and, by identifying an origin, its historical or ethnic context or even parody, interpret its significance. This intensified the impact

Protest

of the Ribbon, making the private translatable to a wider public and connecting makers emotionally through what they had sewed.

The Ribbon attracted scant media attention and had little political impact. President Reagan was reported as having claimed he had not seen it when his helicopter flew over the Pentagon at the very time when thousands of his citizens were engaged in mass peaceful demonstration. But, Justine Merritt attested, political change was never her ambition. She conceived the Ribbon to encourage people to think more about how nuclear weapons affected them on a personal level, and to increase public engagement in the issue.

Protest in the 1980s was characterised by the assembly of multiple textiles to create demonstrations marked by the duality of a personal act and public action. On one hand, there was the vast scale of assembled textiles, which created an extraordinary image of collective concern; on the other were its individual parts, the personal hand-crafted contributions in the campaign for change. This was the approach used by the women of Greenham Common and the participants of the Ribbon, and it was replicated in many other campaigns of the period. But by the 1990s, sewing skills were less in evidence at political rallies. T-shirts, lapel badges and placards had replaced them.

Today, however needlework is emerging once again as a form of political protest. The Craftivist Collective whose strapline is 'changing the world one stitch at a time' was founded by Sarah Corbett in 2009 and follows in the footsteps of the American craftivist Betsy Greer to offer a beguiling alternative to mass demonstrations and the sometimes bully-boy tactics of harassment by political activists. It devises projects of gentle persuasion – deliberately non-threatening and non-violent – to encourage others to think about and support a variety of causes for a fairer, more caring world. With personally crafted pieces of needlework, and the kindness of needlework gifts, the Craftivist Collective creates visually pleasing and surprising appeals.

Sarah Corbett's belief in such tactics was forged when she found her regular email petitioning of her local M.P. to urge her to support a variety of issues met with little response. She decided on a different approach and made her a hand-stitched message on a lilac sprigged handkerchief embroidered with a message about her commitment to social change and the words 'Don't blow it'. At her M.P.'s surgery Corbett handed her the handkerchief, nicely wrapped as a present should be. The M.P. was taken aback but appreciative. She realised that Corbett's emails to her were not just the tokenistic forwarding of online dissent but about issues she cared deeply about, cared enough about to spend time embroidering a different kind of protest, made especially for the M.P. herself. The discussion that followed was more honest, more empathetic on both sides and through the experience Corbett realised that needlework could provide an alternative way to protest, draw public attention to injustice, and engage non-activists in issues they might otherwise find too overwhelming to confront.

The tag label on the Craftivist Collective works reads 'made with courage and care' and that is the key principle behind their projects. Whether it be tying tiny stitched banners to lampposts to alert passers-by to the iniquity of racism, or organising a shop-drop where messages about ethical manufacture are left in the pockets of shirts in a non-ethical retail chain or making bespoke embroidered handkerchiefs for board members and shareholders of a company not yet committed to the Living Wage, the sewn campaigns of the Craftivist Collective might be quiet and small but they still pack an emotional punch. The sewing itself is less important than the thought and the time it represents. It is the latter that allows campaigners to demonstrate their depth of feeling and commitment. Gifts initiate a connection and they are memorable. They elicit support through being witty, thoughtful, targeted, purposeful and hand-made.

10

Loss

My mother has just died, and a member of the hospital staff slips into the room and begins to quietly discuss arrangements with me, my brother and my two sisters. There are various matters to be settled and we do the best we can. Then she asks: 'What would you like your mother to wear?'

We look at each other in confusion. It is a question we have never considered and one to which we have no ready reply. We stumble, grow hesitant and stay silent. 'What about her grey outfit?' my elder sister eventually suggests and we nod in relief. At least the question has been answered. 'Or the green suit', my other sister reflects, 'the one she wore for her eightieth birthday?' We consider the green suit. It was a definite favourite. Yes, maybe the green suit. Other possibilities come to mind. We become distracted by nostalgia as we rummage through a mental inventory of our mother's wardrobe, reminding each other of this dress or that coat: each a memory of childhood or a special occasion, the family times when we were all together.

The decision about what my mother should wear for this, her final journey, was important. It was our final honouring, our last intimate, affectionate act. Since ancient times, we have dressed, wrapped and covered our dead to speak of who they were, to mark out their value to us, to ensure that their worth is recognised in the next world; to show that they were loved. For many people, preparing a body for interment or cremation is the last time they touch the bodies of those they have loved; a final tangible connection. It is the emotional and physical point of separation of the living from the dead, a mother from

143

a daughter, a husband from a wife, the soul from the body. In many cultures, the clothes the deceased are dressed in, or the cloths wound around them, are more than just a final gesture of care and farewell. They are passports to eternal peace, to acceptance in the next world.

In a 2,000-year-old necropolis in the Andes lie hundreds of bodies, some wound in over 250 metres of embroidered cloth, preserved by the arid air around them. The body of a girl has been wrapped and wrapped again in layers of fabric, in embroidered tunics sewn in bright colours of red, blue, yellow, pink and green. The fabric is stitched with sentinel creatures such as serpents, birds of prey and killer whales, fierce escorts to accompany her on her journey to the afterlife. In the burial chamber of the Egyptian pharaoh, Tutankhamun, were twelve bead-shimmering tunics, twenty-four shawls; fifteen sashes; one hundred and fifty-five loin cloths and a robe decorated with 3,000 gold rosettes. They marked him out as a sovereign in this world and announced his status to the spirits of the next. When the tomb of St Cuthbert, who died in 687 AD, was opened at Durham Cathedral in 1827, they found buried with him a set of vestments made of jewelled and embroidered Byzantine silk, which had been deposited by King Aethelstan in the tenth century while the king was on pilgrimage as sewn credentials of the saint's spiritual worth.

Some embroidered textiles follow a person through life to death. In Slovakia, dead men were traditionally buried in the shirt their bride embroidered for their wedding. In northern Russia, the red stitched towel a baby was laid down on at birth would cover its adult face at death. In the Ukraine, a new-born's *rushnyk* (ritual cloth), was kept through life and taken with its owner's body to the cemetery to be destroyed by the elements as part of the funeral rites.

For those left behind, sewing as a mark of grief can be a private way to mourn or used as a public register of loss. The death of George Washington in 1799 caused a contagion of grief. He was the United States' first president, its first national hero, the triumphant general of the American War of Independence. His death led to widespread public mourning. Churches and homes were draped in black. People donned black clothes, black cockades, armbands, gloves and sashes. Manufacturers were quick to exploit the commercial potential of his commemoration. Ceramic plates, cameos, fans, handkerchiefs, even wallpaper featuring portraits of Washington were avidly purchased as patriotic symbols of respect and sorrow.

Samuel Folwell, an artist from Philadelphia, produced a series of designs for mourning embroideries. Others followed suit. Soon, these small sewn memorials appeared in every self-respecting home. For women, they offered a rare opportunity to participate in a national political event. The digital archive of the National Museum of American History in Washington, D.C. has an example of what was sewn. The picture is set in a graveyard with a stitched urn centre-stage on which is inscribed the words: 'Sacred to the Memory of the Illustrious Washington.' Female mourners draped in white, their hair loosed free in free-flowing heartache, are keeping vigil under a weeping willow tree. An angel, descending from an embroidered sky and clasping a laurel wreath, is winging its way to release Washington's soul, a trumpet of glory held to its lips.

The picture is typical of the mourning embroideries which grew in popularity in the aftermath of Washington's death. They followed the conventions of the sentimental silk embroidered pictures that had been sewn by girls and women in Britain and America since the eighteenth century. These were pastoral idylls, pretty and innocuous, often with scenes of rural courtship with a shepherdess or milkmaid as their heroine. But by changing the landscape from the countryside to a graveyard, women could claim a gravitas, transform their sewing from a frivolous pastime to an honourable pursuit and portray themselves as symbols of courage and duty, as the guardians of national or family grief. Mourning embroideries became a needlework craze.

What began as pictorial graveside scenes were simplified into equally sombre but more detailed mourning samplers that functioned as inventories of family bereavement. A list of the names of the dead, alongside the date of their death, was often accompanied by sorrowful verses. Louisa Buchholtz (c.1812-1879) made three stitched epitaphs, two on the death of her mother Susannah in 1823 when Louisa was thirteen and another to mourn the death of her father who died two years later. To commemorate her mother's death she stitched verses in black thread:

> In painful sores long time she bore
> physicians were in vain
> Till God was pleas'd by Death to ease
> And free her from her pains.
> The opening grave receives her dust
> All dark and cold she lies
> But o his spirit with the just
> Lies far above the skies.

> For since she's dead for ever gone
> O god my soul prepare
> To enter into heaven's high gates
> In hopes to meet her there.

In America, women made mourning quilts in dull colours with cloth patches of brown, blue, grey and black. Elizabeth Roseberry Mitchell went further than most. Married at eighteen in 1817 to Shadrach Mitchell, she bore eleven children over the next twenty-four years. In their early married life, Elizabeth not only serviced her growing family, but also helped Shadrach run a small hotel. After seven years of marriage they moved west to Ohio, where they bought some land and set up a general store and another inn. These were difficult times of debt and drought, but they survived and prospered; by 1850 they owned three horses and two cows and were harvesting forty acres of corn and oats.

But there were tragedies along the way. In 1836 her infant son, John Vannatta, died. He was only two years old. Elizabeth began to make a mourning quilt. She gathered up the faded floral sprigs from her daughters' old school dresses and the drab cottons of worn-out family workwear and began to shape them into a cloth replica of the local fenced graveyard. She appliquéd a pathway to the graveyard gate, pairing floral patterns to edge each side. She cut from fabric a small six-sided coffin and sewed it down in the graveyard. She embroidered vines around it and a weeping willow and a red rose bush by the gate. With the help of her daughter Sarah, she pieced, from tiny scraps of fabric, forty-five LeMoyne star blocks to complete the quilt and bordered it in a pieced zig zag design. In 1843 Elizabeth lost another son. Mathias, nicknamed Bub, was only nineteen when he died. She made another slightly larger cloth coffin for him and sewed it in its place in the graveyard. She added stitched inscriptions to the coffins of both of her dead children. But the quilt remained unfinished. It was never quilted or backed.

Instead, Elizabeth began work on something much more ambitious: a graveyard quilt for the whole family. She followed the same design as the first, albeit with more refined stitchery. This had the same central path, the same surround of the LeMoyne star blocks and the two coffins tucked at the back of the graveyard. But this time she embroidered the flowers along the pathway, and arched more decorative vines and flowering white and red rose bushes above the gate. Then she lined the outer pathway with eleven cloth coffins barely sewn in place so that her stitching could be easily unpicked and the coffins moved into the graveyard when death occurred. To these she attached small pieces of paper: seven penned with the names of her remaining children; the other two simply saying 'mother' and 'father'. She embroidered more flowers: a red rose bush beside John and Bub's coffin and a white rose shrub near the named coffins of her other living sons. Around her living baby son Marling's coffin, sewn in its temporary position, she embroidered a thick protective shield of delicate yellow roses. Then she marked within the graveyard, in stitched outline, the final resting place of each coffin. Her daughters Sarah and Lib helped, sewing the sites of their own coffins.

When Elizabeth died in 1857 the thread that anchored her fabric coffin in its temporary location was cut, and the coffin labelled 'mother' was moved to its place beside her two sons. Her daughter Sarah became the guardian of the quilt. As other family members died – Sarah's husband, her baby son, her sister's child, nieces and nephews – more coffins were added to the quilt and laid in a separate row outside the graveyard fence. When Sarah's sister Lib died in 1867, her coffin was snipped free and moved to its allotted place in the graveyard. There would be no more changes made to the quilt. It stayed as it was, with four coffins in the graveyard and twenty-three around its border. Sarah remarried at the age of 50 but her husband died just two years later and, given the property laws at the time which allowed widows a paucity of joint possessions, it seemed that Sarah, fearful the quilt would pass to her husband's relatives, put it into the safe-keeping of her brother Benjamin. It passed through family hands, through generations until in 1959 Nora Mitchell Biggs donated it to the Kentucky Historical Society which has been its guardian ever since.

There is no right or wrong way to grieve; each culture finds its own way to mourn. Romanians decorate graves with the clothes of corpses, while Mongolians keep the clothes of dead relatives as family treasures, the patina of wear imbuing them with an intimate value. A friend told me of a woman she knew who, having cleared out the belongings of her dead father, came across his shirts folded neatly in a drawer. These she kept, cut up and made into a patchwork quilt. It was no act of remembrance or emotional attachment. They had been estranged for many years and he had been a distant and detached figure in her life. But with the heritage of his shirts, she could change their relationship and claim a closeness she had never encountered. Now, after his death, she gave herself the licence to wrap herself in his warmth.

Using the clothing of the dead is a traditional ritual of mourning in many cultures. In South America, an effigy of the deceased, dressed in their own clothes, is laid beside the grave so that mourners can embrace and talk to them for a while longer before the burial takes place. Georgian mourners lay out their loved ones' clothes out on the 'dead man's carpet', arranged as they might have been worn. It allows for a re-animation of sorts, a way of preserving a presence. Mourners feast, sing and entertain the physical representation of their loved one until the corpse is interred. Romanians decorate graves with the clothes of the deceased to allow the last remnants of their identity to disintegrate in the wind.

Many of us find that the hardest thing to do when someone close to us has died is to dispose of their clothes. They are what most vividly express a singular personality, what retain an essence of who a person was. The deceased's lingering presence is held in fabric that has absorbed their shape and smell. So we keep the clothes folded in drawers and hanging in wardrobes, as if our loved one's existence is still present in the clothes they left behind.

Nowhere has the re-animation of the dead through the clothes they wore been used to more dramatic and emotive effect than in the NAMES memorial quilt project, a response to the AIDS epidemic that swept through America like a tsunami in the 1980s. It was in 1981 that medical practitioners in New York,

Los Angeles and San Francisco began to report a mysterious virus that was attacking healthy gay young men. By the following year it had killed 200 and infected 400 more in twenty-four states. Cases were emerging across the world. Health and scientific institutions set to work to try to identify the cause, to detect methods of transmission and provide guidelines for prevention. But their efforts were hampered by a climate of fiscal austerity in the United Sates where, with unemployment and inflation rising, the Reagan government had enforced budget constraints. Politicians prevaricated over dedicating funds to what it deemed a minority affliction. Research, preventative measures and patient care were compromised in the name of national thrift.

The public and the media seemed indifferent to what was known as the 'gay plague' and it was only when haemophiliacs and heterosexuals began to show signs of infection that people became concerned. Meanwhile, numbers were escalating. By 1984, over 3,050 people had died and a further 7,000 were infected. The gay community of America found itself under siege. Firefighters, police officers, medical staff, dentists and prison guards demanded the protection of face masks and rubber gloves. Morticians refused to embalm the corpses of AIDS victims. The public were warned not to share towels, cutlery or drinking vessels with gay people. Even members of the gay community were in denial, wary of limitations to their sexual freedom, protesting proposals to shut down gay bath houses and bars, claiming an infringement of civil rights should the screening of blood donors be imposed.

When Jim Curran, the epidemiologist who led a task force on HIV/AIDS at the Center for Disease Control and Prevention in the United States, warned that, since the number of those infected was doubling month by month and that research had shown that the virus could lie dormant for years thereby harbouring a risk to thousands in the future, and the threat of a global catastrophe, he was accused of grossly exaggerating the problem. In fact, even he had underestimated the scale of the epidemic. By 1985 over 4,000 had died and 9,000 were infected. It was just the tip of the iceberg.

In America, the gay community was becoming bewildered. It had become used to what had seemed to be a generally liberal attitude to homosexuality. Now, in the face of tragedy, bigoted, uncaring, self-protective and at times morally triumphant attitudes were being unmasked. The death from AIDS of Rock Hudson, a popular movie star and icon of heterosexual masculinity, triggered media attention. The pace of concern quickened. More funding was allocated to publish preventative guidelines and increase the research into possible antibodies. But the sense of public and political rejection, of bigotry and betrayal, of isolation continued to be deeply felt by the gay community.

It was this community who had to organise informal rotas of care for the dying when none was available from the health services, to arrange the funerals of lovers estranged from their families, to inform parents of a son's sexuality and his imminent death. Many were barred from sick rooms and deathbeds, not allowed to stay with their loved ones. But their emotional burden hardly registered on the nation's conscience.

The climate of prejudice and avoidance were catalysts in the creation of the NAMES memorial quilt project. Quilts were chosen as a deliberate ploy to evoke a wholesome association with home, family and comfort. It was conceived by Cleve Jones, a gay rights activist who had helped in the campaign to elect Harvey Milk as the first gay supervisor in San Francisco and who had witnessed his assassination in 1978. In 1985, at the annual candlelit vigil in honour of Milk, Cleve Jones had asked participants to bring with them a placard bearing the name of someone who had died of AIDS and post it on the walls of the San Francisco Federal Building. When the placards were grouped together it reminded him of a patchwork quilt, and this triggered the idea of a cloth memorial for the victims of Aids. The following year, when his friend, the actor Marvin Feldman, became yet another victim, Jones made a commemorative panel the size of a burial plot: three foot by six foot. From that grew the idea of creating a textile graveyard of similar panels, each bearing the name of someone who had died of Aids. In 1987 he established the NAMES Project Foundation. Its aim was simple: to invite people to make a sewn panel. Its purpose was more ambitious: to create a fabric requiem that lamented the waste of so many lives through negligence and fear, on a scale and impact that would make its message inescapable and could campaign for more resources to stem the epidemic.

On 11 October 1987, nearly 2,000 panels were laid out on the Mall of Washington D.C., transforming it into an encrusted carpet. The Mall became a tactile garden of remembrance, with the panels purposefully designed to lie on the ground so that people had to kneel to explore each sewn biography. The panels, dedicated to both the famous and the unknown, lay side by side in material democracy. In predominantly male hands, men who were largely inexperienced stitchers, the techniques and materials were improvised. Many of the panels used the clothes of those who had died, sometimes stitched down in their entirety: T-shirts, football strips, ties and jeans. Designer labels, lapel badges, zips and buttons were used as adornments. Unaware of needlework conventions, the makers of many panels were liberated from their constraints and became experimental, finding imaginative ways to encapsulate a person's life in fabric. Its effect was as much to do with tactility as scale, creating a textural and sensory evocation of life as much as a commemoration of death.

The NAMES Memorial Quilt Project was not merely a creative and public way to voice grief. It was a way to challenge the anonymity of the dead, their reduction to statistics. This was emphasised in future displays of the quilt when the names of those represented were read aloud, sometimes with celebrities taking part. By 1992 the roll call took 24 hours. This reading of names and the slow, respectful, ritualistic unfolding of each section at a time transformed the NAMES Memorial Quilt from an object to a performance of loss. Half a million people came to see its first installation in 1987. By the time it was finally seen in its entirety in October 1996, it covered the entire Mall and had received 14 million visitors. There are now 48,000 panels.

Not everyone, however, was convinced of the efficacy of the NAMES Memorial Quilt as a campaigning tool. There were those who saw it as a sanitisation and sentimentalisation of gay culture, who thought that the fund-raising merchandise that accompanied it – books, T-shirts, ornaments, calendars, post-cards, a songbook – trivialised a tragedy and made it into a commodity, encouraging people to support a brand rather than a cause. There were satirical parodies of it, epitomised by the 'gerbil memorial quilt' dedicated to dead pet rodents. The theatricality of its display was criticised for turning a human disaster into a voyeuristic show of loss.

But this mile upon mile of fabric eulogy was an indisputable call to awareness, stitched by those who cared. The NAMES Project ensured that the public was witness to the scale of loss through a haunting and memorable spectacle. Public and governmental attitudes changed. And while the NAMES Memorial Quilt might not have been the trigger, it played its part in raising funds for research, better sex education, preventative measures and effective drugs. Perhaps its main achievement was to realise one of the aims stated in its early publicity: 'to break down bigotry that inhibits global response'.

People in different countries, at different times and in different ways, have used needlework to speak when their voices have been silenced, to speak for those they have lost through social and political upheaval. Women, especially those who are illiterate or living in poverty, have used sewing because it is the most accessible form available to them and used it as their voice.

The military dictatorship in Chile, which followed the overthrow of President Salvador Allende and his democratic government in 1973, ushered in seventeen years of dictatorship, censorship, curfews and the suspension of civil liberty. Under the leadership of General Augusto Pinochet, Chile was silenced. The constitution was suspended, left-wing parties proscribed and the media put under the control of the military government. Those who tried to speak out were arrested and imprisoned. In the first three weeks of the new regime, 1,500 are said to have been killed, and many more thousands were rounded up and taken to the two main sports stadiums in Santiago. Sixteen-year-old Lelia Perez was taken with ten of her classmates to the central stadium, the Estadio Nacional, where 18,000 people were eventually detained. Her hands were tied together and she was held there for the next five days. In 1975 she was arrested again, but this time her eyes were taped over and she was subjected to electric shocks. The singer-songwriter Victor Jarra was arrested in September 1973 and, like Lelia, taken to a football stadium where he was beaten up and his fingers smashed. The guards taunted him, ordering him to play the guitar with his broken hands. He was subsequently shot, his body riddled with bullets. According to Amnesty International, during Pinochet's reign 40,000 people were illegally detained or tortured and up to 3,000 more killed or forcibly disappeared; 30,000 fled the country.

Some of those who were killed, tortured, imprisoned or abducted came from the shanty towns of Santiago. Many were young. Women whose husbands had been abducted or killed became the sole providers for their families. In 1974, the Catholic Church formed the Vicariate of Solidarity as an agent of support and, as part of its aid programme, established a handicraft workshop where women could make products for the Church to sell and provide the women with as an economic lifeline.

Under the guidance of Valentina Bonne, a church official who knew of the appliquéd pictures sewn by women in Isla Negra, the coastal area of Chile, that illustrated their rural fishing community, and aware of the *arpilleras* (embroideries sewn on burlap, a coarse jute cloth) created by the Chilean artist Violeta Parra, who had exhibited in the Louvre in Paris in 1964, the women were encouraged to make their own *arpilleras* with scraps of fabric, and sew the scenes of their lives. The women fashioned small three-dimensional dolls to animate their stitched scenes of rural landscapes and city streets, and they told of a Chile in crisis, a community laid low by water and food short-ages, poverty and prostitution, unemployment and broken homes. They told of their own experiences, of kidnapped sons and daughters, of their search to find them, of the loneliness of not knowing what had befallen loved ones.

Given the paucity of available materials, they recycled old clothes, dressing their scenes and dolls in fabric they brought from home. Some stitched their own hair onto their dolls' heads and, little by little, these cloth figures began to embody those they loved. Their sewing became an act of repossession.

The *arpilleras* depicted domestic scenes of loss: a woman standing by herself in the doorway of her home, a family mealtime with one empty place. There were also exterior scenes: a marketplace with no food on its stalls, unemployed youngsters scavenging for cardboard to sell, policemen making an arrest, a tree with pictures of lost relatives instead of leaves all backgrounded by the Andes mountains and a shining sun or bright moon. They were made in the most cheerful of fabrics, bright colours and pretty fabrics belying the stories of fear and desolation.

Visitors and journalists discovered the *arpilleras* and started buying them. The Church began to smuggle them out of the country through its own network of support. What started as a way for the women to earn some money became a clandestine, political act. At the time, these were the only dissenting voices to reach the outside world. So, the *arpilleras* – layered with emotional meaning – became tactile cloths of resistance and symbols of reunion: the joining together of fabric remnants as a metaphor for the reclamation of family.

With their jaunty colours, rudimentary stitching and worn cloth the *arpilleras* appeared innocuous and were overlooked at first by the regime's officials as tools of subversion, dismissed as women's sewing. They weren't circulated within Chile but exported to other countries as evidence with which to expose the infringements of human rights that were being perpetrated by Pinochet's regime. Exhibitions were held in Washington, D.C.; Amnesty International published greeting cards, a calendar was printed and the *arpilleras* found buyers and collectors among the politically aware and the Chilean diaspora. Purchasing an *arpillera* became an act of solidarity. But the promotion of them by supporters in other countries brought them to the attention of the authorities in Chile itself.

The dictatorship in Chile became incensed. The *arpilleras* were denounced as 'tapestries of infamy'. The women were followed, their homes raided, some had a red cross painted on their door to mark out the home of a workshop member. But the women sewed on. They hid their needlework as they made their way to and from the church. They trained other women and the workshops expanded until there were forty throughout the country. After 1993 and the overthrow of Pinochet's government, their activities became public. The making of *arpilleras* became what it had originally been intended as: an income-generating scheme for the poor. But the original *arpilleristas* continued to stitch their stories of loss, unwilling to relinquish their role as political commentators or allow history to be sanitised. They had been at the forefront of political dissent, not only through their sewing, but also through other political actions such as hunger strikes, chaining themselves to railings and publishing the names of the detained and disappeared and they had done so largely without the support of men who, in a patriarchal society, had been generally dismissive, even critical, of their efforts. Now, even with Pinochet's dictatorship long over, and despite the frailty of their failing sight and ageing hands, they insist on still having a voice, of sewing their laments and testimonies. There is no longer a need or a market for what they make. In Chile, people want to forget. But these women keep faith, denouncing the murderers of their family members, calling them to account, replaying their crimes and documenting the excavation of the mass graves of their loved ones. They are the guardians of a nation's memory, the conscience of Chile.

And women in other countries have adopted the medium of *arpilleras* to tell of community trauma. The Conflict Textiles collection at Ulster University, Northern Ireland, has archived *arpilleras* from Germany, Zimbabwe, Northern Ireland, Argentina, Peru, Colombia, Spain, Ecuador, Brazil and Canada as well as Chile.

In 1973, the year General Pinochet and his military forces took control of Chile, Juan Domingo Peron was re-elected president of Argentina after an exile of eighteen years. His presidency marked the beginning of escalating aggression between the country's right and left-wing factions. When Peron died in 1974, he was succeeded by his wife, Isabel who, as political violence continued, was overthrown by a military coup d'état in 1976. The military dictatorship rounded up and detained hundreds, then thousands of civilians, some of whom were never seen again. As in Chile, many of those abducted were young. In 1977, a group of fourteen mothers converged at the Casa Rosada, the presidential palace in the public square of Buenos Aires, each seeking news of a child who had disappeared. They were told to go home but they refused, and when the guards warned them that it was forbidden for more than three people to gather together in public, they defiantly linked arms and stayed, strolling in pairs around the square.

It was the start of what was to become a thirty-five-year campaign to uncover their children's fate. After that first defiance, the women continued to gather every Thursday in the square, their numbers swelled by other mothers, until there were hundreds of women protesting at the disappearance of their children. They called themselves Las Madres de Plaza de Mayo.

The women donned white headscarves to mark themselves out as mothers, headscarves that mimicked babies' white nappies. On them they embroidered the names and birth dates of their children, not the date of their disappearance, but the day these women had brought them into the world. The headscarves were worn as symbols of their mothering, their responsibility for maternal care and protection of their young. They identified the women publicly as the Mothers of the Disappeared and, more importantly, were evidence of their children's existence when the military guards at detention centres claimed not to have heard of them never mind know of their whereabouts. The mothers were determined not to let their children become statistics but to be known as individuals who belonged to others. Through their headscarves they insisted on their children's presence. The final March of Resistance took place in 2006. By then the Grandmothers of Plaza de Mayo had been formed, demanding to know the fate of the 500 children who had been born in detention camps or prisons, more than half of them already illegally adopted. Their grandmothers' campaign resulted in over 100 children being identified and reunited with their biological parents.

It is extraordinary to know now of the measures the military government took to silence these mothers and stop their efforts to find their children or know of their fate. When Azucena Villaflor De Vincenti, a founder member of Las Madres de Plaza de Mayo, published the names of missing young people in a national newspaper in December 1977, on International Human Rights Day, she was abducted, tortured and taken, it transpired, on what became known as a 'death flight', and tossed into the sea. Two other founder members met a similar death. That same year their bodies were washed ashore but it took until 2005 and DNA testing for their identities to be verified. Azucena's ashes were buried in the Plaza de Mayo. By then, mass graves were being excavated and the bodies of hundreds of young people exhumed: their lives recorded on the headscarves their mothers wore. By the end of the military dictatorship it was estimated that 30,000 had been kidnapped, most presumed dead. 9,000 others remain unaccounted for.

Esther Nisenthal Krinitz knew only too well the cost of war. Born a Jew in the tiny village of Mniszck in Poland, home to just a dozen families, her childhood was shaped by local rural life – tending geese, swimming in the river, going to market, taking part in the rituals of her Jewish faith, the celebrations of Shavuot, Rosh Hashanah and Passover. At nine she learned to sew, taught by the local dressmaker. In 1939, when Esther was twelve years old, Nazi troops arrived at her village. Her grandfather was dragged from his house and badly beaten. His beard, a symbol of his faith, was cut off as a sign to other Jews in the village that their race, their religion, was despised by their oppressors. The troops set the villagers to work. They depleted their food stock by commandeering food for themselves and forbidding the care of livestock. When Esther's family were preparing for Passover with the table set with special dishes, two soldiers came to the house and, incensed by the show of a Jewish ceremony, tugged the cloth from the table, sending its dishes smashing to the floor. On discovering a goose that her family had kept hidden in readiness for the feast, they killed it.

But there was worse to come. In 1942 the Gestapo arrived in

the village at dawn. They marched Esther's entire family in their nightshirts under gunpoint to the river, lined them up and raised their guns. Neighbours pleaded for their lives and they were saved. There were dawn raids when she and her family had to run and stay hidden in the woods. She was struck in the face by a soldier's rifle when he didn't think she had raised her arms high enough when he had ordered her to do so. Then the day came when the Gestapo ordered all Jews to leave the village and join the wagons going to the station at Krasni. Those who disobeyed their orders would be shot. Esther disobeyed. Unlike her parents, who believed they were being sent to a Jewish ghetto, Esther was convinced that the journey would end in imprisonment in a concentration camp and possibly death. She persuaded her parents to let her and her younger sister Mania find a different means of escape. On 15 October, they bid goodbye to their parents, brother, little sisters, aunts, uncle and five cousins. Esther was only fifteen years old and Mania thirteen when they became fugitives. They never saw their family again.

The girls masqueraded as Polish Catholics, changed their names to Josephine and Maria and hid in attics protected by courageous people and they survived the war. After Liberation, in July 1944, Esther went in search of her family. She visited the concentration camp in Maidanek outside Lublin, where she thought they might have been taken. She saw the small hills of shoes and heard about the massacre at nearby Krepicki Forest, where 18,000 Polish Jews were killed in November 1943. She joined the Russian and Polish army as it made its way through a landscape hung with the rotting bodies of German soldiers. She married, gave birth to a daughter and emigrated with her husband to America in 1949 at the age of just twenty-two.

We know this story because Esther sewed it down. She couldn't write it. Writing would not have captured as vividly the pictures she had held in her mind through time. Prose could not have described the contrast between the flowering fields and the barbed wire of a labour camp; nor the intensity of the colours of the fallen autumn leaves on the day her family left on death trucks. It could not have captured the way the patterns of her clothes merged with the meadowed grass, camouflaging her as she crouched in the fields beyond her village. Sewing allowed her to stitch the detail of her girlhood, her terror and escape, acutely remembered: the prettiness of the embroidered cloth her mother laid on the table for Rosh Hashanah; the pattern of the thatched roof of the cottage where she and her sister found refuge. Through her sewing she demonstrated how the adrenaline of fear heightens our senses and fixes a memory. The panels she appliquéd and embroidered, 36 in all, are illustrated like a storybook, pictures above and text below. She set each scene in its specific location – her family home, the field beyond her house, the countryside around it – defined in textured scraps of carefully chosen fabric and embroidered to render the detail of her experiences. Her scene of when the Nazis arrive in Mniszek in September 1939 has her grandmother in a crisp sprigged apron standing on the steps of her lace-curtained house, her grandfather's shoe lying where it fell as he was dragged from his home. Esther and her two sisters are tidy in floral dresses and plaited hair, watching helplessly as their world changes. Around them pansies are in full flower on the verges, the tree outside their grandparent's house is laden with apples and chickens are pecking at the soil. Everything seems just as it ever was but for the four helmeted Nazi soldiers on horseback and the one who has dismounted with his gun in his belt, the one chopping off her grandfather's beard. There is patterned fabric for the floral hedgerows, striped cloth for the garden sheds, both carefully remembered. One sister has a large red bow tied beautifully at her waist, another's dress is collared in lace. She portrays a normality brutally disrupted in horror. Her embroidered personal story of war and the holocaust ends in 1949 with Esther, her husband, child and sister standing in America for the first time, two small suitcases by their side. They are gazing up at the Statue of Liberty, around which seagulls are winging free in the sky.

It would be twenty-eight years after her arrival in America before Esther took up a needle and thread to set down her story. By then she was fifty years old. She embroidered it as a legacy for her daughters, as a textile memoir. The 36 embroidered pictures track the twelve years of her life from when she was ten until she was twenty-two during which she witnessed the cost of human prejudice and greed: a culture and religion humiliated, a village and family destroyed. Her belief in humanity was tested over and over again. But she chose sewing as an act of restoration. Through her sewn picture, she reanimates her parents and siblings, revisits her faith, rebuilds her village, re-plants the fields around her house. Restores a lost life. She goes back home.

Needlework takes time. The choosing of fabric, its cutting out to shape different images – the leaves of a tree, the bright red bow of a girl's dress – have to be carefully done. The needle lingers and the stitcher is forced to pause from time to time to re-thread a needle, pick out and cut a new piece of thread, decide what to embroider next, what colour or stitch to use. It allows space for reminiscing, for remembering. So it must have been for Esther Nisenthal Krinitz on her slow journey of re-creation; one stitch a commemoration, and the next a farewell.

11
Community

It is early afternoon in the Scottish Storytelling Centre Gallery and all the seats are taken. People have come for the Edinbrugh launch of Material Matters, the community textile project I have been working on over the past year with people from Glasgow, Edinburgh and Dundee. Now its results – twelve small textile panels – are to be unveiled, each telling the story of a piece of fabric or embroidery which has special meaning to its maker. One by one, participants remove the red cloth that covers their creation to reveal the story beneath.

Kathleen has chosen the blue and gold ribbon from which hangs the valour medal awarded to her grandfather in the First World War. She inherited it when he died and keeps it in her handbag as a talisman to protect her against her own uncertain courage. Flora is wearing the 200-year-old skirt she inherited, woven and worn by one of her crofting ancestors, before her family were forced off the land at the time of the Highland clearances in the eighteenth century. She has traced their exodus to America, the waves of the Atlantic Ocean embroidered with the Gaelic words for loss. Eve holds up a pair of child's denim dungarees that she re-fashioned in the 1960s from her own pair of jeans. They were made for her toddler son, a task of thrift when she was a young mother struggling to make ends meet. He is pictured on her panel as a child and again fifty years on, surrounded by replicas of the pattern pieces she used, made ghostly in net fabric.

The originators of the final panel, Jim and Bill, cannot be here to unveil their creation. Jim died just two weeks ago at the age of eighty-seven and Bill, now ninety-six, is in hospital after a fall. The young community worker who brought them together, Ryan Mackay, will be their voice to tell us their story. He talks about their experience of growing old, of how in widowhood both men became socially isolated. Jim, in his later years, had been the main carer for his wife until her death. Looking after her had meant relinquishing the social activities and network of friends they had enjoyed over the years. He was devastated by her death and hadn't the spirit to pick up the pieces of his old life. Instead, he got stuck in loneliness. Bill, living alone with his family at a distance, had lost his social confidence bit by bit, until he found himself marooned, cut off from the community life. They had both become members of the Older Men's Health and Well-Being Group run by the Pilmeny Development Project (PDP), a community support organisation based in Leith, a dockland area of Edinburgh just five minutes from the city centre. When the PDP discovered that Leith had the highest suicide rate of men over the age of seventy-five in the Lothian region, it decided it had to find a way to mitigate the social isolation of its ageing male population.

The Older Men's Health and Well-Being Group became a weekly fixture for Jim and Bill. Programmed by the group itself, it ran a range of activities: trips out, quizzes, classes in simple cookery, Desert Island Discs events to which members brought along their eight favourite pieces of music and talked about their lives. Jim, still driving, had offered to collect Bill, who no longer drove, and drop him back home after the group's sessions. They became friends. They came not just to the Older Men's Health and Well-Being Group, but also joined PDP's New Spin inter-generational group, at which teenagers and older residents got together on Friday afternoons to have Lego challenges, play dominos and photograph the local area. When Ryan, then on a student placement, came to run an Anti-Sectarianism Project, Jim and Bill signed up. It turned out that they came from what had once been opposing religions: Jim a Catholic and Bill a Protestant.

It was Bill's story about his mother that had made Ryan suggest they get involved with Material Matters. She had been an ardent follower of John Cormack, the leader of the Scottish Protestant Action Group, which during the 1930s had incited violent riots against Catholics in Scotland's main cities. One of his sharpest memories had been the sash she wore to attend Cormack's meetings and demonstrations. This had cost her ten shillings, an extortionate amount of money in the days when, with the family living in near poverty, ten shillings, as Bill said, 'would have bought a whole lot of stuff.' A sash remembered so acutely because of the family sacrifice it represented.

Jim had his own story, of a sister who, with her sweetheart soldier about to go to war, had agreed to marry him quickly in the Registry Office. When their local priest discovered she had married outside of the church, he excommunicated her. Jim's mother was so outraged by the priest's lack of compassion that she removed them all from the church. Jim was forced to leave his local Catholic Primary School and was sent to the Protestant School down the road. There, he said, he was not shunned, but rather 'set aside.' Like Bill, he came from poverty, recalling having to carry the load of family washing for his mother to the communal wash house each week and, one winter's morning, barefoot and hungry, fainting on the roadside.

The men shared a history of early deprivation, service in the Second World War – Jim to the Air Force, Bill to the Navy – and a return to a world which had little opportunity for either of them. Jim took himself off to Canada for a while but, unable to settle, came back home. Bill found work building the Pitlochry Hydroelectric Dam in Perthshire: two years of sleeping rough in tents with thousands of other men. But somehow they made it through, married, had families, survived, grew old.

They had lived long enough to see religious prejudice if not eradicated, at least no longer a barrier to friendship. This is what they chose to depict on their panel: how divided lives, such as theirs had been in their youth, could come together later in mutual support. They titled their panel IDENTITY. One half had its cream background flecked in green thread, the Catholic colour. It contained images of the Catholic faith, Jim when he was young and Jim and his wife. The other half was flecked in the orange of Protestantism and showed Bill as a young naval serviceman. There was a replica of a poster of John Cormack, his fist raised against Popery. The title was embroidered in the two colours to symbolise a merging, faiths reconciled, sectarianism diminished. At the bottom was a photograph of the two friends sitting side by side, reproduced on fabric. It had been taken by me at one of the early Material Matters workshops. Jim is leaning forward on his stick enthusiastically, Bill is settled back in his chair, more considered, sporting a crisp shirt and well-ironed jumper. Since Material Matters was unveiled, Bill, too, has died.

With the panels unveiled, I invited the audience to tell their own stories of textiles they cherished. People had brought samplers and tray cloths, old dolls and embroidered jeans. Anne Munro of PDP had brought a patchwork panel with eight squares, each depicting a different scene of community life in Leith from thirty years before. I had been involved in its making as a follow-on from a project I did in Leith, a banner that had been my first community commission when I returned to Scotland in 1985.

The Pilmeny Development Project in Leith was set up in 1979 and, during the last thirty years, has remained true to its founding principle of helping local people identify and resolve problems that limit their wellbeing, issues common to many urban neighbourhoods in the western world: inadequate housing, the vulnerability of the elderly, cultural exclusion of immigrants, inter-generational distrust and community stress played out in drug or domestic abuse. These are issues that affect how people feel about themselves, their neighbours and their community. In the forty years since its inception, the PDP has spent its hard-won resources on servicing its community rather than expanding or enriching its own administrative base. It still operates from a small office in Buchanan Street and a one-room drop-in centre a few doors down, which acts as a social hub, meeting room and workshop. It still has Anne Munro, the original community worker, who was only twenty-two when she joined in 1979, now supported by a part-time youth worker, bookkeeper and administrator. It was Anne who helped to organise my first community textile project in Scotland in 1985, a banner for the Buchanan Street Housing Association.

Anne has witnessed the changing fate of Leith over the last three decades, a change in community fortune experienced by working-class inner-city areas throughout the industrialised world. She took up her post the same year that Britain voted in a Conservative government with Margaret Thatcher as its first female Prime Minister. For the next eighteen years, Conservative policies encouraged wealth creation at the expense of those unable to invest in upwardly mobile ambition. The government had inherited rising inflation from a Labour administration and came to power when the world's economy was shifting on its axis. Western manufacturing companies and heavy industries were discovering more profitable enterprise in the east. New technology was speeding up production and drastically reducing workforces. Unemployment in Britain escalated. By 1983 there were over three million people in Britain without jobs.

Young people who had grown up expecting to follow their parents into local work – into the factories and industries which, while low-paid, offered stability – were hit particularly hard. These young people emerged from education into a decimated job market, bereft of opportunity. Without the means to live independent lives within their community or leave, many young people in Leith turned to the salve of heroin, which was readily available through local dockyard imports from Pakistan. Drugs offered an alternative escape route. The experiences of Leith's young unemployed are forever fixed in celluloid in the film adaptation of Irvine Welsh's *Trainspotting*, which used Leith as its backdrop and its young people as its cast of characters to tell a story of nihilistic addiction. To Anne it seemed extraordinary that just five minutes away from the historic commercial honeytrap of Edinburgh's city centre, its young people were living such desperate lives. With no jobs, no money and no sense of their own worth they were roaming the streets, dicing with death on demolition sites, taking whatever drugs they could muster to escape their present and be somewhere else for a brief respite.

But local events such as gala days, street festivals, talent competitions, persisted. Anne remembers a local act that, for her, summed up Leith in those days. He called himself the Burning Buddhist: a hopeless fire-eater who nonetheless was determined to entertain, he walked on burning coals and burnt his feet, he ate fire and torched his mouth. It was, she said, an act of not simple bravado but visible defiance. He seemed to be a symbol of Leith itself.

There were other pressures on the community. Historically, Leith had always been a place of varied cultures. Employment in its docklands had ensured a continuing cultural mix of residents who shared the same working-class experiences, belonged to the same unions, had a similar pattern of working shifts and leisure time. But when the docks closed in 1981 there was no work to share. Immigration continued, largely from Asia, but for these newcomers there was no work-based socialising to ease integration. Instead they became marooned in separate cultures. The social restrictions on Asian women exacerbated their isolation. The community was in danger of becoming fragmented.

It was in housing that the deprivation in Leith was most keenly felt. A programme of demolition of some of the older council housing – the densely populated tenement blocks – led to a rise in homelessness and the dislocation of families. Many of the tenements that remained were unfit for modern living: they were dilapidated, cramped, with outside toilets, no hot water, most without baths or showers. In the Lorne area of Leith, where Buchanan Street is sited, things came to a head in 1979, the year Anne took up her post and Thatcher came to power. For years, the council had been trying to shore up the foundations of its housing stock, foundations that, in the nineteenth century, had been built over streams and, during the Second World War, dug out to create air-raid shelters. But on New Year's Eve in 1979, a stairwell in 2 Buchanan Street crumbled away and the building collapsed. Two streets were certified as unstable, the families living in them evacuated, their homes – 1,000 in all – scheduled for demolition. Overnight, the PDP had queues of people at their door in need of help, a bed for the night, redress from the council, rescue from the loan sharks with whom they had become embroiled to keep the rent paid on time. Anne says that many of the older residents died within six months of their evacuation, and younger residents simply left the area. It was clear how quickly a tight-knit community can become fragmented, the speed at which its emotional investment in the area can falter and family-based infrastructures can break apart. The condemned housing site remained derelict as the council debated its options. It was repossessed by local youth who used it as a drug-making factory.

In the early 1980s, the debris was finally cleared, by which time the Buchanan Street Housing Association had been set up to campaign for redevelopment under community control. It was not interested in a home-for-home reinstatement. It wanted to create housing that was designed to reflect the reality of Leith's changing community, where more people needed a supportive environment. Their vision was to create a housing complex that maintained social diversity in dwellings customised for independent living inclusive of the elderly, disabled and the most vulnerable in their community; a balanced mixture of family provision, sheltered and supportive housing and a women's refuge. The Pilmeny Development Project's offices sat across the road from the gap site. It was the natural support agency in the local campaign for self-improvement.

It wasn't Anne Munro who commissioned me to make a banner in 1985 but the Buchanan Street Housing Association, who thought a banner would be a useful campaigning tool. It was Anne, however, as the PDP's community worker, who was tasked with setting up the banner-making workshops. She remembers being highly sceptical about the project, unconvinced of the usefulness of sewing a banner when there were more urgent tasks: a council to lobby, reports to be written, finance to raise. She was dubious about what level of participation it would attract. Nonetheless, despite her misgivings, she advertised the workshops, encouraged people to come, cleared workshop space in the centre and brought in tea and coffee. When people did come, a motley group of pensioners, unemployed young, local activists and curious residents, Anne got stuck in. While claiming no artistic skills and little interest in needlework, she nonetheless worked alongside us to make a banner that would represent the community-led housing association.

The banner illustrated the hoped-for modernised homes on a satin backdrop of appliquéd low-rise housing traced out by a seventeen-year-old lad using my overhead projector, the projected image of hoped-for homes etching his body in an architectural vision of light-filling windows and own-front-doors that would be his future. I arranged for a photograph to be taken of the core of campaigners as a template for a group portrait to be archived in fabric and stitched onto the banner. People arrived in an array of outfits – some even came in their best formal hats. One woman brought her cat, insisting on its inclusion. The group set to work replicating themselves in cloth, grumbling over the fiddle of it.

Gladys, a formidable presence, exempted herself from the sewing altogether, and instead thumped out Second World War ditties on an old piano to keep up morale. One by one, members of the association and its community were stitched together, standing proudly in front of their proposed homes. We appliquéd 'Buchanan Street Housing Association' in large red letters on an arching scroll and a strap-line, 'Living for the Future', in gold on black satin. We sewed the housing plans in black thread on the cotton pavement upon which the group stood, and we decided to leave a space blank on the banner, ready for the time when – if – the battle was won.

The project changed Anne's view of how the arts could add value to a community endeavour. It had rekindled enthusiasm in what had become a hard-pressed and demoralised campaign, at a time when progress was achingly slow. It provided a different focus, revitalising diminished energies in something achievable and it allowed a moment to rest and review, to re-gather impetus in a project that was sociable and entertaining. Most significantly of all, it enabled the group to make themselves and their ambition more tangible, sewn together on the banner in front of the homes they longed for. It bolstered media interest. Residents unfurled their banner on the steps of the council chambers before important decisions were made, took it to community meetings, hung it up in the PDP window. They used it as an emphatic declaration of community solidarity and local need to further their cause.

Five years later, I went back to Buchanan Street to record the moment when Edinburgh's Lady Provost presented the housing association with the title deeds to what was now community land, and to what was to be the largest new-build in Scotland at the time. The battle had been won. The banner, now complete with its final scene of triumph, was transformed into a testament of community resolve. It marked the long hard journey from local loss to neighbourhood gain.

In the process of working on the Leith banner, Anne and I discovered that we shared the same community values even though we had worked in different spheres, Anne in community work and myself in community arts. For both of us, our mindset and belief in the value of community involvement had been forged by the student unrest of the 1960s and community involvement in the 70s. Anne was the first of her family to access further education. She was training to be a teacher when a student placement in a community centre in Dundee opened her eyes to what poverty could inflict on a community and how community education could make a difference to its fate. A second placement that sought to give purpose to young people far from home or lost in addiction convinced her of the urgent need to keep young people connected to local life. She abandoned her teaching career and pushed at the door of community and youth provision. The Pilmeny Development Project was the first door to open.

I was shaped, like Anne, by campus politics. My route into community arts was via community theatre and local art centres. By the late 1970s, community arts was a growing international movement aimed at providing marginalised communities with creative resources such as artists, art centres, activities and projects, to foster local participation and self-expression through the arts. The social focus differed from country to country. In Australia, the Australia Arts Council created the Arts and Working Life programme to provide artists' residencies in working-class workplaces and encourage the co-production, between artists and communities, of artefacts and exhibitions that reflected a wide diversity of local lives. Banners, large-scale textiles and printed fabric all featured strongly in the art that emerged. In France, the emphasis was on salvaging and rebuilding community identities dislocated by German occupation in the Second World War. Projects were devised to restore a more positive community memory that was celebratory, playful,

respectful of past traditions and artisanal skills. In Italy, anima-
tors in the city called Red Bologna, because of its left-wing
governance and the colour of its buildings and surrounding
hills, prioritised young people and devised a programme of
public artworks, youth-centre provision and workshops in craft
skills to foster a recognition of young people as a resource rather
than a problem, and to give their creativity greater visibility. In
Britain, the agenda was more political. Artists set out to challenge the elitist stronghold of the arts establishment, which
viewed arts institutions and galleries as the only valid and
fundable promoters of art. They created alternative approaches
to local arts development through which artists and community
members could be equal collaborators in the creation of new
neighbourhood-based artworks where the divisions between art
forms and between amateur and professional works were
purposefully blurred.

For the community artists in Britain, it was the process that
was key. Therein lay the politics. While the end product was
important, it was the process of making and exhibiting a creation, and the local response to the artwork or performance, that
were often prioritised. The sharing of the practical tasks like
securing funding, identifying and negotiating the use of unusual
locations, generating participation and promoting events, were
also essential components, vital in the skilling-up of communities to enable them to organise future activities and projects
independent of artists' involvement. It required them to create
art that was authentically authored by community in its design,
purpose, value and impact. We called it cultural democracy: art
shaped by the needs and concerns of local people that serviced
the underprivileged, marginalised and unheard. Critics damned
it as another form of social work; as 'poor art for poor people'.
But it pulled me in.

While the banner for the Buchanan Street Housing Association
had been made in just a few sessions, they were enough to

convince Anne that sewing had something useful to offer Leith's beleaguered community. She decided to organise a more ambitious, longer-term project, something that could keep residents in touch with each other in a creative and sustained way. She called it *Pictures of Leith*, and what she had in mind was a sewn portrait of the neighbourhood, caught at a moment of change. It was its pilot panel she had brought to the launch of Material Matters; the end product was to emerge as a much more eclectic and large-scale affair, driven by the surprising enthusiasm of disparate individuals and groups eager to get involved. By the end, over 300 people contributed to what became a thirty-foot long triptych illustrating local life: Leith's past, present and future, public events and personal memories.

One summer's evening in 2018, Anne and I got together to revisit Pictures of Leith thirty years on. I took along a bottle of Prosecco to aid recall. Anne, much more sensibly, gathered together some photographs, reports and made an audio file of the soundtrack to its unveiling, a soundtrack I had totally forgotten about. She pulled out a photograph of an early workshop in the Buchanan Street centre. There is Gladys, the woman who had played patriotic tunes on the piano during the making of the Buchanan Street Housing Association banner and who, despite her avowals never to sew, did become involved in Pictures of Leith, helping to reconstruct her own community in fabric and thread, muttering criticisms and judgements as she did so. Gladys had been widowed when she was young, left with a family and a household to maintain on native wit alone. She was a woman with no time for nonsense and always ready with an opinion or six, but she was a stalwart in community terms and a fierce defender of local action. Her friend Chrissie is also in the photograph. Her husband had been killed in the Second World War and she, like Gladys, had improvised ways to thwart the threat of poverty. Unlike Gladys, Chrissie was a sociable woman and kept all those around her close. At the Pictures of

Leith workshops she would scurry around sweeping up the debris of creativity, clearing space, clattering in the kitchen to set up another round of tea. She was the one who would bring in the home-made shortbread, the first to come and the last to leave. Nellie – the quiet one – sits beside them in the picture, alongside Rita, who always protested her inability to sew anything well, but would stow away work-in-progress in the depths of her handbag and return it the following week, not only beautifully stitched but also embellished with her own small touches of creative flair. These women were the core of the Pictures of Leith project.

So many different people had a story to tell or a portrait to share: the girls who worked in the chemists, the young mums campaigning for a playpark, the Asian Women's Aid centre. And it wasn't just women who sewed. The local bin men, men from the art club, the brothers who ran the fishmongers, members of the boys' club and the boxing club, they all stitched a piece of their lives to go on the wall hanging. Anne and I sifted through the photographs, remembering local characters, struggling to recall names: Walter, the young unemployed man who came to offer his services as a photographer and stayed on to sew; Mike, the local bin man who became so enthused by the project he self-styled himself as its promoter and convinced others on his rounds to get involved; Mary, a stiff and formal woman who came regularly to the workshops but rarely spoke, applying her expert sewing skills to any task at hand; and there was the young lad whose name we have forgotten who hunted down scraps of leather to intricately fashion the bridle and reins of a fabric horse that represented the one that had once graced local gala days. Anne brought out a list of the panels, nearly 100, made by individuals and 60 local groups. There, among the more predictable images of local landmarks and historic events are more personal pictures: Friend of Alex, Sylvia at Work, Snooker Player, My Wedding.

Anne and I debated what the trigger had been to encourage such enthusiastic and wide-ranging participation from people of all ages, backgrounds, cultures and interests, coming together to create a collective portrait of their neighbourhood. She thinks it was that the project offered not just an alternative, but also a striking contrast to people's everyday lives. It was palpably inclusive, fun and creative, and it provided the opportunity to be active rather than passive, to give rather than receive, which, in a community largely dependent on social benefits, restored dignity and self-esteem. People contributed images that, cumulatively, portrayed their community as having more energy than was usually reported by consultants, councillors and the media. This was not a documentary of a community tainted by the ills of poverty, but a vivid portrait of a place with an interesting history and a dynamic and diverse community life. It was an assertion of local pride. Those involved – no matter their story – shared the same inheritance of a place. The project strengthened their sense of belonging together, of being linked not just by geography but by spirit.

That desire to literally materialise their community led participants to seek out ways of being specific to the place and their experience of it. The exact nature of the fabric, of texture, gained importance: the blue nylon of the overalls of the girls who worked at the chemists; the old-fashioned sprig of a mother's wrap-around apron; the heavy tweed of an old woman's coat as she balanced a tray of fish and chips in the community café; the shiny gleam of a boxer's shorts, all sourced with careful attention to authenticity. Participants were determined to capture the precise detail of what they saw around them: the fish in the fishmonger's window had to have embroidered green parsley strewn across it; the wheels of a new pram had to sport bright silver wheels; a chimney needed smoke; a balloon a tiny gleam of light; the small sensory thrills people noticed in their everyday lives had to be present.

When all the separate parts were finished participants were invited to come and lay their picture wherever they wanted on the blue backcloth donated by the local fabric shop. An eclectic collage of personal and local stories began to emerge on the cloth, images jostling together in neither chronological nor creative order. The logos of local groups, the facades of buildings, were punctuated with the intimacy of personal imagery, of local jokes and characters, animating the wall hanging with wry humour and human poignancy, with insight and care. Nothing that anyone had sewn was discarded, none of their stitching unpicked to make it neater. The finished work was an unedited, sometimes raw, expression of the people of Leith. And with that came a vibrancy that no artist could ever replicate. The middle section of the hanging spelled out L.E.I.T.H. in three-feet high lettering, the 'L' made by Leith's oldest residents in a sepia image from their childhood, and the 'H' by its youngest in a riotous assembly of their ideas for the future garnished in iridescent plastics and sequins. I gathered up the three separate panels of the wall hanging, weighted now by its sewn stories and, with my sewing machine, pushed on through image after image to piece together a local sense of identity.

The Prosecco finished, Anne put on the soundtrack made for the Pictures of Leith's launch. We sat together on the sofa as once-familiar voices told us its story. It began with a group of youngsters chanting a well-known rhyme:

> Everywhere we go-oo, everywhere we go-oo
> People always ask us, people always ask us
> Where do you come fae? Where do you come fae?
> We come fae Leith. We come fae Leith.
> If you cannae hear us. We'll shout a wee bit louder.

Mike, the bin man, next takes up the narration, his voice a touch plummier than usual: 'Like everywhere else Leith is changing. It is a close community, proud of its past, and the memories of its people are important to its history. It's not just a question of being nostalgic. Memories of a livelier past give the people of Leith the optimism to fight for a better future.'

The voices of participants fill the room, talking proudly of their area and what they had sewed in the project. The soundtrack ends in a rap, composed and spoken by Leith's young unemployed, telling of a Leith that offers them little hope. Their words are interspersed with the cut-glass tones of the prime minister of the time, Margaret Thatcher, voicing in repetitive phrasing her uncompromising stand: 'If a man will not work, he will not eat . . . If a man will not work, he cannot eat. Create the necessary wealth . . . create the necessary wealth'.

The wall hanging was unveiled in the local community centre on an evening that felt like a family party, with contributors, relatives and neighbours crowding around it to point out what they had sewn and to discover what others had made. It stayed on display in the community centre for a while before being relocated to the local library, where it remained for the next thirty years.

Anne and I moved on to coffee. I asked her if she thought there was any specific advantage to Pictures of Leith being a sewing project, or would the enthusiasm, the level of involvement, the impact have been the same for a project in another art form, such as a community drama, a photographic exhibition or a street mural? Anne deliberated before she replied. She said that for vulnerable people, the elderly, those on medication, people dealing with a high level of stress in their daily lives, sewing on Pictures of Leith was perhaps more accessible than other kinds of arts projects. It didn't demand a high level of energy. It was sedentary, quiet and manageable for most. People didn't need to talk about themselves; their sewing was the main topic of conversation. They could retain their privacy and still be involved in a public project. Being shy, slow, hesitant in English weren't barriers to inclusion. Not only that, but in a sewing project, elderly women and women from different ethnic backgrounds, women who knew how to sew, were vital assets. Their knowledge of needlework was seized upon gratefully by others who lacked the skill and needed help. These women discovered a community value that boosted their social confidence and connected them, some for first time, to a community they thought had no time for them. There was also something unique in sewing together, about disparate members of the community sitting around the same table, sharing scissors, pooling resources, witnessing each others' efforts. It created a physical proximity that generated good-will and camaraderie in an atmosphere of mutual support, of affection even.

For many of these people, who lived in bleak surroundings, the sensuality of handling colour and varying textures of cloth was soothing. It was pleasurable to smooth out the creases in silk, to untangle a rainbow of embroidery threads, to dip into the rag bag of remnants and search out the exact fabric to use for the bricks of a building or the sails of a ship.

Anne reminded me that, as the number of participants grew, we had to abandon the cramped centre in Buchanan Street and move into the community centre café in the local shopping mall. There the project took on another dimension. People with unstable lives who couldn't have committed themselves to regular sessions could now join in more easily, for a little while. Young mothers with babies in pushchairs, workers on night-shift, children after school curious as to what the hive of activity was in the corner of the café, stayed for an hour or two to contribute. Sometimes they just picked up pins, told their own story, or volunteered to take something away to finish at home, but they all helped in some way. The workshops in the community café gave the project public visibility, and sewers were buoyed up by local interest and admiration. Their loyalty to, and pride in, the project grew exponentially. Even then, Anne didn't underestimate how difficult it was for some to become involved. To step out of their comfort zone, to cross the threshold of their houses and present themselves to a group of strangers was challenging. But many did. They bridged the gap between isolation and involvement because, Anne thinks, the sight of such a mixture of people, of different ages, genders, backgrounds and cultures, sewing companionably was reassuring. It signalled an open door.

When residents in disadvantaged areas have few chances to say who they are, the opportunity to create a self-portrait, to convey what is common among them, is very seductive. Scrutinised as subjects of consultancies and government policies, their problems audited, their deprivation inventoried, what they can offer individually and collectively is often overlooked. A community arts project such as Pictures of Leith can provide a medium through which local people can display imagination, skill and knowledge. For the residents of Leith the project was, at a time of change, a vital affirmation of neighbourhood identity and cohesion.

There have been significant changes in Leith over the past thirty years. The derelict docklands have been transformed into a modern riverscape of smart apartments and expensive restaurants to service a new professional populace and the employees of the Scottish government, whose headquarters stretches in glistening steel and glass along the waterfront. Leith's main street, Leith Walk, seems the same, even though the Asian fabric shops of my memory have changed ownership and are now Polish-run enterprises offering dress alteration services, and the greasy cafes have become trendy eateries serving Portuguese custard tarts. But gentrification is polarising the community and creating a widening chasm between rich and poor, and the community is becoming imbalanced. Property developers are buying up shop units and tracts of land to build student accommodation. What were once family homes are being snapped up to turn into Airbnb lets. In some blocks, a solitary pensioner is the only permanent resident; all the others are just passing through. With an increasingly transient population, it is more and more difficult to anchor emotional investment. In the new flats at Ocean Terminal, each floor has a locked door to keep residents safe; but this also discourages neighbourly interaction. Anne tells me that Leith is the most densely populated community in Scotland, with 26,000 people living within 200 yards of each other, but now a Michelin-starred restaurant shares the same stairwell as a family supported by the local food bank. Undoubtedly regeneration has brought benefits. The streets are cleaner, the housing stock upgraded, the area better cared for and more prosperous, but the young people who were born here can't afford to stay and its elderly don't want to leave. Generations are being separated and the continuum of community life and memory is being disrupted. With community facilities closing, replaced by more up-market cultural venues, there are fewer places for a mixture of residents to be together. The community is being culturally displaced from its own neighbourhood. Locals have little part to play in Leith's regeneration. And, Anne says, if the main players, those who make Leith special – its campaigners, the remnants of its working class, the immigrants who brought its unique character – disappear, then Leith's unique identity will be lost forever.

That identity is preserved, however, on the Pictures of Leith wall hanging. And other communities have realised their own stories, characters and spirit in many local textile projects throughout Britain and those I have been involved with – not least in a project I devised for Glasgow's Year as European City of Culture in 1990, called Keeping Glasgow in Stitches, for which 600 people made twelve fifteen-feet long banners that captured the history, personality, politics and popular culture of their city. It was made in collaboration with Glasgow Museums and, unlike Pictures of Leith, its ownership fell to the city authorities rather than its community. After its launch and three years of touring – when it was exhibited elsewhere in Scotland, in Milan, Rostov-on-Don in Russia and Cyprus – it was folded away and, despite requests that it be put back on public view, it has only been seen once in the last 25 years. It was relegated to being an historical object, with the museum as the guardian of its heritage. But its real heritage is the group of women who met during its making, who continued to contribute to community textile projects in the city as the Glasgow Banner Group, and who still meet every month. For them, their part in the creation of Keeping Glasgow in Stitches was their heirloom to their city, the giving of their time and talent, to ensure a lasting document was made that encapsulated the place they belonged to. And they lament its loss as an alternative public landmark of community life.

Community sewing projects have emotional and metaphorical currency. Much like the Chinese and Japanese idea of creating protective textiles by joining up donated cloth or collecting stitches from many different people, so community textiles are imbued with the spirits of the disparate people who create them, witnessed by others, as unique investments in, and registers of, community worth.

12

Place

One winter in 1994, the singer and story gatherer Alison McMorland travelled to Mull (the second largest island of the Inner Hebrides, off the west coast of Scotland) to record the memories of its oldest residents, now clustered in a care home. Mull is a place of ancient settlement, evidenced by the ruins of brochs (Iron Age towers), stone circles, standing stones and burial cairns. It is close to where Christianity began in Britain with the coming of St Columba, the Irish missionary, in AD 563 to establish his monastery on the nearby island of Iona. A Gaelic kingdom in the sixth century, a Viking stronghold by the ninth, Mull's islanders survived by fishing and farming until, in the eighteenth and nineteenth century, they fell victim to the programme of Highland clearances, when communities were evicted from their crofts and forced off their land to make way for sheep. By the early twentieth century, Mull's population had fallen from 10,000 to 3,000. There were more sheep than people. Tourism saved it from economic collapse. Its deep valleys, long, shimmering lochs, white beaches, profusion of native and naturalised plants, have made it a haven for nature-lovers. Geologists come to study its 20 million-year-old rocks, glaciers and basalt cliffs. Bird watchers visit, hoping for a glimpse of the elusive white-tailed eagle.

Alison collected the stories of Mull's oldest islanders as the wellspring of a community textile. They shared with her their tales of mischief and misadventure and rekindled their sense of community worth as postmistress, ploughman and piper. They spoke of the daily grind of their lives, hardship punctuated by harvests and holidays, and brought their past back into focus, recalling what they held dear.

Their stories were given to the Edinburgh-based artist Kate Downie, whose paintings chart what land clings on to and what it discards, its blight and its blossoming. Kate transformed the elderly voices into images with an artist's sleight of hand, collaging fragments of memory in a sweep of brushstrokes: the slouch of an oil cloth on a kitchen table; the shafts of summer barley bundled in a field; a huddle of sheep in a drift of snow.

Hebridean spinner, weaver and dyer Flora McDonald then worked with local school children to transpose Kate's design into wool and fabric dyed by the flora of Mull. They scavenged the moors and shorelines, the meadows and rock crags to prise the island's colour palette from its natural home. They picked broom blossom and stripped nettles of their jags. They hunted out creviced star flowers and snipped fans of ferns laid low by winter. As the colours of Mull oozed from flower and leaf through chopping, crushing, boiling and simmering, Flora named the rainbow carpet that lay beneath the children's feet: yellow pimpernel, ragged robin, oceanic lichen, wood sorrel, meadow sweet. Their pigments had yielded a rag bag of home.

The dyed cloth, wool and thread were sent to Glasgow, where experienced stitchers pieced back together the lives of Hettie the postmistress and Donald the piper and the rest: stories tinted in the flowers of their youth. The wall hanging returned to Mull, a map of sorts, charting an island's landscape through its human history, telling tales of a lived land in the hues of natural materiality. Measuring over four feet wide and three feet high, the wall hanging is redolent with different textures: the linen weave of an apron, the straw residue of a harvested field realised in long sticks of thick cotton thread. Thistles are tufted in purple wool, the thatch pattern on a cottage roof rendered in quilting and the hills patchworked in a medley of fabrics to capture the diverse colours of heather, gorse and bracken. There are a pair of kilt socks hanging on a washing line, knitted in precise miniature detail, and a vegetable patch planted with tidy rows of three-dimensional embroidered cabbages shaded in the greens of Mull's natural world.

Dyeing is one of the most ancient crafts. Archaeologists have unearthed Neolithic scraps of fabric, colour-clung despite thousands of years spent lingering deep in the earth. Until the invention of aniline dyes in 1856, all the colours for cloth and thread were coaxed from nature. It was not only their hue that was harvested; many of the plants used for dyes were chosen for their additional medicinal and spiritual qualities. The deep red extracted from pomegranates provided a remedy for dysentery as well as being a talisman for fertility; the blue of indigo controlled bleeding and encouraged intuition; the bright yellow of turmeric was an antiseptic and spiritual purifier. Each colour was imbued with the earth's literal and symbolic bounty.

We call the cloth we embroider on the 'ground' and the thread that travels through it makes stitches like footprints, leaving its mark as the needle pushes on from one place to the next. Much traditional embroidery features images of the sun, water, plants, trees, the basic elements of survival: nature gathered into needlework to snare its energy and reflect its spirit. The names of embroidery stitches often honour the natural world, such as seed stitch, fern stitch, coral stitch, feather stitch, cloud filling stitch, star stitch. Others register their source: Algerian eye stitch, Armenian cross stitch, Antwerp edging stitch, Basque knot, Berwick stitch, Berlin plush stitch, Bokhara couching, Ceylon stitch, Croatian stitch, Dutch double cross stitch; cities and nations all mapping their claim on needlework.

Given such a close association between embroidery and the land, it is surprising that so few embroidered maps exist. But when, in the last half of the eighteenth century, girls began to access a more academic education in both Europe and America and geography became an integral part of their curriculum, from 1770 onwards, school-stitched maps in the form of samplers gained popularity. Early map samplers delineated both terrestrial and celestial worlds. Most were copied from printed maps, drawn free-hand on cloth by teachers or by schoolgirls using a pantograph. Publishers began to issue maps printed on cloth, ready for an embroiderer's hand. One of the first was produced by Laurie and Whittle of Fleet Street in London in 1797. It proclaimed in elaborate font: 'A New Map of Scotland for Ladies Needle Work'. In 1798 the same company published a 'Map of the World for Ladies Needle Work and Young Students in Geography.'

In 1790, an anonymous stitcher decided to capture Arnold's Farm in Essex in mathematical and agricultural precision. In the map's cartouche, (the decorative heading that contains the map's title and date) a red-tiled farmhouse has been embroidered by the banks of a flowing river, guarded on each side by family pets languishing on tasselled velvet cushions. Scatters of flowers and foraging birds decorate the cloth. But the real artistry lies in its detailed mapping of the farmland, with each plot precisely demarcated and the acreage of each field, mead and wood faithfully noted. Every stretch of soil is named – gravel pit field, eleven-acre piece, rook tree mead, little moor, upper gate field – and the schedule of their rotation listed. It is an exquisite piece of agricultural history sewn by someone who cared enough to mark it down in stitches. Perhaps this sampler marked a new beginning, embroidered to celebrate a first harvest and the promise of bountiful yields in the years ahead.

Elizabeth Snitch embroidered her Map of the County of Bedford Divided into its Hundreds in 1779 when she was twelve. Her father was a respected butcher and church warden in the Southhill village in Bedfordshire. Born the eldest of four children, she lost two brothers and her mother before she was eight years old. Her father remarried but three of her five half-brothers died in infancy. Her family was connected to the Dilly brothers, who were book and map publishers in London. Elizabeth's map has been traced back to a 1759 map of Bedfordshire produced by Emanuel Bowen, an eighteenth-century print seller known for adding extensive notes and footnotes. Elizabeth has made a faithful copy, replicating his enumeration of houses, rectories, vicarages, parishes, members of parliament, the land acreage and charting the time and distance in minutes from London. The outline of the country is sewn in red silk chenille thread, a form of thick tufted yarn, which provides a strong outline for her inner boundaries that are traced in finer yellow embroidery. Main roads are marked in red thread and the map itself is crammed with the names of villages and churches, market towns, even with market days registered in miniscule black stitchery, accompanied with symbols – tiny spired yellow buildings for churches, a red cross for modern charity schools – and outside of her bordered county the margins of the map are crammed with sewn explanations and descriptions. Her cartouche, on the map's top right is encircled in green thread and wreathed in leaves and flowers. She has a red compass rose at the bottom beside her ruled stitched scale and, at the bottom left in tiny lettering she has signed it 'Eliz[th] Snitch 1779'.

This was an age when there was a growing appetite for lists, for quantitative rather than qualitative data, for precise details of size and scale. It is unsurprising, therefore, that geography was the first science to be included in the schoolgirl curriculum. Geography had the advantage of accumulating facts. It encompassed other kinds of learning: of mathematics, surveying, drawing, anthropology and political economy. At a time of the expansion of the British Empire, mass migration to the American Colonies and dare-devil expeditions to far-flung lands, people's eyes became more keenly fixed on distance. Wars and revolutions were recalibrating the global balance of political and economic power. The educated classes in Europe and the Americas, influenced by the seventeenth and eighteenth-century philosophers of The Enlightenment, who had encouraged the development of intellectual thought and scientific study, began to favour a more extensive academic education for girls as well as boys. There was a major shift in girls' education from the tutelage of mothers and governesses, which focussed on accomplishments such as handwriting, singing, dancing and drawing, to the more formal curriculums of boarding schools and ladies' academies. Girls moved from their homes to schools beyond the village or outside the town gaining greater access to the wider world. Their horizons broadened, physically and socially, through a progressive education in which geography was key.

In America, geography was of even greater importance than in Britain or Europe. This was a country which in 1776 declared its independence from the British Empire and freed itself from colonisation. Now it was forging its own physical, societal and political identity, enshrined in its Bill of Rights in 1791. Embroidery was to play a significant role in recording its altered consciousness. The American geographer Judith Tyner has written a comprehensive and fascinating study of the development of American embroidered geography. Her book *Stitching Up the World* is written with the scientific rigour of a practised geographer and the humanity of a woman whose ancestry is traced in needlework. It documents the part played by schoolgirl cartographers in mapping their new world.

Until independence, education in the United States was laissez-faire. Voluntary, free from federal intervention, education for the most part was left to the guidance of different religious faiths. In 1779 in Virginia the More General Diffusion of Knowledge Bill was adopted. This marked a change in thinking. The bill advocated not just the principle of education for the majority, but also included women in its ambition. Its intention was not gender equality, but rather the better preparation of women to nurture their future children as responsible citizens. The first female academies were founded in the 1790s. Catharine Beecher (sister of Harriet Beecher Stowe, author of *Uncle Tom's Cabin*) was an early pioneer of women's education and in 1821 established the New York Female Seminary. Other academies followed in quick succession. It became a movement to prepare middle and upper-class white girls for their role as the guiding lights for the first American generation to inherit the nation's emerging democracy. Women were to be the moral core of the new nation. The concept was manifested in a different curriculum for women in America from that in Britain. There was to be less emphasis on the niceties and superfluities of drawing-room accomplishments like playing a musical instrument, singing, learning French, and more attention paid to practical skills, such as the keeping of accounts, managing a workforce and maintaining efficiency in family affairs when men were called away. Girls were tasked with developing an emotional attachment in their children to their state and their nation as a way to strengthen national loyalty and embed patriotic pride. This then was the climate in which girls embarked on their further education, not as a route to individual gain but as a service to their country. Through education, girls were invited to have a place in the civic evolution of their country, and it was through embroidery that they first made their mark.

The first American geography book was published in 1784, the first atlas to exclusively chart America and its states in 1795, and it was a woman, Susanna Rowson, who produced the country's first educational geographic textbook in 1805. Her life had been one of difficult adventure. Shipwrecked in horrific circumstances when she was five and poverty-stricken at sixteen, she had become the sole provider for her family. Novelist, actress, poet, lyricist, playwright turned educator, Rowson was a humanitarian, a voice for the women of her century and a fervent advocate of the abolition of slavery. In 1797 she established Miss Rowson's Academy for Young Ladies in Massachusetts.

When she published *Rowson's Abridgement of Universal Geography* in 1805, followed by *Youth's First Steps in Geography* in 1811, Rowson became a trailblazer for girls' geographic education, credited with being the first woman geographer. Her *Abridgement of Universal Geography* contained no maps. Instead, it was a narrative that explored the cultural, economic, religious and hierarchical social organisation of different continents. What she was intent on instilling in her students was an awareness of the country they belonged to in relation to others; she wanted to educate girls about the world beyond themselves, and to understand difference. She dwelled on themes such as the position of women, the nature of tyranny and the concept of liberty, but her dominant theme was that of slavery, what she called the 'barbarous, degrading traffic' of human beings which she denounced as a 'disgrace to humanity'. Her book appeared the same year that Samuel West, a Quaker reformist printer, published *Injured Humanity*, a series of vignettes on the torture, enforced family separation and abuse of slaves. The anti-slavery campaign was gaining ground. By 1805 the trade in, and shipment of, slaves to America was prohibited. But the South still relied on its slave labour. The fight was not totally won.

Through Rowson's exercises (the conversational questions and answers she appended to her first book), students were invited to become part of a discourse on cultural and racial identity, to consider the world outside their classroom and the true value of liberty in the face of the injustice meted out to the disempowered. Her exercises encouraged curiosity and a rigorous interrogation of what they were told. This was geography that embraced social, not just physical, mapping. It introduced the physical world as a place to be experienced, not just measured, a geography which required thinking about the experience and sense of place.

Two of the earliest American map samplers we know of, sewn in 1779 and 1780, come from Mrs Rowson's Academy. They are both of Boston harbour, its dozens of islands and its street plan registered in a density of colours. Boston was a site of triumphant revolutionary progress, from the catalytic Boston Tea Party to a key victory of the Patriots over the British. By the start of the nineteenth century, when these samplers were sewn, Boston had evolved into a wealthy and cosmopolitan port, the centre of America's mercantile trade. The stitchers, Lydia Withington and Sally Dodge, seem eager to lay claim to their national identity. In their cartouches they embroidered the American emblem of the eagle with outstretched wings, its motto *E Pluribus Unum* (Out of Many, One) inscribed on the Great Seal.

In Rowson's school, students first measured their maps out on paper, complete with grids, latitudinal and longitudinal lines and a compass rose. A student might start with the layout of her school grounds, then extend her drawing to include the fields that surrounded it and the patchwork of a neighbouring estate. She might graduate to marking down the stretch of her town, city, then state. Then she might transfer her knowledge to a sampler, expanding her horizons stitch by stitch until she had encompassed her whole nation. While in Britain girls were sewing what had always been there, American schoolgirls were mapping out a New World – marking out boundaries of emerging states, tracking geographic and political change. They couched down state borders and expansions in rows of coloured thread, travelling around them again and again and they documented settlements and named rivers in painstaking cross-stitch that demanded close attention. They tinged their embroidered war-won shorelines with a fade of blue ink stretching out from land to sea to highlight their country's independence. Not just in Susanna Rowson's school in Boston, but in Maryland, New Jersey, Hudson River, Virginia, New York City and elsewhere, girls marked down their destiny on map samplers.

Their needlework was a way not just to record, but also to explore and become familiar with the geography of a United States. When you sew, you must pause when the direction changes, alter the angle of your needle to go around a corner, shorten a stitch to make a sharp turn, lengthen it again to skim along a line. Through sewing, these schoolgirls were feeling out the shape of their country they belonged to. Each stitch was a forward step, traversing their nation slowly, inch by inch, discovering its flow and taking its measure. They were committing to memory the contours and boundaries of a newly-born America and how their own state related physically to others. In doing so they composed a mental grid of where they belonged by stitching it slowly and repetitively on their samplers. For them, it would have been not just a geographic but an emotional journey: discovering new horizons, calculating their own possibilities. These were young women creating a different kind of cartography in a medium that was, at the time, uniquely theirs. Embroidered maps created by women and guided by female teachers, interpreted and charted the nation for which they had been given responsibility of care.

Cecilia Lewis was eighteen in 1809 when she made her silk map sampler at the Pleasant Valley Boarding School at Hudson River. On it she included the names of Native American tribes sourced from an earlier eighteenth-century map. She used silk chenille to thread her way around her new land, sewing from east to west, following the pull of America's expansion from North and South Carolina to Kentucky. Her grandfather had been one of the signatories of the Declaration of Independence and her grandmother a British prisoner during the Revolutionary War. Now she was registering in her own hand the evidence of the independent nation her grandparents had fought for. Later in life, when she moved to Wisconsin, over 1,000 miles away, she journeyed across the terrain she had embroidered many years before: the routes she had outlined in thread, the places she had named, the country she had sewn together.

It was not only maps that were stitched. Schoolgirls also embroidered globes of the world. America was the only country to create them. Manufactured printed and painted globes existed in Britain, but they were inordinately expensive to import to America. Westtown Academy near Philadelphia owned just three, a totally inadequate number to service its many pupils. Three-dimensional globes were thought to be more efficacious in the teaching of geography, since they were accurate miniature representations of the whole earth and gave shape to the world, to its movement and rotating presence. When Westtown Academy needed more, it decided to make its own.

Rachel Cope wrote from the school to her parents in 1816:

I expect to have a good deal of trouble in making [the globes], yet I hope they will recompense me for all my trouble, for they will certainly be a curiosity to you and of considerable use in instructing my brother and sisters, and to strengthen my own memory, respecting the supposed shape of our earth, and the manner in which it moves (or is moved) on its axis, or the line drawn through it, round which it revolves every twenty-four hours.

The schoolgirls cut silk ovals that they stitched together to make spheres which they stuffed with wool. Then, on the silk, they delineated the Arctic and Antarctic circles, the Equator, parallels and meridians, ecliptic and rational horizons, state outlines and grids in stitches; they inked the names of continents and cities and named the surroundings seas and shorelines with goose-quill pens. Their globes were perfect miniature universes realised in the tactility of cloth and thread, the first globes to be manufactured in America. They were only five inches high.

When in 2012 Sotheby's in New York auctioned the Landmark Collection of Betty Ring. the American textile scholar who, along with her two-volume guide *Girlhood Embroidery:*

American Samplers and Pictorial Needlework 1650–1850, published in 1993, did more than most to revive public interest in samplers, the collection of nearly 200 lots sold for over $4 million. There was only one map sampler, spheres of the eastern and western hemispheres stitched in 1809 by Polly Platt while she was attending the Pleasant Valley Boarding School in Hudson River Valley, the source of many extant sewn maps. The sampler was bought for $50,000. It had survived long enough to become collectable. Sadly, it was one of the very few to do so.

In more recent years, local map-making has been a way for communities to record what they most value in their neighbour-hood. Common Ground is an environmental charity founded in 1987 to engage people with the places where they live in imaginative ways. It organises diverse events and participatory projects aimed at the exploration and discovery of local natural and architectural heritage. The Parish Maps Project, begun in 1983, encouraged communities to create their own maps in a variety of mediums that captured not just the layout and features of a physical landscape, but also its emotional value. These were heart maps, a charting of preciousness. In community map-making, time can conflate: it is possible to layer knowledge and memory, insert lost landmarks, reinstate hidden paths, rein-stall the ghosts of vanished architecture.

Some communities emphasised tactility to effectively convey the feeling of home. Community map-makers in Redlynch, Wiltshire, made a three-dimensional soft sculpture landscape based on the local Ordnance Survey map of the area. It is an undulating evocation of natural heritage materialised in velvet, silk, cotton and canvas, criss-crossed with threaded paths along the River Avon, patchworked in a crazy quilt of farms and woodlands. Hedgerows fray along the edges of roads, trees fringe pleated fields. In Thirsk, Yorkshire, the local environment was threatened by development. Their community map courted conservation by detailing everything local people wanted to see protected. It is an inventory of Thirsk's natural beauty, season by season: the sweep of returning birds in spring, the ragged fall of leaves in autumn, the snow-ridged hills of winter, the crowded grassy park in the summer. The sewn Parish Maps Project encouraged communities to seek out local distinctiveness and replicate it in cloth and thread to animate a familiar and often endangered landscape of home.

In the Scottish town of Renfrew, I became involved in the creation of a series of embroidered panels for the town's quincentenary. In the centre of a panel called Sky Above, Earth Below, Still Waters was a densely embroidered streetscape of the town: stitches texturising brick and stone, slate and hedges, iron and grass. Aerial photographs provided the detail from which the initial drawings were made and, the crowded map having been dissected into smaller pieces, people were invited to take home a piece to sew. Most chose a place that had personal resonance: their own street, the place where they worked, their local church. It is one thing to distribute parts of a town, but quite another to join them back together. The pieces came back slowly at first and then in a rush as the deadline loomed. Each edge was coated to prevent fraying and stitched down in its rightful place. As piece by piece was assembled we watched Renfrew grow and take shape again, just as it had done over the centuries, moving out from its historic centre to the post-war estates and spreading further to the more recent out-of-town developments. The participants had re-built the town where they lived, charted a physical intimacy: their routes to work, the school run, the kissing corners, the teenage hang-outs, the marriage venues, the burial grounds.

When we revisit familiar places, particularly the villages, towns or cities that shaped us, they are redolent with memories. And what they rekindle is not just a reminder of an event, an encounter or romance, but past emotions, the reawakening of the feelings of an earlier self. For many of us there are places of which we have no tangible memory, yet they tug us with a frisson of belonging. Experiencing a particular quality of light on a gleam of water or the loom of a distant hill can summon up an unexpected connection. For no matter where we were born or where we grew up, for most of us there are other places, ancestral lands, that somehow still resonate deep in our unconscious.

When I visited Australia in 1991 I was asked if I would like to make a banner with an Aboriginal group. I hesitated at first, aware that I had only a glancing knowledge of Aboriginal life. But I said yes, curious to get closer to an ancient culture that was both fascinating and mysterious. I knew a little about song lines and had a small appreciation of the close Aboriginal affinity with the earth, but that was all. It was hard for me, tightly formed by a Scottish industrial city, to grasp the essence of the Aboriginal spirit, so deeply rooted in an empathy for the land. I did some research on this stricken community, an ancient culture diminished by colonial harm, tribal knowledge lost, spiritual roots virtually destroyed by a programme of displacement and the fragmentation of family through the enforced removal of mixed-race children. No matter that there was now an attempt to restore land to its indigenous people with the Aboriginal Land Rights Act of 1976 – this was a culture severed from its ancestral connection to specific locations. Day by day I saw their people sitting alone or in small clusters on the grass in public parks, like fallen leaves made brittle through lack of sustenance.

When I turned up a couple of weeks later at Melbourne's Arts Access workshop for the first session, no one appeared. The staff were unperturbed. This was normal. It wasn't a matter of lack of interest or respect, they told me, but of what feels right at the time. Today obviously was not the right time. The next day, however, they came: a group of eight women from the

Aboriginal Drug and Alcohol Rehab Unit. They seemed a small army of resistance, bonded by their own boundaries, known to each other, some inter-related, watchful of their space, guarding their territory, and wary of me. These were chain-smoking, tough-talking women. I had worked in many poor areas of Glasgow with the roughest and the toughest – or so I had thought – but this group seemed like hewn rock. They had little appetite for chit chat, listened to my spiel about banners with seemingly scant interest. I presumed that, in lives taut with addictive difficulty, time spent with others stretched their attention beyond its limit.

But we blundered on. We devised a structure, a vertical triptych. Its themes were simple: land, loss and hope. We cut out the Aboriginal symbol for a women's meeting place, we appliquéd lost children, we stitched the strips of the Aboriginal flag, and while we worked the women shared current news of abuse, imprisoned relatives, conflict with authority, careless violence, oppression, racism: everyday tales of their lives. I listened with incredulity. As they pinned and sewed, the air became clouded in thicker and thicker layers of smoke from their cigarettes. The smoke seemed to drift, like them, in a separate world upon which they had no hold, no security, no direction. But as the banner took shape there was a loosening and the odd burst of laughter. Creative confidence and interest took a tentative hold. These were women coming up for air.

The banner they made was called Keep the Circle Strong in lettering cut from cloth in the Aboriginal colours of red, black and yellow, claiming solidarity, cleaving to each other to keep a grip on themselves. Their displacement wasn't a symptom of addiction; it went much deeper than that. They could not be emotionally sustained by the culture they had been forced to adopt. They had lost their anchor – their land – and its strength to draw on. They had lost the preciousness of a natural world to which their spirits were tethered.

Once the banner was completed the women departed. There were smiles but no effusive thank yous. Later that week I went to a concert given by the Aboriginal musician Archie Roach. A friend of mine who knew him took me backstage and there, in the dressing room, were some of the women I had worked with. They greeted me like a member of the family, as someone who had crossed a line with them.

Later, back in Glasgow, I invited a group of Highland-born Gaelic women to make their own banner in response to the one created by Aboriginal group. They immediately identified with the Aboriginal women's banner and its themes of emotional anchorage to the land, of social and spiritual displacement and the subsequent diminution of an indigenous identity whose reclamation had never been fully realised. They decided on a visual echo, using the same format as that made by the Aboriginal women in Australia to tell their similar story. At the top they sewed a Celtic knot, the ancient symbol of connection. Below it they appliquéd a sheep, the animal with which the English replaced people in the Highlands in the eighteenth century. Its body was crowded in imagery: of forced evictions, burning crofts, an emigrant ship sailing away from Scotland, the British flag. They marked down the fate of those who were forced off the land, symbolised in hands holding the Gaelic words for loss and home. And, in their last section, they registered the retrieval of a proscribed language. Across continents, the story is the same: displacement bringing a loss of self and the disorientation of a community. But the sense of connection persists. The banners were a dialogue between two groups of women distanced by geography but bound together by a common experience, a textile duet of tactile empathy. Both maps of sorts, they charted how intrinsically people are bound to their place of origin. For both groups, removal had altered their sense of home – no longer physical but emotional, no longer experienced but remembered – an attachment conserved in myths, songs and stories and through words that no longer conveyed the depth of meaning they once had.

Like the Aboriginal people and Gaels, many Africans lost their culture when they were forcibly removed from their homeland and shipped as slaves to Europe and the New World. The American slave trade began in Virginia in 1619. By the time of the Declaration of Independence in 1776, it was legal in all thirteen colonies. Most American slaves were black Africans captured in west Africa, 700,000 brought to America by 1790, 3.2 million registered by 1850. Among the captured slaves were skilled agriculturalists and artisans. Dragged from the natural world in which their spiritual beliefs were rooted, black African slaves tried to safeguard their cultural identity, an identity that had been shaped by a different landscape. With most forbidden to read or write, slaves hoarded the fragments of their traditions through oral storytelling and scraps of songs. But such mediums were limited. They could not preserve the rich, symbolic visual language through which many African magical and tribal beliefs were transmitted, meanings too important or too sacred to be imparted through text or speech or singing.

Bereft of possessions and traditional talismans of protection, black slaves improvised with what materials they could, with bits of wood and off-cuts of fabric, to reclaim elements of their lost material and symbolic world. When a language is lost, or forbidden, people find ways to keep it in circulation. They don't relinquish it, but translate it into other forms that can escape confiscation. So it was with African American slaves: they kept hold of cultural memory by translating it into mediums where it could be kept safe.

Quilts became one way to keep hold of Africa. Slaves plucked cotton from the snag of bushes or its wayward escape on a wired fence, enough to pad a quilt. They gathered bark and indigo, berries and blossom for dyeing and unpicked grain sacks and worn-out clothes. They were glad of the bits of cloth their white mistresses permitted them to keep once the dressmaking was done. With these they made patchwork quilts to piece together a heritage.

Their quilts did not mimic the traditional patchwork of white American women, which were stitched in orderly arrangements. Slave quilts were improvised like music: syncopated, free-spirited, with asymmetrical staggerings of texture and shade to create an abstract whole. Fabrics were cut in strips and sewn together in different lengths, down and across, vertically and horizontally. When they were done, they looked like patches of earth or plots of ground as seen from the sky.

In 2000 Jacqueline Tobin and Raymond Dobard published *Hidden in Plain View: A Secret Story of Quilts and the Underground Railroad,* based on the narrative of the African American quilter Ozella McDaniel. Their book was an exploration of the use of sewn quilts made by slaves as mnemonic codes on the Underground Railroad, the routes that guided slaves to freedom from the south to the north. These quilts, McDaniel had claimed, held encoded information which, when hung on a washing line or draped over a fence, signalled a safe house or danger ahead. They carried topographical data in a deceptive but decipherable arrangement of knots, stitches and symbols. The book was highly controversial. An Underground Railroad expert dismissed the findings as folklore, pointing to the absence of any account of such quilts in slave memoirs, diaries or in the oral testimonies collected in the 1930s. Many American textile curators and quilt historians were equally sceptical given the lack of evidence, either stitched or spoken. But the image of a slave touching out a rise of stitches to trace a route to safety in the moonless dark is so seductive that I, like many others, would wish it true.

Some slave quilts have survived, although they are rare. Most were made with cheap or already worn fabric, and therefore faded, frayed and thinned through constant use in the comfort-less climate of plantation life. There are, however, two that have lasted. They were made by Harriet Powers, born in 1837 into slavery in Georgia, as were two of her nine children. Her quilts, known as The Bible Quilt and The Pictorial Quilt, offer a unique insight into the visual vocabulary of enslaved women in the nineteenth century and provide indisputable evidence that African American slaves carried their visual culture with them and, as Harriet did, used their sewing to preserve it.

Harriet Powers was freed in the 1880s after the Civil War and, for a while, seems to have been reasonably comfortable, tending a small farm of four acres. It is thought that she became a seamstress to supplement the family's farming income. In 1886 she began to exhibit her quilts at the rural cotton fairs that were popular in America at the time. Such fairs were a useful way for women to see each other's needlework and share tech-niques. Possibly, for Harriet, they offered an opportunity to market her skills and drum up business. Her Bible Quilt was exhibited at the Athens Cotton Fair in 1886 and an artist, Jennie Smith, offered to buy it but Harriet was reluctant to sell. This quilt seemed to have had a special significance for her. But Jennie kept in contact and, five years later, when Harriet and her husband fell into financial difficulties, Harriet finally sold it to her. She asked for ten dollars but was beaten down to five. Jennie wrote down her version of the conversation she had with Harriet at the time of her purchase when she explained the quilt's themes. Useful though it is to have this record, it is probable that Jennie was an unreliable witness. Her version emphasises Harriet's Christian motives in making her quilt and supplies a patronising and possibly sanitised, portrayal of Harriet herself.

The second quilt was displayed at the Cotton State Exhibition in Atlanta in 1895, by which time Harriet had separated from her husband. It is thought it was either commissioned or purchased by wives of the faculty members of Atlanta University as a leaving present for the Reverend Charles Cuthbert Hall of New York City, the vice-chair of the university's board of trustees. There is written evidence that Harriet made more quilts but none of these have survived.

Harriet's quilts are a fusion of American quilt-making, Christian imagery and African traditions. While they seem at first to ape the traditional quilts of white Americans in neat blocks of appliqué, illustrating biblical stories – apparently as visual evidence of Christian lessons piously learned – close examination reveals a more subversive message. Many of the biblical stories Harriet chose for her quilts dwell on themes of loss and escape: Adam and Eve, Job, Cain and Abel, Jonah and the Whale, Christ's ascent to heaven. The fabric strips that divide her blocks are not symmetrical, but staggered. Her quilts, while pictorial, are also symbolic, rooted in the African tradition of a coded visual language. They seem to have had a personal resonance for Harriet herself. Unwilling at first to sell her Bible Quilt to Jennie Smith, when she did so she still could not fully relinquish it but went back to see it several times. It seemed from her first refusal to sell, and her later visitations, that the quilt held a special emotional and possibly spiritual significance. It was precious: a talisman of survival, a connection to where she belonged.

The style of her quilts is typical of the west African textiles made by the Fon in Benin and the Fante of Ghana. Like them Harriet uses bold shapes, simple cut-outs of human figures, animals and birds with no character detail. Her quilts appear to be created from cultural memory, although she had no direct experience of Africa and was, most probably, a second, or even third, generation slave. They suggest that the African visual language was conserved over time and space and able to be safeguarded by a woman who did not inherit it directly from her ancestors. If so, it increases the meaning and poignancy of her quilts as examples of what has been called 'ancestral reverie'.

This might have been all we would ever know of Harriet Powers, but for a letter discovered in 2009. In the letter Harriet outlines her life as a slave, shares her story of becoming literate and describes four quilts she sewed. And there is one further tantalising clue of Harriet herself in a photograph taken in around 1897, when she would have been about sixty years old. It shows a plump woman wearing a ceremonial apron on which are appliquéd mystical signs and masonic symbols. They suggest that she might have been a conjure woman, someone who people believed could enlist the help of spiritual agents to activate charms and cure emotional or physical sickness. The zigzag design sewn along the apron's hem is undeniably African in origin and echoes an ancient ritual symbol of African protection much used in the ritual textiles of west Africa.

African traditions also survive in the remote world of Gee's Bend in Boykin, Alabama, where the descendants of African America slaves are making strip quilts – not in nostalgic or sentimental homage for an Africa they have never known, but as the continuation of a textile practice that has been passed down, generation to generation, in this same place since the sowing of the first cotton plantation in 1816. It is an isolated area just a few miles long, bordered on three sides by the Alabama River with only one mud road going elsewhere and an erratic ferry service. Even this was disbanded in the 1960s in retaliation for the community's attempt to register their vote in the nearby town during the Civil Rights Movement. It took forty years before it was reinstated. Such poor transport links have meant that for centuries there has been limited contact with white American culture.

What the women in Gee's Bend sew originates in their inherited slave culture, and through this to their more ancient African ancestry. Their quilts resonate with echoes of the woven kente cloth patterns of the Ashanti and Ewe tribes of Ghana. Through a ridge of corduroy and the rough of denim they piece back the texture of a lost land: scrub-faded, sun-baked, ploughed and furrowed. One of their favourite patchwork blocks is the Log Cabin pattern, which, according to Scottish quilt historian Janet Rae, has its origin in the earliest system of land cultivation in which dry and wet fields were butted together in horizontal and vertical strips. The block has been given a second name in America. It is also called 'The Underground Railroad'.

The geographer and map-sampler sleuth Judith Tyner discovered, as she was writing her book, that her great-great-great aunt had sewn a map sampler. She'd had no idea, but thought it was strange how strongly she felt the pull of map samplers over the years. The African American quilts of today often mirror the textile traditions of an Africa from centuries ago. Needlework can take us far away from where we are in our imagination, but it can also lead us back to where we belong.

On one of Harriet Power's quilts is a scene from Jacob and his ladder, a popular bible story. Only when you connect it to its source do you fully understand its import and the probable reason she chose it:

I will give you and your descendants the land on which you are lying. Your descendants will be like the dust of the earth, and you will spread out to the west and to the east, to the north and to the south. All people on earth will be blessed through you and your offspring. I am with you and will watch over you wherever you go, and I will bring you back to this land. (Genesis 28:10–17)

13
Value

A guest writer has been invited to host the creative writing group I have recently joined. He asks us to introduce ourselves and say a little about what we are working on. As each member outlines their memoir, crime thriller, historical novel or their collection of short stories the writer nods encouragingly. Then it is my turn. I tell him I am writing a book about the social, emotional and political significance of sewing. The writer doesn't nod. Instead he pauses, leans forward and places his elbows on the table, then slowly interlaces his fingers. 'Ah yes', he says. 'I can just see me asking my local bookstore if they have that bestseller on social, emotional and political sewing'. His look towards me is pitying.

We read extracts from our work: the memoir, the thriller, the short story. Certain of further ridicule, I read what I have brought, the opening of the *Connections* chapter, where I describe my discovery of an old patchwork quilt. To my, and the writer's, surprise he finds it moving and interesting. He says it reveals a world he knows little about. He says the writing is beautiful. My faith in the book is restored. It has passed an important test: to undo a prejudice and to enlighten. The following week the leader of the group asks me how my book on knitting is coming along. I leave the group. There are only so many battles I have the spirit to fight.

It all began with string. Its invention changed the history of humanity. Once the craft of turning plant fibres into thread and twisting them to make string was discovered, animals could be caught, tethered and domesticated; objects could be tied together and carried; fishing nets could be fashioned; babies could be cradled on their mother's backs and women could walk further to collect plants for food or medicine. Crucially, from string came thread and from thread came cloth. It fell to women to spin the thread and weave the cloth because it was something they could do near or at home. It was compatible with child rearing and cooking.

The earliest evidence of string, from around 15,000 BCE, was found in the painted caves of Lascaux in France, but its invention was even earlier, as shown by the survival of a small Palaeolithic Venus figure carved in stone in around 20,000 BCE. She is wearing a skirt of cords suspended from a hip belt. Archaeologists discovered that such skirts continued to be used through the Palaeolithic, Neolithic and Bronze Ages, evidenced not only by ancient artefacts, but in actual remnants found in burial sites. The skirts seem to have had little practical purpose. Some only drape over the buttocks, others barely screen the sexual organs. It seems their function was cultural, a form of communication. They were made to signal messages about a woman's fertility. Decorated, knotted and weighted, they became agents of sexual attraction in the competition for virile partners, crucial to societies whose clan survival was dependent on successful procreation. The making of string and its skirts became associated with fecundity and childbirth – with a woman's ability to create life.

Spinning thread and weaving cloth, the bringing of something into existence where nothing had been before was, like conception and childbirth, mysterious to ancient tribes, even magical. Around such crafts, rituals developed to protect their efficacy. Myths evolved, stories of women whose power lay in their use of thread: the Trojan princess Andromache weaving protective roses to make a cloak for her husband, Hector; Ariadne leading Theseus to the centre of the labyrinth and back to safety with her ball of red thread and the Moirai (the three Fates) of Greek mythology, who controlled human destiny: one spinning the thread of life, another measuring it out and the third choosing when to cut it. In the symbolic, metaphorical rhetoric of past cultures, thread became a symbol for time, but it also represented the path a soul took to journey between temporal and spiritual worlds. The needle also was endowed with magical power. It signified a strong union because of its ability to join separate elements and create a whole. Its eye was thought to represent the gateway to heaven.

Embroidery is an ancient craft. Archaeologists have found examples of it in the Cro-Magnon culture in France, in the fossilised remains of clothing, boots and hats from 30,000 BCE. In Siberia, they discovered remnants of stitched decorative designs dating back to 5,000-6,000 BCE and a tomb in the Hubei province of China disclosed silk embroidery from 5th-3rd century BCE. This historical evidence doesn't establish who were the makers of such embroidery, men or women. While men are recorded as embroiderers in imperial and ecclesiastical workshops – at the courts of Moghul emperors and in the Medieval guilds of Europe – it was primarily women who were responsible for the creation of domestic, tribal and ceremonial cloths. In many traditional cultures, specific designs for embroidery and the ritual acts involved in its sewing were passed on from woman to woman, connecting mother and daughter, grandmother and granddaughter as continuums of cultural and emotional value.

The wedding dress of a Karakalpak bride in Uzbekistan was sewn in patterns that symbolised mothers and daughters. In Tajikistan, a woman who had lived a long life would cut out a bride's dress for younger women to sew. A mother and her daughter worked together embroidering the daughter's wedding *suzani* (a tribal textile from Central Asia), with other female relatives helping as the marriage day approached. In Bangladeshi culture, a mother would sew blessings for her daughter into the *nakshi kantha* (an embroidered cloth traditionally made from old saris) she made for her marriage. In the Punjab, a grand-mother embroidered a silk cloth (*phulkari bagh*) for her granddaughter, sewn with symbols and colours of family signif-icance, to be held above her head as she processed to her wedding. Stitched textiles quite literally kept women in touch with one another.

Such textiles also had monetary value. In earlier centuries, a girl's dowry was a significant part of an arranged marriage and part of its barter system as an important element of property transfer. The more valuable the textiles were, the greater chance of a good match. A family would invest heavily in cloth and thread to ensure a better marriage for a daughter, and the financial outlay could be substantial. In Hungary, a girl's dowry might contain up to 300 items, from bedcovers to fabric cases for mirrors and combs, cradle covers, doorway hangings, table-cloths, pillowcases and towels, as well as her own bridal attire. In Transylvania, a dowry might represent more than 500 metres of cloth. The quality of the needlework was as important as its quantity, as evidence of a girl's proficiency. Started when she was seven or eight years old, a dowry could take a girl at least ten years to complete. Dowries, as brides-wealth, have a long history in Europe, South Asia and Africa as well as other parts of the world but in modern times they have been reinvented as bridal shows, the pre-marriage gift-giving, or wedding lists sent out by the couple-to-be. But the dowry tradition persists. It is still practised across all sectors of Indian society, for example, and in Bangladesh and Pakistan. But it has become discredited; blackmail and wife-burning as retaliation for what are claimed to be insufficient dowry settlements have corrupted its original purpose. Today, most governments no longer sanction it and girls contest having their value measured out in property. The dowry system has, by and large, come to an end. But with its demise goes the emotional connection it harboured between women of different generations.

Women's needlework has incrementally lost economic and cultural value through the centuries. In the thirteenth century, the work of professional women embroiderers was recorded in official documents. The needlewoman Mabel of Bury St Edmunds was noted for her services to Henry III, for whom she embroidered a chasuble in 1239 and an embroidered standard for Westminster Abbey in 1234. Her skill was so appreciated that the king commanded she be given six measures of cloth and a length of rabbit fur as a reward, an honour usually reserved for knights of the realm. Nuns, too, were celebrated for their needlework, not necessarily individually but through the reputation of their nunnery. But, in the Middle Ages, merchants increasingly took over the negotiation of embroidery commissions and women's names began to disappear from official order books. When the Black Plague wiped out a vast swathe of the populations of Europe and Asia, the final death toll included many of the wealthy patrons on whom embroiderers relied for commissions. Facing a sharp decline in business, the London Worshipful Guild of Broderers, the trade guild for professional embroiderers, decided on damage limitation. Male embroiderers kept the more lucrative work, such as goldwork, for themselves, and women embroiderers were delegated less skilled needlework. They began to lose status. By the sixteenth century, women were excluded from official positions within the Guild altogether. In 1609 they were barred from guild apprenticeships and, if they were found to be undertaking any 'unlawful work', such as commissions of higher status that guild members felt should be their preserve, they were heavily fined. Without access to professional training, no longer having an equal role in managing the affairs of the guild and lacking the stamp of quality conferred through guild membership, the value of women's needlework diminished. It became seen as unskilled and amateur.

While there were undoubtedly women still employed as embroiderers, with no official status in the commercial world, they moved into the shadows.

When the sumptuary laws (those that governed the quality and consumption of cloth and dress and other products) were revoked in 1630, the Worshipful Guild of Broderers lost its legal power over the training or employment of embroiderers and its authority to legislate over quality. Embroidery was no longer a status symbol as the public indicator of wealth and power. Instead, these were evidenced through a person's personal circumstances. A prosperous merchant and administrative class was on the rise, investing in property as the visible marker of their success. They could afford to separate the workplace from the home and, housed in different physical spheres, men's and women's worlds divided. Men appropriated the external world of politics, trade and commerce, while women were relegated to the internal realm of house and family: still sociable, still influential, but contained. The difference between masculine and feminine activities became more marked. As it did so, a new construct of masculine and feminine qualities began to emerge. Women's needlework, now home-based, became associated with family care and its accompanying virtues of duty, decency and morality. As femininity and domesticity became more intertwined, needlework became their tangible expression, and women compounded the association. Faced with economic and social sequestration, increasingly through the seventeenth and eighteenth centuries, they used their needlework to bolster their presence. They crafted furnishings, clothing and accessories that evidenced skill, elevated status and good taste. They adorned their homes and dressed themselves and their families in the trappings of upward mobility. A delicately embroidered pair of gloves signalled liberation from the grime of agricultural toil and indicated conspicuous leisure. An ornate assembly of embroidered household linens demonstrated household wealth and a wife's capacity for good stewardship. Largely excluded from the world of letters, women used textiles to demonstrate their knowledge and intellect, sewing emblems of personal significance, flowers that held meaning and tales of stoical biblical heroines such as Susanna, Rebecca, Judith and Ruth, women who had committed courageous acts or displayed power within marriage. Just as Mary, Queen of Scots, had used the content of her embroidery to affirm her sovereign power when in captivity, so women made visible their attributes of strength and command diminished by their consignment to a domestic realm.

Women's attention to home-crafted textiles served to widen the gap between professional and amateur needlework. Domestic and decorative sewing became divorced from the professions of tailors, seamstresses and ceremonial embroiderers. An economic and social divide emerged between working women who sewed to earn money and those middle and upper-class women who chose sewing to signal their freedom from paid work. But their home-based needlework did more than create a class divide. It encouraged the idea, the ideal, of the feminine and of decorative sewing as a feminine craft.

Outside the home, a hierarchy was developing between art and craft. With the revocation of the sumptuary laws, embroidery lost its position as a high art, the place it had held since medieval times. It was diminished both economically and culturally. With gender divides more accentuated and the increased feminisation of sewing, men were not interested in compromising their gender identity by associating themselves with needlework. Their lack of participation served to annex sewing further into a woman's realm. Tailors, who had hitherto enjoyed the prestige as skilled craftsmen, began to be ridiculed as effeminate. They were increasingly the butt of male scorn. One tailor protested that his trade had become 'the byword for effeminate helplessness'. In the tailors' trade journal *The London Tailor* John Pallister complained that the 'the association of sewing with femininity' was marking tailors out for contempt.

A similar prejudice was at work in the world of art. The Renaissance of the fourteenth to seventeenth century saw a shift from the role of the artist as craftsman and designer to that of inspired individual artist. This was a role that brought greater status and financial return, both for artists and for those who commissioned, exhibited and collected their work. Artists, culturally and physically, separated themselves from craft workers. They promoted themselves as concerned with heart and mind rather the labour of the hands. They had studios rather than workshops and established their own exclusively male societies. The Royal Academy of London, founded in 1768, was one. Craft, seen as functional and manual, moved down the artistic pecking order. It became a working-class occupation and its economic worth lessened exponentially. Needlework – at best a cottage industry, at worst a domestic diversion for female amateurs – moved down even further. Robbed of cultural import, it was no longer deemed a worthy occupation but increasingly dismissed, even ridiculed, as mindless. Its antecedents were forgotten and the demotion of needlework became increasingly directed and interpreted through a masculine prism.

In the latter half of the seventeenth century in England there was a short-lived burst of creative rebellion against the strictures of women's functional needlework as clothing and furnishings in the sudden and short-lived insurrection of riotous stitchery. Called 'embosted work' (what we now call stump work), it was a curious form of sewn picture-making that seemed to erupt from the restraint of domestic sewing and satisfy a long-quelled craving for creative freedom. Using bright colours and deploying a wide variety of stitches and materials, such as wire, feathers, beads, ribbon, metal threads, seashells and leather, home embroiderers fashioned three-dimensional human figures, buildings, flowers, insects and animals with joyful negligence of the rules of perspective. Some imagery was wildly exotic, like birds with men's heads and strangely shaped plants. Made as separate elements, the disparate figures, birds, trees, or whatever else took women's fancy, were collaged and grouped to tell a story, or randomly bunched together to decorate a border. Some declared royalist allegiance to the deposed Charles I, acorns, butterflies (the symbol of reincarnation) and royal emblems secreted among the seemingly haphazard crowd of motifs. The eccentric concoctions of stump work had no functional use in themselves, but were applied to useful items like mirrors, boxes, trays and small caskets. While so much of what was then sewn has disintegrated or vanished, the survival of stump work is testament to its appeal. Many examples of it still exist; animated, robust, anarchic, indulgent and entertaining as evidence of women's yearning for greater creative expression.

It is thought that the ingredients of stump work, the exotic and seductive miscellany of materials, were pedalled door to door by itinerant travellers. This was just one opportunity seized by a growing needlecraft market. By the eighteenth century, women's needlework might have lost its economic value as a product, but it was becoming hugely profitable as a process. Male manufacturers had a gendered target market and seized the opportunity to direct its tastes. They adopted the role of mentors and designers and flooded the market with paper patterns, kits, transfers, accessories, magazines, pamphlets and books to tell women not just what they should sew but how they should sew. Encouraging dependency was good for business. Women were disarmed of their creative confidence, their sewing skills corralled into uniformity, usually requiring the materials advertised by specialist suppliers. Independent design or, worse, experimentation were discouraged. Women now sewed what other women sewed: distinctiveness now more usually discernible in the quality of their stitching.

Clearly, the belittling of sewing has been centuries in the making. In Britain, even now it is almost culturally ingrained. When I've been involved in a community textile project in a public place I have always been amazed by how cheerful it makes some men to stop by the table, survey the group of women embroidering some intricate appliqué in exquisite fabrics and joke 'I've got some trousers that need taking up', or 'Can you sew a button on my jacket?' Many men, particularly older ones, love this joke and take astonishing glee in reducing the obvious artistry in front of their eyes to a mundanity But their reaction cannot be dismissed as simple misogyny. Such attitudes are not necessarily about women, but about sewing. They stem from the centuries of class, gender, aesthetic and artistic separation that demoted sewing and deprived it of its value. And there is something else at play: the exclusion of men, the claim women themselves have made on sewing as a medium under the control of women's culture. Women appropriated its tactile, sensory world for themselves and were complicit in evolving its feminine connotations. Educational institutions reinforced needlework's feminine branding, making it an essential part of a girl's school curriculum. Since the 1860 Education Act, only girls were taught how to sew in state schools.

In the eighteenth century, however, a new phenomenon challenged the demotion of needlework and its exclusion from what had become the male preserve of visual arts. These were the needle painters who replicated famous paintings in embroidery. Needle painting was a form of embroidery that emulated the brushstrokes of a painter using shaded silk thread and long and short stitches worked alongside each other to create a realistic portrayal of their subjects. The most celebrated exponents were three Marys: Mary Knowles who used it for her portraits, Mary Delany who translated her botanical paintings in needlework and Mary Linwood who took on the challenge of replicating old masters with her own sewn versions. Their artistry flourished under the patronage of Queen Charlotte, who became the consort of George III in 1762 and, once queen, took it upon herself to champion women artists. She was not the only

European monarch to do so. Marie Antoinette in France, Maria Carolina of Naples and Maria Theresa of Austria all supported women artists, commissioning them to paint their portraits, visiting their exhibitions, receiving them at court. At a time when female artists were bereft of the opportunities of their male peers, excluded from membership of the Royal Academy, unable, on grounds of propriety, to attend life drawing classes and discouraged from working from a studio outside of their home, the encouragement of Queen Charlotte provided valuable and visible endorsement with which to progress their careers.

The Queen was particularly fond of embroidery. A needle-woman herself, she employed her own female court embroiderer, Mrs Phoebe Wright. In 1772 she tasked Mrs Wright with establishing the School of Female Embroiderers to create employment for respectable girls who had fallen on hard times and gave her £500 as an annual subscription. She commissioned the school to make bed hangings for her own state bed at Windsor Castle. Its density of flowers took six years to complete and is still on show at Hampton Court Palace.

Although all three Marys enjoyed the attention of Queen Charlotte, it was Mary Delany who became the Queen's close associate. She taught the royal children botany and sewed alongside them. The queen gave her a locket containing a lock of her hair as a token of intimacy and George III commissioned a portrait of her as a gift to Charlotte, which hung in the Queen's bedchamber. When Mary Delany became elderly, the royal couple provided her with a summer house at Windsor and an annual allowance of £300 a year.

Mary Delany's father was Colonel Bernard Granville, who had been Lieutenant Governor of Hull and a Member of Parliament in Cornwall. His sister, Lady Stanley, had served as a Maid of Honour to Queen Mary. It was to Lady Stanley that Mary was sent as a young girl to be trained for a future of royal service. She therefore spent her early years in the social melee of London being versed in history, dancing, needlework and music. The composer Frederick Handel was one of her teachers. But the death of Queen Anne in 1714 and the ensuing political power shift from Jacobite to Whig ended Mary's idyll and any hope of a position at court. The Granvilles had been supporters of the defeated Jacobite party. They were no longer welcome in royal circles and in 1715 Mary found herself transplanted to a remote village in Gloucestershire and social isolation. In 1718, at the age of seventeen, she was married against her will in an arrangement the family hoped would restore its political influence. She later said of her wedding day:

I was married with great pomp. Never was woe drest out in gayer colours, and when I had been led to the altar, I wished from my soul, I had been led, as Iphigenia was, to be sacrificed. I was sacrificed. I lost, not life indeed, but I lost all that makes life desirable – joy and peace of mind.

Her bridegroom, Alexander Pendarves, was a fat, unkempt, sixty-year old member of Parliament with a regrettable fondness for drink. Mary was destined for a life of perpetual unhappiness. In the second year of her marriage, her husband became unwell, immobilised by gout. She nursed him patiently, teeth chattering in the freeze of an unheated house, distanced from her family and the culture upon which she had thrived. To fill her hours, she immersed herself in needlework and botanical painting Her husband's sudden death in 1724 brought liberation, but not the salve of wealth. Alexander Pendarves had omitted to alter his will on their marriage and Mary was left comfortable, but compared to her aristocratic peers, un-wealthy. She relied on the kindness of relatives and friends to keep in the social swim, moving from place to place as a house guest. Luckily for Mary, one of her closest friends was the Duchess of Portland, one of the richest women in England, and she offered her a home amid the creative hubbub of her eclectic artistic and scientific friends.

Their group was christened the Hive because of its siren appeal to the most celebrated writers, painters, scientists and botanists of the day. Here, Mary flourished. She became acquainted with the great plant collector and man of science Joseph Banks and visited his house in London to see his collection of plant specimens and seeds and pore over the illustrations he had made during his voyage with Captain Cook. She began to not just study plants but to propagate and grow exotic species which she replicated in different mediums, including needlework.

In 1743, Mary remarried, finding a convivial and supportive companion in an Irish clergyman, Patrick Delaney, who had cultivated a beautiful garden at Glasnevin, just outside of Dublin. There they redesigned the eleven-acre garden to make it one of the most beautiful in Ireland. Her botanical paintings and their translation into embroidery were admired by those who saw them and won her the attention of Queen Charlotte.

Little of her needlework has survived. There is a white coverlet made for her godson which is preserved in Ulster Museum. It has a central medallion of entwining leaves and trellised knot work interspersed with floral motifs, and its intricate embroidery is testimony to her skill with needle and thread. There are decorative aprons in heavy silk, one decorated with white and purple violets, another with auriculas and geraniums and neckerchiefs embossed with raised poppies or ornamented with Madonna lilies. We know from her own letters that she made church furnishings with 'a border of oak leaves and all sorts of roses', and that she covered the seats of the chairs in her Irish home with embroidered cloth: for winter use an assortment of flowers on a brilliant blue background; for summer husks and leaves on cream linen.

In the age of the Enlightenment, where intellectual attention was on the real world, where valued knowledge came from actual experience and observation, Mary Delany's botanical paintings and needlework were no idle pastime but a mindful exploration of nature. It was through her painting and her sewing that she disseminated her discoveries of plant forms using the skills she felt best equipped her to share their complexities.

Her botanical paintings were set on a black background the better to accentuate the detailed tones of each flower and leaf and each curving stem. Her needlework similarly and meticulously described the minutiae of living plants. Hers was no sentimental floral art, but a scientific scrutiny and presentation of the detail of plant forms. She would sketch flowers from life, dissect them and note each element. And she transferred her passion and knowledge of them onto the clothes that she wore. Her most celebrated masterpiece was a court dress which she wore, it is thought, at the grand Birthday Ball of Frederick Prince of Wales in 1751. Its bodice has a central row of pinks, flanked by lily of the valley. Its hem is a riot of flowers. But it is the overskirt which is the real triumph, made in black silk, it has over 200 species of embroidered flowers scattered in naturalistic abandon: winter jasmine, sweat peas, love-in-a-mist, anemones, tulips, bluebells, forget-me-nots, all drawn from life, each stem and stamen, each twist of leaf, each curling petal replicated in an undulation of shaded silk threads.

It is now thought that while she would have been its designer, and indeed an extant sketchbook testifies to that fact, she might not have been the exclusive author of the needlework. The nature of its techniques – the padding of flowers to give a three-dimensional effect – point to more professional hands. But what is irrefutable is that its genesis originated in her knowledge and appreciation of plant forms and her vision of how best to transpose them into embroidery.

When Patrick died in 1768, Mary Delany moved back to England and, now over seventy, began what proved to be an extraordinary legacy: the creation of a detailed and precise botanical encyclopaedia in which each plant specimen was reconstructed in layers of fine coloured paper, some with hundreds of small pieces. Plant collectors, gardeners and amateur botanists sent her unusual specimens to ensure their unique properties would be preserved in her paper mosaics. She was overwhelmed with botanical donations. Queen Charlotte even arranged for her to be sent interesting plant specimens from her own garden at Kew. She eventually filled ten volumes of what is called *Flora Delanica*, a compendium of 1,000 paper flowers. She died at the age of eighty-eight and, in 1897, her *Flora Delanica* was donated to the British Museum by her great niece, where it can still be viewed by appointment. Two examples of her work are on permanent display in the museum's Enlightenment Gallery.

Another needle painter, Mary Knowles, was a Quaker, poet, abolitionist, feminist, garden designer, botanical enthusiast and the celebrated exponent of 'perfection in needlework'. Hearing of her talent in 1771, Queen Charlotte asked her to undertake a stitched version of Johann Zoffany's portrait of the king. When it was completed, it was reported to be to the 'entire satisfaction' of the royal couple. Not undertaken as a commission, the Queen nevertheless pressed £800 on Mary, not as a fee but as a gift – as a gift it carried more meaning, representing a greater cache of royal intimacy and personal admiration. The sewn portrait of the king was treasured, remaining on display at Kew Palace for over 200 years. It is still safeguarded as part of the Royal Collection.

The most applauded of all the eighteenth-century needle artists, however, was undoubtedly Mary Linwood. Her father was a bankrupt wine merchant, her mother the founder of a private boarding school for girls in Leicester, which Mary took over after her mother's death and ran for the next fifty years. Mary sewed her first embroidered picture when she was just thirteen. Seven years later she was gaining a reputation as the finest needle painter of her day. She reproduced a painter's art through sewing, imitating their brush strokes in specially dyed gradated shades of wool, overlaid with a lustre of silk thread. She copied the popular masterpieces of her day, including works by Raphael, Rubens, Reynolds, Gainsborough and Stubbs, with a sensual materiality that entranced the public. Her sewing skills won her a medal from the Society for the Encouragement of Arts for her 'excellent imitation of pictures in needlework.' British nobility invited her to make sewn copies of the works of art they harboured in their stately homes. John Constable, the celebrated landscape painter, had as his first commission the painting of one of her backgrounds. Queen Charlotte invited her to Windsor Castle and Napoleon was so pleased with two embroidered portraits of himself that he conferred on her the honour of the Freedom of Paris as an acknowledgement of her talent. The King of Poland was an admirer. Empress Catherine the Great of Russia was so taken with the exquisiteness of Mary Linwood's needlework that she offered her £40,000 for her entire collection, but Mary refused, saying she preferred her work to remain in Britain.

And so it did, touring the country to great acclaim in the first ever exhibition to be lit by gaslight, which enabled visitors to see it by night as well as by day. Excluded, because of her gender and medium, from exhibiting at the Royal Academy, she mounted a permanent exhibition of her own work in London's Leicester Square in 1809. With galleries draped in scarlet and gold and silver cloth, her pictures were installed as centrepieces to thrillingly theatrical scenes. Her *Lady Jane Grey Visited by the Abbot and the Keeper of the Throne at Night* was staged in a prison cell, only accessed through a purposefully dark passageway. To see her sewn rendition of Gainsborough's *Cottage Children,* visitors had to peer through the window of a reconstructed country cottage, complete with chimney. Her catalogue boasted that she had been 'honoured with the most encouraging Commendation from Her Majesty and the Princesses'. The exhibition became an annual sensation, attracting over 40,000 paying customers each year and rivalling Madame Tussaud's as a visitor attraction. It remained on display for thirty-six years. The *Ladies Monthly Review* described it as a triumph of 'ingenuity and indefatigable industry . . . the taste and judgement, the variety and graduation of tints cannot possibly be exceeded in effort by the pencil'. Yet it was with pencil in hand that Mary Linwood chose to be depicted for her portrait, a portfolio tucked under her arm. She defiantly claimed the role of artist, not needlewoman, for posterity.

By the end of her life, at the age of ninety, public and artistic taste had changed. The British Museum declined Mary Linwood's proffered donation of her remaining embroidered works. The House of Lords rejected a similar offer. What remained of her collection was sold at Christie's Auction House in 1846, with the collection of 100 pieces fetching a mere £300. Her most celebrated work, *The Judgement of Cain*, which had taken her ten years to complete, went under the hammer for just £64. She was buried in Leicester, the city of her childhood, in a tomb erected by her friends. It praised her talents for shedding 'a lustre on her age, her country and her sex'.

These three artists – Delany, Knowles and Linwood – are scarcely remembered today, and yet, certainly Knowles and Linwod were household names in their time, women who crossed the threshold of the exclusive world of male fine art to revitalise the artistic and commercial value of sewn art. They attracted royal patronage, exhibited widely, made money and reputations as artists. But their time in the sun was temporary, their fame ephemeral, their sewn masterpieces now all but forgotten. Charles Dickens penned a poignant elegy to the transient fame of Mary Linwood. Writing of a visit he made to see her by then neglected exquisite embroideries, he lamented:

I myself was one of the last visitors to that awful storehouse of thy life's work, where an anchorite old man and woman took my shilling with a solemn wonder, and conducting me to a gloomy sepulchre of needlework dropping to pieces with dust and age and shrouded in twilight at high noon, left me there, chilled, frightened and alone. And now, in ghostly letters on all the dead walls of this dead town, I read thy honoured name, and find thy Last Supper, worked in Berlin Wool, invites inspection as a powerful excitement!

Dickens was misguided in associating Linwood's needle painting with what had become a national obsession: a craze for Berlin wool work. The finesse of her careful artistry, her assiduous supervision of the delicate gradated dyeing of fine wools, had little in common with the mass manufacture of wool-worked kits that inveigled their way into the homes, hands and hearts of Victorian womanhood. They had first appeared at the start of the nineteenth century and became so popular that by 1840 there were 14,000 designs in circulation. Berlin wool work, like the embroideries of Knowles and Linwood, emulated famous paintings. But there the comparison ended. The kits were accompanied with a chart for stitchers to follow, a simplified, reductive version of its original masterpiece. The skill required was minimal, the technique diminished to just one or two kinds of stitches. Sewn on coarse cloth, by the late 1850s they offered the spectacularly harsh colour range of the newly invented sharp-bright synthetic wool threads. They featured sentimental subjects like weary puppies, wistful children, cornucopias of flowers that were eagerly seized upon by women of all classes, keen to claim artistic credentials and parade their 'art' in the cram of their over-adorned houses. Looking back on the heyday of Berlin wool work, the author Emily Leigh Lowes was scathing in her assessment of its dubious charms, declaring in her popular classic of 1908, *Chats on Old Lace and Needlework*:

When one think of those years which English women have spent over those wickedly hideous Berlin wool-work pictures, working their bad drawings and vividly crude colour into those awful canvases, and imagining that they were earning undying fame as notable women for all the succeeding ages, death was too good for Mary Linwood.

Of course, it wasn't Mary Linwood's fault. Berlin wool embroidery had none of the textural re-interpretation of the masterpieces of Gainsborough or Rubens offered by her needle painting. Instead, the kits reduced the artistic genius of old masters and contemporary artworks to pixelated pastiches of the originals. The fad for Berlin wool work was a symptom of how far the creative nerve of domestic needlewomen had been crushed; extinguished to the point when women were seduced by the manufacturers' insinuation that it was more artistic to imitate the paintings of celebrated male artists in an excess of lurid stitches than to devise original embroidery of their own – embroidery which, through the centuries, had become devalued as merely 'women's work'.

It was nineteenth century soldiers and tailors who, for a little while, restored needlework's value as an artistic pursuit. And it was the Great Exhibition of 1851, the brainchild of Prince Albert, Queen Victoria's consort, which showcased their masterpieces of intarsia patchwork (an intricately inlaid appliqué technique where tiny pieces of fabric are sewn together edge to edge, in imperceptible stitches, like a form of marquetry).

These men did not call themselves 'embroiderers.' Steven Stokes titled himself '*inventor*'. John Brayshaw, another exhibitor, dubbed himself '*producer*' and John Munro '*artist-tailor.*' They were intent on displaying how superior their needlecraft was compared to the domestic sewing of women. Tailors especially with their trade threatened by the increasing competition of seamstresses, were determined to evidence their creative and technological acumen by allying themselves to the commercial world of inventors and the male domain of artists.

J. Johnstone, from Aidrie in Scotland, exhibited a patchwork composed of 2,000 pieces depicting 21 historical scenes which had taken him eighteen years to assemble. The invalided soldier S. Stokes's counterpane, ten by forty feet, illustrated *The Battle of Cairo* in nearly 10,000 scraps of fabric, which he had stitched together while '*in a lying position.*' The Paisley tailor John Munro spent years creating his 'The Royal Clothograph' a darkly-wrought work made from thousands of woollen offcuts and sewn with the names of hundreds of men of learning and genius. On it he embroidered his message to the working man in just seven words: '*Push, Piety, Patience, Perseverance, Punctuality, Penetrate*' and '*Please.*'

These quilts served a dual purpose. Not only were they exemplars of male artistry and industry, they were made to support the current temperance movement which advocated sobriety amongst the working classes. It was a crusade endorsed by the British military who, in the aftermath of the Crimean War (1853–1856), between Russian and European armies, a war in which both sides suffered cataclysmic losses, was faced with escalating alcohol addiction amongst convalescing and serving soldiers. Needlework, unlikely as it seems, was fostered as an alternative to drink. Soldiers, tutored by military tailors, used the off cuts of uniforms to sew patriotic portraits of military leaders and military victories. Their quilts were made to inspire fellow soldiers to abandon drink and, to this end, they not only exhibited their work at the 1851 exhibition but at the Soldiers' Industrial Exhibitions which were held throughout the country.

Tailors were also supporters of the temperance movement. The Paisley tailor John Munro toured his quilt around Scotland and Ireland and at the Belfast Revival Temperance Association, he urged his audience to practise the seven words he had embroidered on his quilt. A local newspaper of 1860 reported that he: '. . . illustrated therefrom what patience and perseverance could be accomplished and urged upon the young men present to practise these virtues and in order to do so, they should become total abstainers'. A Scottish tailor from Biggar, Menzies Moffat, included scenes from Robert Burns' poem *Tam O' Shanter* on his Star Tablecover. He featured the witch-dancing nightmare Tam encountered on his drink-fuelled journey home from a night out on the tiles as a palpable lesson to men tempted by alcohol. Menzies' intarsia patchwork also carried a political message. He was a Chartist, a campaigner for electoral reform, and, on the back of his Star Tablecover, he beaded the slogan: '*The Reform Bill is the Tailor's Will.*' He carried his quilt as a banner in the 1845 reform demonstrations.

Menzies Moffat toured his Star Tablecloth and another of his creations the Royal Crimean Patchwork Tablecover around the country. The latter was a remarkable tour de force in needlework, with eighty-one figures pieced on its backcloth composed of tiny pieces arranged in precise geometric symmetry. His chosen characters included Napoleon, Rob Roy, William Wallace, Tom Thumb and Robin Hood: outlaws turned champions, battle commanders and popular heroes. It took him seven years to sew the 5,000 and more scraps of cloth together. A splendid typographical poster announced the display of his quilts in his home town of Biggar. It is a triumph of eclectic Victorian fonts.

Menzies Moffat's claim of 'Works of Art' was endorsed elsewhere on his poster as he boasted that the exhibition 'had been patronised by the nobility, gentry, clergy and a good many eminent painters'. It demonstrated his hope that his quilts would secure him a more elevated reputation than that of 'tailor,' garnering critical acclaim and bringing him a welcome financial return. Like the soldiers, many tailors toured and exhibited their intarsia patchworks, charging an entry fee for admission. John Brayshaw, a tailor from Lancaster, toured his quilt around the country, charging 6d for entry. When he attracted one thousand paying customers in Penrith he netted twenty-five pounds, a tidy sum in the days when the weekly wage for a working man was scarcely one pound.

THE WORLD'S WONDER
GRAND EXHIBITION

of the

FINEST SEWED WORKS OF
ART IN CLOTH

Mr. Menzies Moffat begs respectfully to intimate to the inhabitants of Biggar and vicinity, that he will exhibit his Works of Art

IN THE
MASONIC HALL, BIGGAR

On SATURDAY, 20th November
WHEN HE TRUSTS THAT A VISIT WILL BE AMPLY REPAID

OPEN from Two p.m. till Ten p.m.
ADMISSION SIXPENCE

Many of the quilts displayed at the Great Exhibition of 1851 did not survive. Prince Albert's Crystal Palace was flawed: leaks appeared, and water dripped down onto most of the masterpieces made by men, causing irreparable damage. But those that escaped, and others made later, give us a glimpse of a rare excursion by men of the nineteenth-century to promote patience, industry and sobriety and restore their social values through needlework.

14
Art

It was the staff and students of the Department of Needlework at Glasgow School of Art, who, at the end of the nineteenth century and the beginning of the twentieth, scooped embroidery from its undervalued past and set it firmly in the future as a stand-alone art form. They didn't use their needlework to register status, to honour tradition or to send out a message. Instead they experimented with its potential as art. They explored its sensuality, the visual impact of its techniques and the possibilities of combining fabrics, colours and textures to create an unexpected harmony. One of the artists to emerge from that time was Margaret Macdonald. She was the most adventurous. She incorporated string, beads, cardboard, braid and leather into her embroideries and integrated them into artwork that was bold and unlike anything that had gone before.

Margaret Macdonald enrolled as a student at the Glasgow School of Art in 1890 with her sister Frances. They had relocated from England where, given the maturity of their student work, it is likely they had already received some art tuition. They arrived in a Glasgow that was reaching the zenith of its industrial and manufacturing power. With its expanding coastal and international trade, the city was fast becoming one of the richest in the world, dubbed the 'second city of the Empire'. Glasgow's prosperity and aspiration was evident in the development of middle-class districts of distinction and discernment. Booming trade and burgeoning consumerism encouraged stylish department stores to open in the city centre and impressive new educational, manufacturing and recreational buildings to be constructed. Electric street lighting, an underground railway system and a pedestrian tunnel under Glasgow's River Clyde were all underway. This was a city confident about its future.

The relationship between Glasgow's industrial, manufacturing, and artistic sectors was a close one. In a city lacking an aristocracy, it was the industrialists who were its cultural patrons. The Glasgow School of Art had been established in 1845, originally as a seed bed of technical design, innovation and quality to feed into the city's commercial world. Its emerging skilled creators were being schooled to ensure that the city continued to foster a profitable advantage. In 1882 the school was given the largest government grant of any art school in Great Britain, a sum calculated on the number of prizes it had been awarded the previous year – more awards than anywhere else in Scotland.

When the Macdonald sisters arrived, the school was under the enlightened and dynamic directorship of Fra Newbery. He was an enthusiastic socialist who was convinced of the agency of the arts as a tool of cultural, economic and social progress determined through collaboration between consumer, creator and manufacturer. In 1892, two years after the sisters arrived at the school, Newbery took advantage of a new source of grant-aid made available by the 1890 Government Act that redirected the tax on alcohol to invest in the technical and manual instruction of workers. He secured funding to establish a Technical Art Studio at the art school to provide students with a thorough induction not only in technical processes of a wide range of crafts, but also to the necessity of vision, innovation and experiment in design and production. He believed in a collective vision in which exterior and interior design were inter-dependent and, more radically, in which gender and genre were intermixed. The result was a vigorous new artistic expression that brought men and women together in experimental creative enterprise. What they eventually produced became known as the Glasgow Style, a form of decorative arts that represented the talents of a group of young designers and artists, men and women, from the West of Scotland. Though they were influenced by contemporary movements – European Art Nouveau and the Aesthetic Movement – they forged their own distinctive approach. Working in a wide range of materials, their style was epitomised by the contrast of strong verticals and sinuous curves, a stylisation of nature – birds, roses, leaves – into simple shapes and their referencing of Celtic motifs.

Newbery, eschewing the separation of the sexes enforced by other art schools, proffered a challenge to the long-held discrimination against women's involvement in fine art. At Glasgow School of Art, male and female students shared the same studio space, attended joint lectures and were encouraged to collaborate on projects. Women could also attend life-drawing classes, albeit separated from their male peers. It was a daring move, criticised by some. In Sir William Fettes Douglas's prize-giving speech to the students of Edinburgh College of Arts in 1885, the self-taught painter, art connoisseur and eminent president of the Royal Scottish Academy was scathing of women's entry to art colleges, declaring that they 'rarely if ever applied themselves' and ridiculing their presence, saying that 'they go about dressed to look as much like men as possible and miserable, puny, little men they make . . . [and] their works are like them.' Fra Newbery, however, was undaunted. He not only encouraged equal participation of women students, but also employed female teachers at the school, including former student Jessie Rowat, who became Jessie Newbery when they married in 1889.

Contemporary male attitudes typified by those of Sir William Fettes Douglas prevailed in the male-dominated arts world of the late nineteenth century. Women were excluded from full-time attendance at art colleges (even the Ecole des Beaux-Arts in Paris, the heartbeat of contemporary art, did not open its doors to women as full-time students until 1897) and were confined to the limited arts curriculum their schools or private tutors deemed appropriate for their sex: pastels, watercolours, drawing and miniatures. Few worked in oils or on a large scale. Those women who did gain a modicum of access to advanced arts tuition – permitted from the 1850s onwards to attend art colleges' day or evening classes – did so on the understanding that they were fostering a career in teaching or following their own amateur enthusiasm, and that they were in no way aspiring to a professional status. This was emphatically a male preserve. Women were barred from membership of art institutions, societies and clubs and excluded from the Royal Academy, the main platform in Britain from which to secure an artistic reputation. And women exerted no influence over the exhibiting, commissioning, collecting or critiquing of works of art. What was even more pernicious was that they had little opportunity to represent themselves publicly through art. In a male-controlled artistic culture, the image of women was interpreted through the lens of masculinity. Even the paintings of the Pre-Raphaelite Brotherhood – the group of English painters founded in 1848 by William Holman Hunt, John Everett Millais and Dante Gabriel Rossetti, who set out to challenge the stale academia of art with their new style of detailed realism, depicted women as victims of sexual transgression or of a love betrayed. Their women were largely solitary, isolated from the world, portrayed as martyrs to a tragic fate. There was little imagery in the art of the late nineteenth century that conveyed women's actual experiences or emotions, that expressed female sexuality or interrogated the strictures of women's domestic constraints. And most women, with limited social mobility and often chaperoned, were restricted as observers of the world they lived in, with few opportunities to witness the world independently, never mind interpret it through their art.

The female artists of Glasgow School of Art were the first women in Scotland to encroach on its hitherto masculine artistic stronghold. Dubbed the 'Glasgow Girls' in the 1960s, (not with derogatory implications, but to place them on par with the Glasgow Boys, a collective of male painters who were their peers) these women were pioneers. They were educated, middle-class and independent. Women who had no financial need to storm the barricades of a defensive male art elite and no need to risk ridicule as women artists in a precarious, prejudiced world. But they were on a mission to demonstrate that their interpretations of crafts such as book-binding, metalwork, enamelling as well as needlework were as valid as artistic expressions as paint, as worthy of judgement alongside its male counterparts of sculpture and painting. These women established their own studios, exhibited internationally, submitted work for competitions, gave lectures, wrote articles, taught other women, enlightened men and claimed their place in the art world. They won awards, critical acclaim, international recognition, admiration and artistic equality by putting on an indisputably professional show.

In 1892 they set up the Glasgow Society of Women Artists, the first of its kind in Scotland. Lucy Raeburn (1869–1952) founded *The Magazine* which was published from 1893–1896 and became a platform for original writings and designs by students at Glasgow School of Art. Jessie M. King (1875–1949) designed for Liberty, illustrated over 70 books and exhibited widely in India, Germany, Italy and elsewhere. Margaret Gilmour (1860–1942) and De Courcy Lewthwaite Dewar (1878–1959) took on the male preserve of metalworking with Gilmour mounting her own display of beaten brass and copperwork at the Glasgow International Exhibition of 1901. Their achievements mirrored the progress of other women in other male-held fields such as science, medicine and education. Women on the cusp of the twentieth century were intent on broadening their professional and political horizons and with the suffragette movement gathering momentum, the endeavours of Glasgow's aspiring women artists were lending support to a wider social change by using their art to make the talents and achievements of women more visible.

Unlike the female artists of earlier times, such as the needle-painter Mary Linwood of the eighteenth century, the embroidery students of Glasgow School of Art were not interested in aping a male artistry. Instead, they were determined to have needlework accepted as a distinct art form, worthy of critical attention alongside painting and sculpture and removed from its limiting association with a constructed view of the 'feminine'. Margaret Macdonald was one of those students intent on change. By 1902 the department was rewarded with government approval and the embroidery course at Glasgow School of Art was certificated with its own diploma. Needlework became the most important feature of the school's Department of Applied Arts.

There were precedents to the elevation of needlework to art needlework, but their aim had been restorative rather than truly innovatory. The Arts and Crafts movement of the mid-nineteenth century, led by the designer William Morris and the writer John Ruskin, was anti-machine. It championed needlework as a complaint against the mechanical reproduction of ancient hand crafts, the conditions of home workers and the brain numbing craze for Berlin wool work. They had the philanthropic vision of stemming the mass migration from the countryside of workers seeking new opportunities in the expanding industrial cities by revitalising the market for rural artisan skills. Morris pined for a return to the chivalric splendour of medieval crafts, when embroidery had status and commissionable value. His textile designs, did not mimic but deferred to the imagery of the past and found favour with the Gothic revivalist architecture of the day. His company Morris and Co., established in 1875, employed artists as designers. Yet, while he did learn to sew, it was the women of Morris's family and employees at the Royal School of Needlework who stitched his designs. Despite being a noted campaigner for women's suffrage, he maintained the gendered conception of men as designers and artists and women as executors of their vision.

The philanthropic Royal School of Needlework had been established in 1882 to provide employment for impecunious gentlewomen. A reference from a clergyman was an entry requirement. Its aim was ambitious: 'to restore ornamental needlework to the high place it once held among the decorative arts and advance the employment of women in those arts in which they are best able to excel.' Students sewed for seven hours a day and were paid five shillings for the privilege. Individuality was frowned upon. Precision of stitchery and a schooled uniformity was its ideal: to each woman the same stitch, to each stitch the same method, to each method the same execution. Its aim was to ensure that if one stitcher left off and another took her place, it would be impossible to detect the change. Sewers had to faithfully copy what was placed before them. Such disciplined considerations won commissions, royal patronage and the involvement of the most celebrated male artists of the day, including William Morris, of course, but also Edward Burne-Jones, Dante Gabriel Rossetti and Walter Crane. By 1883 the school had 200 employees.

But it was not all plain sailing. Despite the eagle eye of its supervisor, Miss Higgins, who gamely tried to keep up standards, there were errors in 'the taking of orders', the 'spoiling of materials' and the 'misdirecting of parcels'. Its early travails were surmounted, however, and the school proved so successful that it was soon emulated elsewhere. The Fisherton de la Mere Industries in Wiltshire created employment for disabled women and the Leek School of Embroidery in Staffordshire ran embroidery classes, exhibited its products, supplied London stores and designed its own kits. The Haslemere Peasant Industries established in Surrey combined the designs of artists with the skills of locally taught weavers and embroiderers to produce a range of high quality embroidered and woven textiles. Three similar schools were established in Scotland. Art needlework was born.

In America, the forty-nine-year old Candace Wheeler, visiting the Philadelphia Centennial Exhibition in 1876, was inspired by the work of the Royal School of Needlework. She used it as a model that she adapted to meet the needs of impoverished women in the United States, particularly those affected by the death or injury of their husbands or fathers during the Civil War. A feminist, Candace Wheeler thought that financial independence rather than political emancipation was the priority for women's social progress. To this end, she founded the Society of Decorative Arts in New York in 1877 to offer women artists and artisans training in the applied arts, and create markets for their work. In 1878 she set up the New York Exchange for Women's Work, a pioneering enterprise through which women could sell any of their home-produced products, needlework included. The following year she co-founded the interior design firm Tiffany & Wheeler with Louis Comfort Tiffany and became the first woman in America to have interior design as her profession. In 1883 she formed her own company, Associated Artists, run entirely by women. Wheeler transformed American taste by introducing uniquely American designs inspired by native plants and the nature of an American light. In 1892 she established a creative colony in the Catskill Mountains, which became a haven for single women artists and writers. Throughout her career her main purpose was to provide a platform for women's talents and art though which women could realise not just professional worth, but also financial power.

The Royal School of Needlework, meanwhile, went from strength to strength. In 1879 it expanded its operation and opened a school in Glasgow. But the Glasgow students proved wayward and dilettante. Miss Higgins, London's doughty workshop supervisor, was despatched to muster discipline but even she could not enforce the required control. Princess Charlotte was persuaded to administer encouragement but her efforts proved equally ineffectual. The school closed in 1885, the same year Fra Newbery took up his post as the new Director of the Glasgow School of Art. Seven years later, under the leadership of his wife, Jessie Newbery, the School established its own embroidery department, the Department of Needlework, to foster a very different approach to the teaching of sewing than that promulgated by London's Royal School of Needlework. It was a radical departure from anything that had gone before, encouraging an individualistic stamp and exploration of materials and their effect. It was Jessie Newbery who heralded a new consciousness of the sensual potential of surface stitchery, unloosed from tradition, not looking back like Morris, but forward. Embroidery would never be the same again.

As its champion, Jessie Newbery embedded art needlework at the heart of the design curriculum of Glasgow's School of Art, insisting that her female students be exposed to the same curriculum as men. Women investigated botanical forms through dissection and drawing. They attended life-drawing classes, sketching live models to become better acquainted with the structure and spatial presence of the human body. Nature as a subject was reduced to its most basic elements – the bend of a stem, the curl of a leaf, the curve of a spine or the incline of a head – and the relationship between each. What she was interested in was the possibility of balance between apparent opposites and between linear and circular forms.

Newbery advocated a new, subtler colour palette in antithesis to the sharp colours of Berlin wools: pale lilacs, pinks, greys and greens backgrounded in cream or dark colours. The rose, the traditional symbol of femininity, was her main emblem, but not the rose in full bloom beloved by traditional embroiderers or its geometrically rendered abstraction found in Muslim embroidery. She simplified its petals in appliqué as connected segments of flattened curves with no attempt at naturalism, shading or ornamentation. Her rose, with its strong, clear structure, became a new contemporary interpretation of the bolder feminine. It became known as the Glasgow Rose.

In their needlework, her students were encouraged to ensure that each element of their work had a role in its design. Hems were not just a neatening of frayed edges, but an integral part of the whole, folded back and stitched in contrasting colours or studded in glass beads. The stitching used to outline and anchor an appliquéd shape on its background was sewn in a contrasting colour or with braid to add definition and emphasise the shape itself. Beads, ribbons, paper and card were incorporated to introduce a variety of surfaces and weights, a variance of textures that Margaret Macdonald was to adopt so enthusiastically in her subsequent work. Image was married to text. Nothing was hidden from view; everything was arranged in relation to something else. This was not sewing as a philanthropic salve to middle-class women who had fallen on hard times, but the elevation of needlework as a textural art form, an assertion of its rightful place as a higher art.

The *Studio* magazine, the influential illustrated magazine devoted to decorative art published from 1893 onwards, applauded their efforts:

It is not founded on tradition and has no resemblance to any style that preceded it. The new embroidery is common in this respect to the oldest arts. It takes the everyday things in life, and by the simple individualistic process, seeks to make them beautiful as well as useful.

Jessie Newbery's aim was to recalibrate the prevailing attitude to needlework and demonstrate that utility and beauty were not irreconcilable. She became a proselytiser of its agency, wanting it to be within everyone's reach, to all classes and both genders. By using the most basic of fabrics, such as linen cotton, calico, flannel and hessian, she showed how affordable it was. By adopting simple designs and the easier technique of appliqué (where the use of shapes cut out of fabric, their outline sewn onto the backing cloth, saved stitchers the time and effort to embroider the whole of a motif) she made needlework more accessible. Always a zealous educator, in the 1890s she set up needlework and design courses that ran every Saturday, open to all at a small cost. Over 100 women attended. More classes were organised for workers in thread mills, in factories, for women in the co-operative guilds and for 'commercial men engaged in textile and allied trades'. The latter course attracted manufacturers, calico printers and salesmen. There was also a course for teachers to work towards a Certificate in Art Needlework and Embroidery.

Jessie Newbery was an active supporter of the suffragette cause and became involved in other initiatives to bolster the place of women in society and secure visibility for women's art. She became a member of the Glasgow Society of Women Artists, which, by 1895, had sufficient funds to purchase its own head-quarters becoming the first women artists' residential club in the country. In 1910 she helped the Women's Social and Political Union organise a Grand Bazaar of women's craft: women's art made by women and bought by women. In a world where consumerism was on the rise, the agency of women as consumers purchasing items to be displayed in their homes offered a new market and a much-needed platform for women's art and crafts.

It was not only through what she did that Jessie Newbery promoted the new artistry of needlework, but also through what she wore. She abandoned corsets in favour of a looser style of 'artistic dress', which allowed fabric to fall naturally rather than being manipulated into the tight, uncomfortable shapes that fashion dictated. She embellished her dresses with embroidered collars and belts and decorative hems. For my wedding I emulated her and, on a dress of dark forest-green velvet, I sewed a deep curve of cream silk around its neckline on which I appliquéd a crust of pale pink Glasgow roses lying among embroidered leaves. It was my way of claiming my city and my heritage: the heritage of the independent and imaginative Glasgow Girls whose mission was to create beauty and art through simple embroidery on cloth.

Ann Macbeth, another embroidery student, became Jessie Newbery's assistant in 1901. Together they made suffragette banners and co-produced a banner for the city that was emblazoned with its coat of arms. It won a silver medal at the First International Exhibition of Modern and Decorative Art in Turin in 1902. One of Ann Macbeth's banners, originally made as a quilt, was embroidered with eighty signatures of suffragettes who had been incarcerated and force fed in Holloway Prison. It was carried aloft in the From Prison to Citizenship Rally of 1911. She herself went through the same ordeal, an experience which compromised her health thereafter. Like Jessie Newbery, she wore artistic dress decorated with deep appliquéd collars and, like her, she was an impassioned teacher. She developed a unique approach to needlework education and in 1911, with a fellow teacher Margaret Swanson, published *Educational Needlework*, a textbook for teaching needlework to children. It was as revolutionary as the embroidery emerging from Glasgow School of Art. With their mission to 'take Needlecraft from its humble place as the Cinderella of manual arts and to show how it may become a means of general and even of higher education' they declared that 'the boy or girl who uses material and needle freely in independent design . . . ranks on a plane with the scientist who makes a hypothesis, with the artist who makes an experiment'. Macbeth and Swanson discarded the concept of needlework being a tool of discipline and duty and instead advocated a delight and ease with sewing. They based their educational theories on the physiological realities of the development of children's eyesight and hand-to-eye co-ordination. Children, working with simple stitches in brightly coloured thread, were taught to fashion something both practical and decorative: a small bag, a pen wiper, a needle case. The emphasis was on incremental creativity: technical competence and design confidence, coaxed step by step through pleasurable small projects. The book heralded the end of samplers as the best method of needlework education. Macbeth and Swanson's innovative sewing curriculum was adopted throughout the country and overseas and it became the mainstay of needlework education until the late 1950s.

Of all the Glasgow Girls, it was Margaret Macdonald who was the most courageous and inventive in her needlework, and who had the most inquiring mind of them all. She was not the most prolific of the embroiderers to emerge from Glasgow School of Art, nor the most celebrated, but her work was the most experimental. I have a photograph of her pinned on my workshop wall. She is my chosen muse, my guide. As I have threaded my way through a professional life in textiles, it is to her I turn to tug on my sleeve and egg me on.

Margaret and her sister Frances made their mark early at Glasgow School of Art, with a fellow student describing them as the 'brilliant Macdonald sisters'. They embraced a wide variety of media, from poster art to bookbinding, metalwork, panels fashioned from gesso (a thick plaster medium generally used for priming paintings), watercolours and embroidery. Their watercolours dwelled on themes of women's choices, constraint and relationships; emotion and experiences were abstracted to symbolic interpretation implied by the balance of colour and composition. In 1892 they met two male students who were attending night classes. Herbert MacNair was an apprentice with the Glasgow architect John Honeyman and Charles Rennie Mackintosh – the son of a police superintendent and the fourth of eleven children – was a draughtsman with the same firm. The quartet, encouraged by Fra Newbery, began to collaborate on projects. The strange, androgynous and elongated figures that featured in their work earned them the nickname 'The Spook School'. Eventually they became known simply as 'The Four', carving out a reputation that was both non-conformist and, to many, eccentric.

In 1896 the sisters set up their own studio in the city centre, although they continued to work with Herbert MacNair and Charles Rennie Mackintosh on specific projects. That same year, Charles painted a watercolour entitled *Part Seen, Imagined Past*. It is thought to be a full-length portrait of Margaret in profile, her thick hair swept in a dark drape around her head. Her body is undefined, wrapped in a tangle of rose briars that flower at their upper stems, and behind her head is a sphere of iridescent turquoise. In 1899 Frances and Herbert got married and moved to Liverpool, and Charles saw his design for a new art school become a reality. The following year, Margaret and Charles got married. But the four still worked together. They were invited to participate in the VIIIth Secession Exhibition in Vienna in 1900, an international exhibition organised by a group of Austrian painters, architects and sculptors who had formed a movement called the Vienna Secession as a rejection of the confines of art as dictated by academic and nationalistic tradition. The Austrian symbolist artist Gustav Klimt was its first President. The exhibition focussed on the Applied Arts and called for individual pieces of artistic craftsmanship. Margaret and Charles accepted the all-expenses-paid invitation to display their work, and although Frances and Herbert, now new parents, had to forgo the adventure of travel, they joined in its execution. Together they created *The Scottish Room*. Its white interior accentuated the timbre of the objects it contained fashioned in wood, metal, glass, fabric and gesso and in a collective ideal of simplicity and textured harmony. *The Scottish Room* caused a sensation and everything in it sold. While some critics found the stark interior unsettling, most were fulsome in their praise for a design that could 'animate the inanimate', appear both 'personal and curious' and achieve 'a strange accord'. Margaret was admired for the 'jewel-like embroidery' of the appliquéd curtains she exhibited. She and Charles were led through the streets of Vienna by admiring students in a cart strewn with flowers, and Margaret's work had a strong influence on Gustav Klimt. It spurred him into an even more robust experimentation with pattern and texture, of the play of light on sheens of gold, an approach that rewarded him with fame and eventual fortune.

As the MacNairs immersed themselves in impressing their innovative style on Liverpool, Margaret and Charles' creativity became evermore closely intertwined. Following their triumph in Vienna, they were commissioned to design a music salon for Fritz Waerndorfer, a major Viennese arts patron, and as her contribution Margaret began work on a series of ambitious gesso panels called *The Seven Princesses*. Her use of gesso was unusual. Rather than employing its thick consistency as a base for paint, she manipulated it as a three-dimensional medium, piping it onto canvas to create raised linear sweeps and moulding it to fashion a crust of roses. Under her hands, her gesso panels became more like appliqué, heavily textured, studded with glass beads and inlaid with mother of pearl.

In 1901 Margaret and Charles submitted a joint design for *House for an Arts Lover* to a competition organised by the German design magazine *Zeitschrift Für Innendekoration*, which invited entries only of 'genuinely original modern designs'. It was conceived with The Four's trademark white backdrop, its long side windows accentuated by a series of twelve identical fabric hangings, each containing a solitary female figure, her hair running the length of her body, her disembodied frame demarcated by linear vertical lines punctuated in small roundels. Their design didn't win the competition, but it won the Mackintoshes plaudits and increased international interest.

In 1988, NeedleWorks, the company I ran in Glasgow, was

invited to realise Margaret Macdonald's textile designs for a *House for an Art Lover*. A consulting engineer, Graham Roxburgh, had decided on a venture to turn the Mackintosh drawings into bricks and mortar as a piece of creative research that would animate the vision behind it. As part of her research, Amanda Thompson, one of our team, visited the Glasgow School of Art's archives, where its curator let her study the only extant embroidered panels created by Margaret, thought to be replicas of the curtains she created for the VIIIth Vienna Secession. While different, aspects of the design were similar and the techniques she used would undoubtedly have been replicated on those of the *House for an Art Lover* had they ever been created.

The two panels, mirror images of one another, were over five feet long and just sixteen inches wide. Each contained the abstracted figure of a woman. There was no detailing of her arms, legs or breasts; instead her body was indicated in a simple oval of deep pink, heavy silk. Each head, with its moon-white face, was inclined towards the other. The eyes were closed, the lips sensual and the heads haloed in a circle of silk, a shape repeated around her upper half by two leafed and curving stems which encased it, and by a single beaded circle around her lower limbs. Her hair, realised in bronze fabric, flowed down from the top of her head to merge with her outer body and frame it in a gleam of silk. To it was pinned a solitary cream circle, from which fell a heavy vertical band made of different braids that led to other small circles enclosing a vaginal design. Similar circles were laid within her body. The panels' outermost borders were inlaid with deep, thick, pillar-like strips of braid that had, at their top, inward-facing pennants, each displaying two eyes, set one below the other. Margaret used a plethora of materials to achieve textural impact: linen, silk, metal threads, braid, ribbon, glass beads, white kid stretched over card for her faces. What they suggested were different weights of emotion: the steadfastness of the sentinel eye – watching braid pillars; the protectiveness of the inner circles; the self-containment of the women themselves, with their inner sensuality of silk enclosed in the strength of robust braid. Desire was hemmed in glass beads, hinted at with vaginal references: dark with light, line with curve, silk with thick braid, all creating a physical and emotive art that spoke of a woman's inner experience as an independent and self-protected spirit. It was art of a kind never achieved before in needlework.

With these as her guide, Amanda set to work to source vintage braid and beads and dye silk to match those in the original design. It was patient work. Precise tones were vital: the pink not too pink, nor too sharp, having depth but carrying light; the gold not too lustrous, muted but not overly subtle. Once the materials were reproduced, the team set to work on specially constructed frames to hand stitch Margaret's never-materialised masterpieces. We couched down the thick lines of black braid, appliquéd the cream and pink circles that lay staggered along linear lines, trying to find her own hand by using a style of stitching that emulated Margaret's own: not so fine that they hardly registered, yet avoiding a coarseness that might seem crude. By the time the panels were completed, the project had run out of money and it was shelved. It was resuscitated, however, in 1994, by which time Amanda had died tragically young of cancer. Two of the panels had disappeared. I was tasked with replacing them and, having kept Amanda's original dye recipes, I resuscitated the hues that Margaret might have had in mind. It was all for naught in the end, as the panels, large though they were, did not cover their allotted spaces. In 1988 their measurements had had to be estimated as the building wasn't yet constructed. Our embroidered panels were abandoned and the artist Claire Heminsley was commissioned to stitch just one exemplar piece of the correct dimensions to hang alongside its now-stencilled fellows. But I was glad of the small part I played in their genesis. It allowed me to replay Margaret's techniques, her instinctive placing of circles along a line of containment; the intuitive rise and fall of flat and raised texture to let the eye rest and lift again; of the way she sewed a bottom stem, separated it as it rose to leaf and tripled it across a woman's face to become a grounded symbol of growth and renewal. If I had never had the opportunity to stitch what she might have sewn, I would never have got as close to her process of making art.

In 1902 Margaret won the Diploma of Honour at the International Decorative Arts Exhibition in Turin for her gesso panel *The White Rose and the Red Rose*. The following year she and Charles were commissioned to create the Willow Tea Rooms in Glasgow's Sauchiehall Street, and chose to reference its street name, which in Scottish Gaelic translates as 'the alley of the willows'. In their collaborative work there was always a story, albeit distilled into abstracted imagery and atmosphere. The tea room's proprietor, Kate Cranston – not just a commercial but also a cultural entrepreneur – had already worked with Charles on her other tearoom establishments. A champion of the temperance movement and women's suffrage, her tea rooms were ultra-modern both in style and social opportunity. Here were places where women could go unescorted to meet other women and share the same social space as men.

The Mackintoshes were to be given free rein on a four-storey building. They designed not only the exterior façade and interior backdrop, but also the furniture, cutlery, vases and staff uniforms – even, it is said, the way a waitress's apron bow was tied.

They had also begun to design Hill House, a commission to create a new home for the publisher Walter Blackie. Like the Willow Tea Rooms, Margaret and Charles were responsible for both its exterior and interior design. They had responsibility for every detail of its domestic environment. In the bedroom,

they installed appliquéd panels of dreaming women, the upholstery was embroidered with roses, the lampshades fashioned in
cream silk, braided in black and adorned with Glasgow Roses
and black veined leaves. For the drawing room, Margaret made
an antimacassar (a rectangle of fabric laid over the back of a
chair to protect it). It is an audacious piece of needlework for
its time: abstract art in stitching. On a black background flecked
with white, she criss-crossed green velvet and lilac ribbon with
cream braid, lines of different thicknesses woven in and out of
each other in an intuitive reach for balance. At its centre is a
small rectangle of striped fabric with an inverted 'V' of ribbon
travelling though it to reach, at its base a small roundel filled
with tiny pearl beads. It is arresting and complex, fashioned in
unusual colour combinations and intentional contrasts: weight,
texture, open and closed space. It is, for me, her signature piece.
When Hill House was completed, it was hailed as a domestic
masterpiece, an inspired fusion of traditional Scottish architecture and contemporary artistic ideals.

Margaret continued to work on the *Seven Princesses* commission for Fritz Waerndorfer's music salon, and she and Charles
both continued to exhibit internationally and receive commissions and favourable reviews. In 1908, Margaret's sister Frances
returned to Glasgow following the breakdown of her marriage
to Herbert MacNair. She found part-time work at the Glasgow
School of Art, teaching embroidery and enamelling design. Her
watercolours trace an ever-deepening depression. In 1921 she
died, most likely by suicide. MacNair destroyed all her letters
and artwork in his possession. The same year, Margaret and
Charles sold their house in Glasgow for a mere £400. It had
been a celebrated showcase of their innovative style (eventually
saved for posterity by the Hunterian Museum in Glasgow).
Their glory days were fading. Charles had tried to set up an
architectural practice in the city but, with limited funds, it proved
impossible. In 1914 the couple moved to Suffolk, where they

painted a series of exquisite botanical studies, jointly signed, and then to London, where again Charles tried to establish his own practice. A photograph of one of Margaret's watercolours, *The Sleeper,* bears witness to their wanderings, with addresses written on the back in pencil, each crossed out as they moved: 120 Main Street; 78 Ann Street; 43a Glebe Place, Chelsea. In London, they existed on small commissions: a textile design for a handkerchief, another one for fabric, graphics for a menu. But this celebrated architect of Glasgow's new School of Art, whose work was acclaimed on the European stage, was little known in London and his efforts to set up a practice failed. There was a brief glimmer of possibility when in 1916 they were invited to undertake their first English commission, a house in Northampton at 78 Derngate. Despite its bold interiors of black woodwork, walls and ceilings and striking furnishings of shot purple edged in emerald-green ribbon and black-and-white striped wallpaper edged in bright blue braid, it made little stir in a nation now beleaguered by the First World War.

Margaret's last recorded works were two watercolours. *La Parfumée Mort* was exhibited at the Royal Scottish Academy of Painters in Watercolours in 1921. Against a dark, almost black, background, a woman's corpse is heaped high in roses. A sweep of five spectral female figures stretch skeletal arms out protectively across her body. It seemed an omen of her sister's death. *The Legend of the Blackthorns,* painted in 1922, just after her sister died, is even darker, showing two bowed women draped in black cloaks and suffused in the delicate white blossom of the blackthorn, the flower of grief. The Mackintoshes left London and moved to France, where they could live more cheaply. They exiled themselves from Glasgow and from Britain, and concentrated on being together.

In France, they lived a hand-to-mouth existence, eventually settling at the Hotel du Commerce in Port Vendres in the south of France, where Charles continued to paint. There is no trace of Margaret. For the next four years, she disappeared from public view. There is only a glimpse of her in the small bundle of twenty-three letters Charles sent to her in 1927 when she had to return to London for six weeks of medical treatment. His letters are written on wafer-thin paper, the earliest ones in pencil. He tells her how he has discovered that by not leaning too heavily on the lead he can keep the cost of postage down. His letters speak of his need of her, of shared delights of black cherries and ripe figs. He sends tales of the family and staff at the Hotel du Commerce and their fondness for her. He goes down to the harbour by himself in the early morning and finds that the quiet singing of its waters reminds him of the soft whirring of her sewing machine. So Margaret was still sewing. Whatever she was creating, however, has long since disappeared. He writes of his love of her, his debt to her creativity which was, he insists, three-quarters of his own achievement. He did not know then that the growth on his nose, which he describes to her, was the beginning of a cancerous tumour that would kill him some months later. On Margaret's return, Charles became terminally ill and they moved back to London, where he died in 1928. There were brief mentions of his death in *The Times* and *The Glasgow Herald*. The letters he wrote to Margaret in 1927 were kept by her, tied up in a faded blue ribbon.

Margaret died five years later, on 7 January 1933, of a cardiac arrest. The Hunterian Art Gallery and Museum Archive is guardian not only to some of her paintings, but also to her remaining few possessions. I went to see them, laid out by their curator on isolated tables. There were the contents of her work-basket: a few yards of metallic thread wrapped around a twist of paper; two bundles of cream and white braid; small scraps of velvet in apricot, purple, pale pink, cream, rose; a fold of cerise-pink silk; an offcut of brown and cream organza and another of black voile flecked with cream; and a length of violet ribbon edged in black. That was all, less than a metre of fabric all told and assorted thread and braid. The colours echoed the palette she had used for much of her needlework, the pinks, purples, cream and black. On another table lay her bank book. Her outgoings were circumspect: ten pounds taken out here and there, a doctor paid, the radium laboratory's bill settled, payments for what turned out to be ineffectual remedies to Boots the Chemists, the Herb Farm Shop and Hampstead Health Food Stores. She moved from place to place, from the Belgrave Club to London's Ladies Dwellings to Falmouth Hotel. Payments to Thomas Cook's travel agency are evidence of her journeying further afield.

When she died, her cousin Joseph Tilly Hardeman wrote to her executor, her brother Archibald Macdonald, to say that he had registered her death and at her flat he had gone through the letters he found in a suitcase and destroyed those that were 'of no use', keeping a few he thought might be of interest. He had also locked away three rings and the only money he found: £1.2s 9d. When he went through her handbag he discovered a rough draft of her will, which he attached. In it she asked to be cremated 'in the simplest and cheapest manner' and that her ashes be 'cast to the winds'. The contents of her studio were to be sold or dispersed by William Davidson, a loyal friend of both her and Charles, who was to keep or give them away to those who would 'care for the reputation of the Artists who made them'. There were a few itemised bequests: to her cousin, her silver cake dish; to her nephew's wife, her jewellery; to Desmond Chapman-Huston, the Irish writer, her silver grapefruit spoons with M. M. M. on their handles and Charles's silver salad fork and spoon. The last item I viewed was her inventory, dated 13 February 1933. It listed her furniture, jewellery, plate, glass, pottery, clothes and the other effects Margaret left behind. Among them was an 'old sewing machine'. The valuator estimated their total value at £88 16s 2d.

Her obituary in *The Times* referred to her as Mrs Charles Rennie Mackintosh and Glasgow, the city that had spawned their talent, later reclaimed Charles but not Margaret. After her death, a retrospective of Charles's work was quickly organised. The influential London critic P. Morton Shane dismissed Margaret's work as being of 'decidedly inferior artistic calibre' and accused her of leading Mackintosh into 'a usurious ornamental vulgarity'. She was not just marginalised, but eradicated. The male world of art had claimed Mackintosh as their own, untainted by the artistic influence of a woman. Over the next few decades, as Charles Rennie Mackintosh became lionised, Margaret Macdonald's art and Margaret herself faded in his shadow. The artist who made visible the psychological world of women, interpreted inner thoughts and feelings through the textured mediums of needlework and gesso, and used the symbolism in her watercolours to transmit the atmosphere and mood of women's experiences; who was thought to be, in her time, one of the most talented artists of her generation and who so defiantly transgressed the conventions of embroidery, became a footnote in the history of art.

The Willow Tea Rooms on Glasgow's Sauchiehall Street are now being restored. The renovations are screened by large hoardings that feature full-size portraits of Charles Rennie Mackintosh and Kate Cranston. There are none of Margaret. Inside there is an information desk serviced by women eager to market the revival of a commercial attraction for the city. I ask about Margaret Macdonald; why is she not pictured outside? The woman I speak to is confused. She has never heard of her. 'This was her work too,' I say, 'as much her work as that of Rennie Mackintosh.' I am aware that my outrage is verging on the confrontational, and that the woman is only hearing my tone, not my information. I modify my tone. 'Look her up on Google', I suggest, and walk away. 'I'll do that,' the woman's conciliatory voice follows me as I walk disconsolately down Sauchiehall

Street. How long does it have to take, I wonder to myself, for women artists to be properly and fairly acknowledged?

In 2002 Margaret Macdonald's gesso panel *The White Rose and the Red Rose* sold at Christie's Auction House in New York for £1.7 million. The ascendency of the Glasgow Girls was short lived. The First World War and its sad depletion of a generation of young men saw creative momentum and artistic opportunity recede. Books, magazines, transfer companies and pattern makers dominated the world of sewing once more. The term 'art needlework' disappeared from the sewing lexicon and, in time, from the curriculum of the Glasgow School of Art. By the end of the First World War, Ann Macbeth was pragmatic:

But the pendulum must swing back again soon and the women of canteens and munitions works, of the farm-yard and motor-van will turn again, though with a difference, to the more leisured work of gentler days as a relief from war and its huge transformation of all our former habits and fashions. We shall be changed, women and men, will stand partners together in works of all kinds . . .

But women artists created a climate of exploration at Glasgow School of Arts, and a tradition of innovative needlework. While they didn't succeed in completely eradicating the gender-based discrimination needlework faced, they were active agents in demonstrating how sewing could be central to an artistic movement. Margaret's story mirrored that of other women artists of the time, women who used needlework to create a different kind of art – Pheobe Traquair, Mary Lowndes, Margaret Gilmore, Muriel Boyd – and who are now all but forgotten. But the Glasgow School of Art continued their spirit, with others, such as Kathleen Mann, Kath Whyte, Hannah Frew Paterson and Malcolm Lochhead, following in the footsteps of the pioneering embroiderers who made their reputation through imaginative use of fabric and thread. Through their art and their teaching, they continued to inspire men as well as women to experiment with needlework design and make of it an art.

In the revamped Glasgow Style Gallery at Kelvingrove Museum, the works of the city's early twentieth-century artists, designers and architects are on display. Glasgow owes the major share of its international reputation and visitor appeal to their artistic flair. It was these artists who fed the cultural ambitions of Glasgow, rescuing it from being cast as a gloomy industrial sprawl mired by colonial trade and elevating it to a city that offered style and sensuality. Their experiments with simplicity and the inherent quality of materials – the glow of burnished copper, the gleam of silver, the bloom of glass, the rise of a stitch – celebrate a fusion of art and craft, of function and beauty. The artistry and intellect of these artists brought accolades to Glasgow. Now in their gallery I was surrounded by their elegant furniture, bold ceramics, textured wall panels, exquisite jewellery, streamlined cutlery and book bindings. I am, of course, trying to find embroideries, especially those of Jessie Newbery, Margaret Macdonald, Ann Macbeth and others who played such a major part in their triumph. But I cannot find a single stitch. There are gesso panels by the Macdonald sisters, illustrations by Jessie Newbery, the ground-breaking book on educational needlework penned by Anne Macbeth and Margaret Swanson but there is no sewing. It is as if all the ambition of the Glasgow embroiderers to elevate needlework and promote its capacity as an art form had come to naught. But they left a legacy, the legacy of textile art, a term coined later, which others would embrace, experiment with and explore, investigating the limitless possibilities of needlework's materials and techniques to express their professional art.

15
Work

In my late teens, I went out to work for the first time and found a part-time summer job at my local dry cleaners. It offered a variety of tariffs, from 'same day' to 'super valet service'. The latter involved not just the laundering and pressing of clothes but the meticulous overhaul of garments. A dress shirt would have all its buttons removed and reattached by hand; an unravelling hem would be resewn; missing hooks or eyes would be replaced and stains removed by a cocktail of chemicals; seams would be tested and over-sewn for strength.

This tending of clothes was done in the very last hour of the day. We would leave the steaming, ironing and big dry-cleaning machines and gather at the back of the shop, where an assortment of needles, threads, pins, buttons and stain removers awaited us. Duties were apportioned according to skill. As the student, I was designated the task of sewing on buttons. Once everyone was settled, the talking began.

I had fallen into the best of company: the world of hardworking women who told it like it was with humour and wisdom. Conscious that I was only seventeen, the women were keen to induct me in what lay ahead: a world of predatory men, disappointing sex, painful childbirth, harried motherhood and constant care. I have never laughed so much in my life. I loved those hours we spent together sewing. I loved these strong women who gathered me into their world and helped prepare me for mine. Even today, the sudden waft of dry-cleaning vapour brings a momentary thrill, evoking memories of being clustered around that large table with the marooned boxes of threads and buttons, our laps piled high with fabric as our hands darted to and fro in a deftness of sewing.

Just before I left the job, the women told me to bring in the clothes I was taking with me on a holiday break before I went to university. When I came in for my last shift, they presented me with them not just laundered, but folded round cardboard, wrapped in tissue, their loose buttons reattached, dipping hems realigned, each and every piece protected in cellophane. It was their gift to mark my departure to another world, divorced from theirs, a world of university and opportunity. But the greater gift had been their companionship and ribald welcome to their world.

The industrialisation of Britain brought with it a major shift in the working lives of people who sewed on buttons and hand-stitched the other laborious processes involved in garment-making. Since the first steam-driven piston engine had been invented in 1712, the acceleration of mechanised production transformed the location and nature of work. There was a major expansion of roads and canals to link the emerging centres of industry where populations were growing exponentially to service industrial progress. By the mid-eighteenth century, textile production was the dominant industry of Britain, resourced by the energy provided by its plentiful rivers and mines of coal. Cottage industries declined as vast numbers of the rural poor moved to newly forged industrial cities, lured by the promise of more stable work. The population grew as families discovered that their pooled income could be increased by having more children, deemed fit to work by the age of seven or even younger. But 'the sweated industries' didn't bring a hoped-for prosperity to the poor. Instead they found themselves exploited with low pay, long hours and unsafe working conditions. Many became pieceworkers, operating from home, paid for the number of items sewn. They were dependent on contractors who could set whatever terms of employment they chose and change them whenever they pleased. In the textile industries, women predominated as the labour required little physical strength. Women were also cheaper and largely un-unionised. Textile pieceworkers often had to pay a deposit for the fabric their contractor provided and cover the cost of needles and thread from their own pockets. In inadequate housing, over-crowded and insanitary conditions (in 1840s Manchester, nearly 15,000 people lived in cellars), workers lived in constant dread of their work being spoiled, since any damage was deducted from their pay. But there was no redress to exploitation and, for women, little alternative employment, bar prostitution. When a widowed seamstress, Mrs Biddell, was charged with theft and sent to the workhouse after she had pawned the cloth supplied by her employer to buy food for her starving children, the poet and author Thomas Hood was so moved by her situation that he wrote eleven verses describing her toil and poverty. *The Song of the Shirt* was published in the 1843 Christmas edition of *Punch*, the British weekly satirical magazine:

> With fingers weary and worn,
> With eyelids heavy and red,
> A woman sat in unwomanly rags,
> Paying her needle and thread –
> Stitch! Stitch! Stitch!
> In poverty, hunger, and dirt,
> And still with a voice of dolorous pitch
> She sang The Song of the Shirt!

The poem fanned the flames of an already increasing public concern about the inhumane conditions suffered by the working poor. But Mrs Biddell was only one of the thousands of textile workers, many of them children, who, despite having employment, lived in poverty. In parts of England, but predominantly in Ireland and Scotland, a new, insidious kind of piecework was introduced. White-work embroidery, or 'flowering' as it became known, involved embroidering floral and other patterns on white muslin in white thread. It looked like lace, but its open areas were created through stitching. White-work could be produced and bought far more cheaply than lace itself but it offered the same delicacy. Its desirability and marketability increased when Queen Victoria commissioned it for christening gowns for the Princess Royal and the Prince of Wales. Business boomed. At the height of its popularity over 80,000 women and chidren were employed as 'flowerers' in Scotland, and an estimated 400,000 more in Ireland. But the stitching of white on white is one of the most taxing kinds of embroidery. For the flowerers its incessant sewing, invariably in poor light, risked injury to their eyesight. A girl could go blind by the time she turned twenty. A supposed remedy was whisky poured directly into the eyes to alleviate tiredness. A Nottinghamshire doctor noted in his submission to the Children's Employment Commission of 1843 than in ten years of practice he had treated over 10,000 women and girls for eye damage.

By 1906, conditions for pieceworkers had scarcely changed. The *Daily News*, a radical and reformist daily newspaper founded in 1846, decided to champion piecework reform. It mounted an exhibition in London called The Daily News Sweated Industries' Exhibition with the aim of 'acquainting the public with the evils of Sweating in Home Industries.' There were stalls displaying products that pieceworkers had made and photographs of their working conditions. Many focused on the textile trades: dressmaking, shirt making, umbrella covering, coffin tassel making, tennis ball covering, sack sewing, glove stitching and military embroidery. There was an accompanying handbook which quoted from government and independent reports. These exposed the paucity of workers' lives and how widespread their exploitation had become. Margaret H. Irwin is cited from her *The Problem of Home Workers* report published in the Westminster Review in 1897. She describes the conditions endured by shirt hand-finishers and the financial and time pressure they were under:

For shirt finishing at 9d a dozen, one woman had to put on each shirt 2 rows of feather stitching down the breast, sew on 8 buttons, make 6 button-holes, 'bridge' the seams, and stitch any part the machine had missed. In order to complete her dozen of shirts she was obliged to sit at the work from 8 a.m. until 1 the next morning. 'She was not greedy', she said, and would have been content if she could only have made her full shilling a day. Owing to the irregularity of her work her earnings varied from 2s 6d to 4s a week.

The sewing machine was meant to be these women's saviour. Different versions of a mechanical aid to sewing had begun to appear from the 1840s onwards. The Americans Walter Hunt and Elias Howe led the way, coming closest to creating a workable sewing machine, but although their inventions, and those of their competitors, did reach the factory floor and tailors' workshops, these early machines were notoriously unreliable. It was a fellow American, Isaac Merritt Singer, who was to devise dependability: a sewing machine that lived up to its promise of continually sewing pieces of fabric together. His rags-to-riches story epitomised the American dream.

Born in 1811 to poor German immigrant parents, it is thought in the small town of Schaghticoke, NY, Singer was abandoned by his mother at the age of ten and left home at the age of twelve. His two main attributes were his dual love of engineering and showmanship. In moral terms, his commercial rise was inglorious. Singer's story is one of ruthless betrayals – of women, friends, business partners and family – of predatory sexual liaisons with many – usually young – women, and an immoral, at times illegal, contempt of patent law. But he steered the sewing machine not only into the newly forged garment-making factories of 1850s America and elsewhere in the world but into the homes of thousands. For all his personal and commercial faults, he was driven by an engineer's curiosity as well as financial gain. He was determined to design a sewing machine that was efficient, durable and affordable.

Singer lived by his wits. Badly schooled, barely able to write or spell, he spent his early years on the road, finding work where he could, as a joiner, a lathe operator, a pitchman in a funfair. The latter gave him a taste for theatrics and he joined the Rochester Players. At nineteen he married the fifteen-year-old Catharine Maria Haley. They had two children before Singer took to the road again, signing up with the Baltimore Strolling Players. When he espied the attractive Mary Ann Sponsler in the audience, he made her his mistress and she was soon pregnant, During their twenty-five-year liaison they were to produce ten children together. He and Mary Ann established their own company, The Merritt Players, but its financial precariousness led Singer to disband the company in the early 1840s and concentrate on the more lucrative potential of inventions. His prototype for a machine to carve printers' letter blocks caught the interest of the publisher George Zieber who thought that it had enough potential to warrant the investment of his money, time and a workshop space for Singer to hone the prototype into a marketable product. When catastrophe struck in 1850 and a boiler exploded in the building where Singer was working destroying his work-in-progress, he relocated to another workshop in Boston. It was already inhabited by Orson Phelps, a scientific instrument maker to trade, who had once advised Elias Howe on the mechanism for his sewing machine invention, patented in 1845. Phelps had a contract with the sewing machine manufacturer, Blodgett and Lerow. But both Elias Howe's and Blodgett and Lerow's machines were temperamental. The company of tailors who rented the workshop at the top of the Boston building were constantly in need of Phelps' expertise to repair their machines. They broke down with such regularity that

Singer, appalled at their inefficiency, declared he could create a much more dependable alternative. Zieber bet him $40 to do just that, adding that if he did succeed then he, Singer and Phelps would form a tripartite company to market his improved model. Singer set to work and, so the myth goes, in just eleven days had cannibalised the disparate machine parts Phelps put at his disposal and assembled a machine that performed continuous and reliable stitching and surpassed its predecessors. His breakthrough had been achieved by lateral thinking. Instead of attempting to devise a machine that emulated the movement of hand-stitchers in a mechanical way, as other designs had done, Singer concentrated on the machine's purpose: the joining of two pieces of fabric. Through small adjustments, such as using a straight rather than curved needle and making its movement linear rather than circular, he achieved an exactitude and continuity of stitching that hitherto had been elusive.

The three men agreed on a partnership. At first it worked well. Zieber provided the investment in materials and patent costs, Phelps supplied the skilled team of mechanics and Singer the attention to engineering detail. But Singer wanted more than his fair share. He saw off Zieber first, convincing him that he was terminally ill and could better provide for his family after his death by relinquishing his partnership in the company for a lump sum. He bullied Phelps into giving up his shares but retained his services as a salesman on the Singer team. He enlisted as a more useful partner a hot-shot lawyer, Edward Clark, to fight off the plethora of lawsuits from competitors for infringement of their patent rights. His Singer No.1, an industrial model, was finally patented in 1851, and in 1856 Edward Clark finally managed to broker a deal to bring several competitors together to form a patent pool. The cartel, called the Sewing Machine Combination, was the first multinational conglomerate. Walter Hunt, who had invented but not patented a locksmith sewing machine in 1833, was bought off by being enticed onto Singer's payroll and even Elias Howe came on board, comforted by a royalty on every Singer machine sold. Singer and Clark were ready to conquer the world.

In the Clydebank Museum in Scotland, the site of Singer's first overseas factory in 1885 – which was to become the largest sewing machine factory in the world – there is a gleam of Singer sewing machines, a display of different models through the ages. Singer's first model, the Singer No.1, takes pride of place. It is a surprisingly rough-hewn affair, its base a simple wooden box encasing a functionally designed foot pedal (later be re-fashioned as an elegant, intricately interlaced wrought-iron affair). On top is a sturdy sewing machine, its shape not dissimilar to contemporary machines, with a familiar arching sewing arm, top bobbin and side wheel. But its various pulleys and tension wheels, which draw the thread through, lack the finesse of subsequent models. Beside it is displayed the Turtleneck, which Singer designed in 1856 as his first domestic sewing machine. It sits in striking contrast to his Singer No.1, with a compact, box-like structure and small flourishes of gold patterning on its wheel, its body inlaid with a tidy mother-of-pearl posy of flowers. Originally priced at $100, the Turtleneck had to be reduced to $50 because of poor sales, and even then it wasn't popular. It was only when Singer brought out his Letter A family model in 1858 that sales took off. Larger and more robust, the Letter A, even at a price of $75, became a best seller. Singer had found his niche in the market.

The Letter A was targeted at the middle and upper classes. Singer was determined to persuade them to install sewing machines in pride of place above stairs. His improved family machine was a much grander version than the Turtleneck. This was a machine designed to exude domestic desirability as 'a beautiful ornament in the parlour or boudoir' Its body was finished in a gleam of black 'Japan' lacquer liberally ornamented with intricate gold scrolling; its metal plates were engraved and its base hewn from highly polished wood. Here was a machine of elegance, a piece of fine furniture with the added appeal of functionality. Its marketing was deliberately gendered to reinforce the stereotype of sewing as an exclusively female occupation. This is borne out by some early examples of the company's advertisements in Clydebank Museum. They depict a beautifully dressed woman, sometimes with a daughter by her side, sitting serenely stitching on her Singer sewing machine: the light is soft, the scene refined and the mood peaceful. Such marketing was effective. Mechanised sewing relocated the chore of sewing: it moved it from the servant's quarters and brought it into the drawing room.

Singer and Clark's legal and financial acumen was accompanied by marketing genius. With the price of a sewing machine beyond the reach of many, Edward Clark persuaded Singer to introduce the first ever hire-purchase scheme. For a mere three dollars a month, people could take home a brand new machine, guaranteed for a year, and pay it up over subsequent years. Purchasers made their payments locally at a Singer store, and received an official payment book that was stamped each month. Other innovative purchasing schemes were introduced. Schools, neighbours, families could group together to buy a shared machine; people could trade in their inferior models, invariably made by Singer's competitors, and become owners of his latest model.

Always the showman, Singer sent his salesmen on the road to promote his invention in factories, theatres and at church gatherings. He installed attractive young women in the shop windows of department stores to demonstrate his machines where they drew so much attention that the pavements became blocked by riveted bystanders. He set up human-against-machine sewing competitions. One, in New York's largest garment-making factory, had an official-time keeper operating a stopwatch as three of the factory's fastest hand stitchers were pitted against a solitary sewer on a Singer machine. The latter won hands-down and, the media having been invited out in force to witness the battle, reported that the factory had ordered, there and then, several of Singer's machines. Some cynics said it had already been a done deal.

By 1885, Singer was selling 900 sewing machines, by 1859 the *Scientific American*, a popular science magazine, was declaring that it was: 'astonishing how, in a few years the sewing machine has made such strides in popular favour, going from a mechanical worker to a domestic necessity', by 1886, sales had reached over 250,000. They continued to escalate and Singer continued to improve his models, adding other customised products to his profits: needles, threads, attachments and polished cabinets. He marketed his sewing machine as 'the most potent factor in promoting the happiness of mankind all over the world'. By 1906, annual sales of Singer's sewing machines reached one million units and Singer's company had secured 80 percent of the world market.

Singer had become a very rich man. He flaunted his success by building a state-of-the-art factory in New York City, the most modern yet seen in the world, eight floors high. Sporting white marble and walnut wood, it was a palace of industry where potential purchasers could view his latest machines in ornate splendour. He drove his family through Central Park in a specially built bright yellow carriage pulled by six black horses. Thirty feet long, it boasted toilets, a bar, smoking room and nursery as well as a comfortable seating area for sixteen passengers. It was an advertisement for how far Singer had come in the world.

But, for all his commercial achievement, Singer was spurned by those he most wanted to impress: the cream of New York society. The newspapers had a field day exposing the minutiae of his legal and romantic entanglements. Not content with a wife and mistress, he had taken up with Mary Eastwood Walters, a machine demonstrator, with whom he had fathered a daughter, then with another of his demonstrators, Mary McGonigal, and then with her sister Kate. He divorced Catharine in 1860 and, when his first son William spoke out in court in his mother's defence, Singer cast him aside. In 1861 he appeared in court again, this time accused of violently abusing his mistress, Mary Ann Sponsler, and their daughter Violetta. An out-of-court settlement was reached, but Mary remained vengeful and wrote a biography of Singer in which she did her best to destroy his reputation. That same year, 1861, when he was fifty, he met a married nineteen-year old, the French beauty Isabella Eugenie Boyer who, it is said, was the model for New York's Statue of Liberty. By 1863 she had divorced her husband and married Singer. Edward Clark, always alert to market downfalls and the corrupting influence of bad press, persuaded Singer that he had become a liability, a barrier to commercial growth. Singer left America with a 40 percent stake in Singer shares and remained on its Board of Directors. He and Isabella settled in Paignton in Torquay, where they had six children and where Singer built a 110-roomed palace with a hall of mirrors, a maze and grotto garden. The area became nicknamed 'Singerton'.

He died in 1875, shortly after his daughter Alice, by Mary Eastwood Walters, walked down the aisle wearing a dress that cost the equivalent of a London apartment. Singer had drawn up his own designs for his interment. There were to be three coffins, each inside the next: an inner coffin made in cedar and lined in white satin, a middle coffin of lead and an outer coffin of English oak decorated with silver filigree, all encased within a marble tomb. Eighty horse-pulled carriages led his cortege to the cemetery, the river of mourners, 2,000 or more, stretched from the seafront to the cemetery.

Twenty of his children were named individually in his will. To his son William, who had spoken against him in the divorce case from his first wife, Catharine, he deliberately left the meagre amount of $500. He died a multi-millionaire, leaving a fortune of over $14 million: a handsome dividend for a man whose life's work had been to find the most expedient way to speed up sewing.

A shirt could be stitched by a Singer machine in an hour, compared to the fifteen hours it would have taken to sew it by hand. But the machine's arrival did not bring the expected liberation from toil for hand-stitching pieceworkers. Ready-made clothes still required hand finishing. Sewing machines rather than alleviating exploitation, exacerbated it by churning out more clothes at more speed, all in need of finishing. The glut pushed prices down, which in turn drove down wages for pieceworkers, their numbers swelled by the unemployed garment makers who had been replaced by machinery.

In his book *Das Kapital*, written in the 1860s, the German philosopher and economist Karl Marx foresaw the devastation the arrival of the sewing machine would wreak on textile workers and railed against its coming:

The hour of the machine has struck for the advent of machinery. The decisively revolutionary machine, the machine which attacks in an equal degree the whole of the numberless branches of this sphere of production, dressmaking, tailoring, shoemaking, sewing, hat-making and many others, is the sewing machine.

Until the invention of the sewing machine, sewing had been companionable. Whether grouped with other women or sitting with the family, a woman could sew and still converse. The advent of the sewing machine changed how and where sewing was done. It became a solitary occupation at home, the silent chore of home workers or the toil of factory workers sewing in places where, amid the clang and clatter of machinery, conversation was impossible. The nature of industrial garment making also changed. Processes were separated: the hemming done on one machine, collars fixed by another. It now required several people to assemble a shirt, each one responsible for just one aspect of its making. Time became more pressurised. Rather than being meditative or mindful, factory machining turned sewing into an activity that was mind numbing, robbed of a stitcher's satisfaction of producing something from start to finish.

But the domestic sewing machine revolutionised the opportunities for women to have independence and financial freedom. They could now set themselves up in a respectable career as dressmakers and, for a small monthly outlay, run their own business at home, no longer prey to the vagaries and exploitation of employers. In Scotland, by 1861 over 62,000 women were registered as dressmakers, and by the 1890s in America there were over 300,000, 70 percent of whom were single.

Philanthropic ventures proliferated to support impoverished gentlewomen and girls in need of respectable employment as alternatives to factory exploitation. While these focussed on decorative hand-stitching, the sewing machine provided them with the means to manufacture at greater volume, and produce marketable items with profitable potential. The Ladies Work Society was one such charity, established in 1875 to develop a 'useful and elevating character for ladies dependent on their own exertions'. The Association for the Sale of Works of Ladies of Limited Means and the Co-operative Needlewoman's Society were among other charitable enterprises. For the women who created them, such organisations gave them a creative and economic role in public life. Women and their needlework moved out of the home and into the public arena under the guise of good works. A plethora of needlework schools followed providing training, sales outlets and reliable employment. Some, however, became almost interchangeable with the sweatshops their charitable founders had so condemned. The only difference being the perceived superiority of their guiding class.

By the late nineteenth century a middle-class culture had begun to dominate the needlework market. Women's magazines and needlework publications emphasised well-kept interiors, home-making and maternal care. I have a book of the time written by Emilie called *Everywoman's Guide to Home Dressmaking* in which she advised new mothers on what to sew in preparation for their babies:

Three sets of vests, long flannels, flannel bands, white petticoats, day gowns and woollen shoes; two sets of binders; four pairs of white sewn shoes; six nightgowns; one silk robe; one woollen shawl; three dozen napkins; one coat; one cloak and one silk bonnet or hat.

As an occupation, needlework became even more nuanced by the class division between women themselves. Middle and upper-class women emphatically dissociated themselves from the toil of functional industrialised stitching and claimed decorative embroidery as their own relaxing pastime. They were encouraged by an expansion of products specifically designed to facilitate their hobby – embroidery made easy – with kits, transfers and cloths pre-stamped with designs. An excess of unnecessary fancy-work began to appear in peoples' homes: table runners, nightdress cases, handkerchief sachets, bottle wraps and finger napkins.

But by the Second World War the consequences of all this inconsequential sewing were keenly felt. With clothes rationed and textile factories requisitioned to produce fabric and uniforms for army use, the government ushered in fashion austerity. Decorative embroidery was banned on lingerie and sleepwear and the recycling and repairing of clothes was encouraged – a skill, it was then discovered, that many women lacked. The widespread provision of kits and patterns had robbed them of the knowledge of basic sewing. The government launched its Make Do and Mend Scheme to reintroduce women to the techniques of simple needlework. With the aim of ensuring that 'no material should lie idle' it set up community mending clubs, organised exhibitions of recycled fashion in London underground stations and city high street stores, retrained teachers in sewing techniques and established sewing classes throughout the country. By 1943 there were over 24,000 sewing classes being run in Britain. The 1944 Education Act made it compulsory for girls in state schools to learn practical dressmaking, not as a decorative skill, but as part of their education in home-making, a subject newly termed Domestic Science.

In the Domestic Science Laboratory, as it was called in my all-girls school, a row of old-fashioned treadle sewing machines – dark lines of silent servants – waited for our young hands and feet to put them to work. I dreaded their ominous presence. I couldn't get the hang of how to co-ordinate my feet see-sawing the heavy metal plate while my hands steadied the fabric through the treadle's chomping teeth. I would push down determinedly on the footplate, rocking it back and forward for a skitter of stitches, lose momentum and watch in alarm as the wheel rolled into reverse, etching out a crazed path of haphazard sewing. My friend Elizabeth agreed to give me illicit lessons and we would creep into the sewing room during our lunch breaks until, eventually, I thudded my way to treadle mastery.

Looking to the future, in the 1950s the Singer company identified teenage girls as its future consumers. It organised Singer Teen-Age Sewing Classes and mounted advertising campaigns that used the Cinderella story as its key marketing tool, a story in which the sewing machine was a girl's Fairy Godmother, transforming her lack-lustre wardrobe into wondrous fashions through which she would find true romance. I was one of the many seduced by Singer's propaganda. From the age of twelve I made most of my own clothes. In what was then, for young people, a fashion-starved Glasgow, if you couldn't sew your own clothes you were dressed like your mother. I made my own, cutting out a dress one night and sewing and wearing it the next. If time was limited, I would dispense with fastenings altogether and get my sister or mother to sew me into it. At home most evenings, with the family grouped around the television, I was to be found crouched on the floor, pinning paper patterns to bargain-bought fabric. Yards of cheap buttermilk muslin could fashion a float of romance, crisp sprigged cottons be tiered into rustic skirts. When I discovered a shop selling cut-price furnishing fabrics I decked myself out in Jacobean splendour. A friend called it my 'upholstery period'.

I decided to pursue a career in sewing. I had the dream of becoming a couturier or costume designer perhaps. At my high school, however, the teachers were scandalised when I proffered Art and Domestic Science as my specialist subject choices. If I had the latter, I explained, I could go to Glasgow's Domestic Science College, called the 'Dough School', and study pattern-cutting and dressmaking. The Dough School, they instructed me, was somewhere you went when you had no other options. As a bright student, I was destined for university. Despite my protests, a curriculum was arranged: Italian, Latin, French, History and English. I went to university. It was to be another fifteen years before I reclaimed needlework as a profession. By then I was an arts consultant working in London, using my sewing skills as a second string in community arts projects. But my experience of making banners for the miners' strike and visiting Greenham Common, where women used needlework to voice protest, developed into an idea to use sewing as a vehicle to publicly promote communities' unacknowledged creativity. I left London, returned to Scotland and, with the help of the Gulbenkian Foundation, embarked on a feasibility study to explore the potential of establishing a community sewing enterprise. A year later, in 1985, I set up NeedleWorks in Glasgow.

At first it was just a name on a headed piece of paper, my sewing machine, me and the £40 a week provided by the Job Creation Scheme, which supported business start-ups. I became very, very poor, selling my bike and my books to keep myself afloat. The rewarding experience of early community projects, such as those in Leith, strengthened my resolve. Commissions began to trickle in. They caught media interest. NeedleWorks' reputation began to build. Strathclyde Community Business agreed to fund the enterprise for its first three years. Within eighteen months, NeedleWorks had a constitution, a board, its own professional workshop and its first employees.

An exhibition of community textiles NeedleWorks mounted in 1986 called A Stitch in Time at Glasgow's local history museum, the Peoples' Palace, was an unexpected success with over 100,000 people flocking to see it. It proved to me that there was an untapped audience for needlework of scale and meaning. But it was harder work than I could ever have imagined. The team worked flat out to keep up with corporate orders, community commissions and the ambitious projects spawned by the company's success. Days became blurred with the loading and unloading of sewing machines and sewing tool kits; evenings became filled with machining to get orders completed on time. Sewing through the night became a regular occurrence. The inevitable happened: I collapsed from exhaustion. Shortly after my recovery, NeedleWorks won the 'Arts Working for Cities' award of £10,000 from the Arts Council of Great Britain. An official from the Economic Development Unit of Glasgow City Council came to see me. He suggested that rather than producing caviar – his description of the imaginative, large-scale artworks NeedleWorks was making with communities and for corporate clients – what we should have been producing all along was beans, by which he meant high volume, batch-produced goods. I thanked him for his time and advice, inwardly mourning that for all its success, all the fantastic displays of extraordinary needlework created by local people, the enthusiastic media response and the thousands who came to our exhibitions, NeedleWorks was still, in the world of commerce, seen as just women's work. It was a sobering and disheartening moment.

After a decade of projects and commissions, NeedleWorks

was voluntarily liquidated in 1996. It had served its time. It had spent ten years creating public sewing artworks, finding public platforms for the communities it worked with, in museums, shopping malls, community centres and public halls, and in attracting admiration for the skills and imagination of the people most marginalised from civic life. That was its work and the sewing was its medium, re-valued as an expressive narrative of predominantly women's lives. It provided employment, training and involvement and it was, in the end, a worthwhile venture.

In the aftermath of NeedleWorks, I decided to design, make and market my own range of textiles, to attempt batch production. As I had little experience of how to maximise volume and minimise labour, I went to work as a machinist for a small company that made silk velvet scarves. My job was to sew down the middle seam, sew across the bottom seam, turn the scarf to its right side, carefully hand-stitch the other bottom seam, press and fold. What seemed straightforward turned out to be surprisingly stressful. Each hand-printed scarf was precious, the velvet expensive. Any waste represented a loss of income and time. But a momentary distraction could cause a seam to go awry and it would have to be unpicked. Unpicking left tell-tale perforations on the fabric, which then needed re-seaming a little further in, which meant losing a sliver of the design. One slip of the iron, a setting too high, and the velvet would be indelibly marked. I was not very good at either the sewing or the pressure. I grew bored with the monotony of repetitive stitching at the sewing machine, my back to the workroom. After a few weeks, I handed in my notice and abandoned the idea of batch production.

In 1911, a fire had broken out at the Triangle Shirtwaist Factory in New York City. The owners had bolted the doors to keep out inspectors and interfering union members. People watched horrified as sixty-two workers leapt to their death from its upper floors and others were consumed in the blaze; 140 people died. It marked a greater awareness of the need for safer working environments for textile workers. In 2012, the tragedy at the Shirtwaist Factory was echoed when 117 people lost their lives and another 200 were injured in a fire at the Tazreen Fashion Factory in Dhaka, Bangladesh. The ills of the sweatshop system in the west had been transferred to poorer countries in the east.

Throughout the twentieth century, textile companies increasingly set up satellite factories in countries where labour was cheaper and where managers and owners were less exercised by employment laws and workers' rights. Today, textiles continue to be made by the world's poorest and most vulnerable – children, women and migrants – people who have no unions to safeguard them from abuse, no means of alternative employment and whose employers have scant regard for their safety. Low pay and poor working conditions continue to haunt the industry. As recently as 2013, it was discovered that many of the 11,000 textile workers in the East Midlands in the UK were being paid as little as £3 an hour, well below the required national minimum wage. That same year, the International Labour Office reported that there were 170 million children working in the textile and garment industries worldwide.

Textile workers, however, have a long history of industrial action, campaigning to improve their conditions and pay with sit-ins, strikes, marches and demonstrations. In 1968 the 'Dagenham Girls', women who stitched car seat covers alongside men at the Ford Motor Company Limited's plant, went on strike. A new pay deal proposed that the women should be paid 15 percent less than their male counterparts for the same work. The women protested and galvanised the support of their fellow-workers. Their three-week strike brought Ford's car production in Britain to a total standstill. The women's determination to be awarded the same pay as men was backed by the then Secretary of State for Employment and Productivity, Barbara

Castle. They won their case. Two years later, in 1970, The Equal Pay Act came into force.

Today there are a growing number of organisations attempting to end exploitation in the textile industry, such as the Clean Clothes Campaign, Global Exchange, No Sweat, Stop Child Labour, Fairtrade, Fair Wear Foundation, all campaigning for ethical trade and protective practices that support and value workers. The Alta Gracia factory in the Dominican Republic is a new kind of anti-sweatshop, an innovative model of textile production that combines financial profit with social justice. In an alliance between its workers, management and experts in the apparel industry, it championed full participation of its workers to develop a company that treated them fairly and rewarded them with an adequate and reliable income, well above normal rates. It has published a book, *Sewing Hope*, about its ambition and its achievement, told by those involved. It is inspirational, and sets a new standard for what can be done successfully to establish a profitable textile enterprise that values and promotes the skills and input of all its stakeholders.

Such cooperative working in textile production is not a new concept. In parts of the world where war, famine and ethnic cleansing have devastated communities, needlework has often been used and continues to be used by aid agencies as a tool to help women whose need for income is urgent, to set up their own cooperatives or social enterprises. Sewing offers advantages for women in desperate circumstances. Its raw materials are cheap and readily sourced. It requires no equipment or electricity and is easily accommodated when living conditions are cramped. Moreover, it can be done at any time of day and be fitted around domestic chores and child care.

When Liz Kemp, a craft and design consultant based in Scotland, was invited to Peshawar in northwest Pakistan in 2004 to work with female Afghan refugees, she met women traumatised by war, sequestered in heavily guarded compounds. With social contact limited to their immediate families, living under the strict control of their husbands, they lived claustrophobic lives in which divisions and rivalries were common. To alleviate the stress and tedium, many young women had turned to drugs, and it was the United Office of Drug Control that invited Liz to run needlework design workshops with the women in the hope that an enterprise based on sewing – an activity allowed by their husbands and fathers – might relieve these women of boredom, bring them a small independent income and, in time, alleviate their drug dependency.

The women were well versed in the intricacies of embroidery, since Afghanistan has an extraordinarily rich textile heritage. What they lacked was commercial insight. Using fewer colours and less surface decoration, the women created designs that could be transferred from product to product, to bags, shawls and cushions. They made samples and test-marketed them at local shops, the bazaar and through charitable agencies. The feedback was positive. The Nomad Gallery in Islamabad put in an order. Sales increased and earning money brought unexpected side benefits: it raised the status of the women in the eyes of their husbands and won them a small relaxation of social control.

The project in Peshwar is just one of the many that have been and are organised to assist beleaguered communities find an economic and social lifeline through needlework. Organisations like Common Threads and Clothroads provide training, workshop space, business skills, outlets and an environment where women can debate issues which prevent them seizing a better way to live their lives. And yet, and yet. There is always the threat of cultural colonialisation: of women being persuaded to relinquish sewing traditions and techniques to manufacture products the west will buy: fabric accessories like bags, spectacle cases, purses, covers for iPads, computers and mobile phones

– products that many of the women who sew them cannot afford to possess. This is especially at odds with the cultural and emotional needs of refugees, for whom community upheaval often strengthens the urge to keep traditions intact. The repetition of pattern and the certainty of design offer visual continuity in communities broken apart by social or political change. How to retain the integrity and authenticity of traditional embroidery while meeting the demands of a competitive market is a continuing dilemma. Commercial imperatives mean that the replication of traditional needlework is often not economically viable: it simply takes too long to sew. Moreover, many traditional textiles, especially densely embroidered clothes, while beautiful, hold little interest for the modern consumer or tourist. With an urgent need to sell, adaptation is essential, a compromise found for the rich, ceremonial and meaningful embroidery to be truncated into more marketable goods that are quicker to create, easier to display and meet the needs and tastes of consumers. The sacrifice is a trade-off for other benefits, other vital forms of support, such as credit banks, child care, health clinics, literacy and numeracy education and business skills. Needlework is often used as a first step to empowering women to determine ways to improve their status and diminish the social controls and economic dependency that limit their well-being and progress.

This is the motivation behind the Sughar Empowerment Society which has twenty-five embroidery and cultural centres in rural Pakistan. It was set up by an eighteen-year-old, Khalida Brohi, who was determined to challenge the lack of equality between men and women, an inequality exacerbated by a male culture which condoned practices such as arranged marriages and honour killings. Through the project, which reproduces tribal designs in traditional ways, embroidery heritage and skills are not only respected but also safeguarded. The Sughar Empowerment Society values the talents and traditions of the women involved. An embroidered purse might take eleven hours to sew, but it retains the integrity of its roots. It places a high price on their worth, selling them to Pakistan's burgeoning fashion industry, marketing not just an embroidered product but the traditions they conserve. Their centres provide a place for women to be together, to talk about their rights, the issues that restrict them and how best to improve their standing without rejecting or destroying precious community traditions. These women are the archivists of some of needlework's most ancient patterns and techniques. Without their labours, the needlework heritage of their culture would become extinct as has happened elsewhere. They are conserving not just traditional skills and patterns but the heartbeat of needlework itself: its emotional purpose.

At the Sughar Empowerment Society, one woman was confused about how she could transfer the honour she had sewed into a garment for her daughter's dowry to a handbag she made for a stranger. How could she sew into her product its personal message of protection, her blessings? In her questioning lies a challenge to the textile industries of the future of how can they best endow what they sew with honour?

16

Voice

From when I was very young my mother lured me into a love of sewing. She bought me little linen cloths, already stamped with designs, and packets of gold tipped needles; scissors shaped like birds with folded wings and skeins of embroidery thread in hues, softer and richer than anything I had ever seen. My mother taught me how to carefully draw out a length of thread from its looped skein, cut it, then separate its six strands into divisions of ones, twos or threes depending on the desired delicacy of stitches. And she showed me the basic repertoire of strangely named stitches – stem, blanket, fern, lazy daisy, chain and French knot.

I would spend hours coaxing a flat cloth to yield to my design jabbing the needle in and out and untangling the thread that twisted and knotted until, eventually, I found a rhythm of my own that could settle smooth in my hands. Then the cloth became pliant, absorbing all that I stitched into it until, little by little, it became what it was meant to be: a pretty tray cloth, or a tablecloth festooned in blossom. In my memory, all the stencilled cloths, and those I later inked with transfers, were always floral. I would delve into my hoard of threads and select a bouquet of colour, sensing harmony. At the time, it seemed to me that this embroidering of flowers was not just a pastime but a portal to another way of life. My designs held the essence of luxury, of dressing tables strewn with perfume bottles, of tea sipped from porcelain cups amongst a friendship of women. It wasn't that I yearned to be part of such a world but, from the austerity of my own life in post-war Glasgow, it seemed a comfort that it might exist at all.

But why did my mother, so hard-pressed with the toil of

housework and the rearing of four children, take time to sit patiently by my side and induct me in the intricacies of embroidery? With finances already stretched why did she invest in skeins of thread and linen cloth to feed my flickering interest in needlework? I believe now that she wanted to find a way to keep me occupied. Although never boisterous, I was forged from a curious spirit, ever questioning, wanting to explore the small world around me. My inquisitiveness claimed an excessive share of her attention. The absorption of needlework encouraged me to be stiller, quieter. But it also gave me another way to express myself.

Sewing is a visual language. It has a voice. It has been used by people to communicate something of themselves – their history, beliefs, prayers and protests. For some, it is the only means to tell of what matters to them: those who are imprisoned or censored; those who do not know how or are not allowed to write of their lives. For them needlework can carry their autobiographies and testimonies, registering their origin and fate. Using patterns as its syntax, symbols and motifs as its vocabulary, the arrangement of both as its grammar, sewing is a graphic way to add information and meaning. But it is not a monologue, it is part of a conversation, a dialogue, a correspondence only fully realised once it is seen and its messages are read. It connects the maker to the viewer across time, cultures, generations and geographies. As a shared language, needlework transmits – through techniques, coded symbols, fabrics and colour – the unedited stories not just of women, but often of those marginalised by oppression and prejudice. And sewers use it – adapting it to their own circumstances, concerns and cultures – to provide a continuum of traditions, values and perceptions, in a world in which their influence is all too often deemed superfluous. It has evolved, primarily, as the voice of women who, through the centuries with limited access to literacy, or little assurance that if they did write, their words would be preserved, chose needlework as a medium to assert their presence in the hope that it, at least, might persist and, in time, be heard.

But oppressors have also appropriated sewing to disempower and diminish others: the German missionaries in Namibia who replaced Herero tribal dress with European fashion, the Soviet regime which neutered the traditional embroidery of Ukraine. It was, however, the Nazis, who as part of Hitler's Final Solution – his ambition to eradicate the Jewish race – used sewing to silence a people.

One of the Nazis' strategies for Jewish genocide was called 'Vernichtung durch Arbeit', destruction through work. In 1940 the Nazis set up sewing workshops in the Polish Jewish ghetto of Lodz, called the Litzmannstadt Ghetto. Here they corralled over 160,000 local Jews, men, women and children, into an area four-mile square. Imprisoned behind high walls patrolled by German guards, the Jewish community was cut off from the outside world with no access to food beyond what their captors permitted them: a daily ration of little more than 700 calories a day, inadequate to sustain health. In the first year 18,000 died from famine. Others, those deemed unproductive, predominantly children under the age of nine and the elderly, were deported to concentration camps. The rest became slave labour. Sewing machines were requisitioned from plundered Jewish properties and despatched to Lodz where they were stamped with a metal Star of David, the word 'ghetto' engraved at its centre. The Jews in Lodz worked from 7 in the morning until 7 at night in over-crowded and scarcely ventilated rooms, sewing German uniforms, corsets and luxury textile goods for German stores. The hundreds of child workers, those over the age of nine, made dolls dresses for German toy shops and learnt tailoring and machining from their elders. Like the adults they toiled as pieceworkers, repetitively sewing the same kind of seam, or attaching the same kind of collar for hours, for months, for years on end. A quota not reached would be punished with a reduction in food rations, any dip in production could mean deportation and certain death. These were children sewing for their lives. Survivor Josef Zelkowicz described in secret diaries the effect on the children in the ghetto: 'The machine digests their young tender bodies, squeezes them, and turns them into waste . . . [they] have twisted, stooped spines, sunken chests, and subdued, dejected eyes that drift off a distant, alien, cold gaze . . .' When the ghetto was liberated in 1944 the Soviet troops found 877 Jewish survivors who had hidden in the ghetto itself or had been hidden in the town by Polish families. Only twelve of them were children.

Needlework has duality: the ability to show one thing and tell of another. The seemingly joyous, brightly-coloured patchwork pictures made by women in Chile during Pinochet's dictatorship sent word to the outside world of deprivation and the suppression of human rights; the embroidered flowers on the patchwork quilts made by women in Changi prison were unreadable to their guards but conveyed messages of hope, love and undented patriotism to male relatives in the adjoining camp; the embroidered story cloths of the Miao were visual translations of a forbidden language, history and myth conserved in stitches. In the Hunan province of China over 1,000 years ago women used needlework to write their own secret language, Nüshu, a phonetic code based on the local proscribed dialect. They embroidered their thoughts and feelings onto handkerchiefs and pillowcases and wrote with a needle and thread on cloth books made as gifts of female friendship and given to a new bride when she left the village. It was a script which men could not read, passed on from woman to woman, the only gender specific language known to exist in the world. Amongst words of advice: 'Be a good wife, do lots of embroidery and try your best to tolerate your husband's family,' women also sewed laments at losing a friend, recorded their resignation to an arranged marriage, told of their frustration at the lack of control over their fate. These little books of embroidered stitches were created as covert intimate conversations between women.

It is not just through stitching that needlework articulates emotion and correspondence. The nature of what is made, and the choice of colour, its use, offer opportunities to provide a complex and multi-layered form of communication. As a coded language, needlework can embed dialogues directed at specific people and convey secret messages unknown to those lacking the knowledge or culture to understand its material nuances. The African American slave Harriet Powers used her seemingly innocuous bible quilts to sew themes of oppression and freedom and conserve an African visual language only decipherable by other slaves. Another slave in the mid-nineteenth century used a non descript cotton seed sack to gift her spirit to the generations who followed.

The sack was discovered in a flea market in Nashville in 2007. It had belonged to Rose, an African slave, who gave it to her nine-year-old daughter Ashley when she was separated from her mother, sold by her owner's family after his death. Seventy years after their separation, in 1921, Ashley's granddaughter, Ruth Middleton, embroidered eight lines of text, which she signed and dated, on the bag to record the story of the sack: of how Rose had given the sack to Ashley as a farewell gift, that it had contained a tattered dress, a braid of Rose's hair and a handful of pecan nuts. But the way the story is stitched, has a deeper resonance than its basic narrative. The words are set out with different lengths of spaces between them as if to mimic the pauses for breath in human speech; some phrases are written in an African vernacular 'It be filled with my Love always,' the word 'Love' sewn in larger text to emphasise its message of kinship. This is a tangible form of storytelling, a way of transcribing oral speech into stitched spacing and colour. Ruth's embroidery carries the voices of her great-grandmother, and her mother's conserving them in her sewing, as she has had it conserved for her by her mother telling her its tale. The sack itself has been carefully patched and mended over time, a sign of how it has been cherished, not just as a family heirloom but as a form of tangible connection, a continuing dialogue between generations. Its safe-guarding represents more than that of a sentimental keepsake, because the sack was in fact a form of niksi, or mojo (a prayer in a bag), a magical amulet in West African culture. Most usually manifested by a bundle of herbs and roots, or a carved figurine which contained symbols of protection, the tattered dress in Ashley's sack was an embodiment of Rose herself, her gift of her hair, traditionally in Africa invested with a person's power, was the gift of her own spirit; the pecan nuts a symbol of growth and nourishment. Rose's sack, made from rough cotton in what was then called 'negro cloth' was emblematic of her life as a slave and her powerlessness. By filling it with objects of magical significance, Rose transformed it into a powerful talisman to protect her daughter, to provide her and subsequent generations with the tools of survival. Ruth, a single mother at the age of fifteen, embroidered Rose's story directly onto the cloth itself, to add to its protective power, investing it with her own personal spirit and transmitting it to her daughter, just as Rose had done for Ashley. Her embroidery ensured that the cultural and spiritual value of the sack was preserved. The sack is now on display at the Smithsonian National Museum of African American History and Culture in Washington D.C., a rare material testimony of the cultural transference between slaves and their descendants, an invisible correspondence, only meaningful to those who can understand its layered messages.

When a cultural language is threatened, or forbidden, its distinct vocabulary is often preserved through needlework as an alternative visual script. When the Welsh language was banned in Welsh schools, people conserved it on sewn samplers. When Catholicism was outlawed in Reformation Britain, Helena Wintour, the daughter and niece of two of the Gunpowder Plot conspirators who were executed for their plan to blow up the King and the houses of Parliament in 1605, risked imprisonment not only by harbouring fugitive Jesuit priests, but by articulating her clandestine faith – its meditations, devotions and hallelujahs – on exquisitely embroidered vestments encrusted with coded imagery which paid homage to martyred saints and called upon the Virgin Mary to hear her prayers. She signed her needlework: 'Orate per me, Helena Wintour,' 'Pray for me, Helena Wintour.'

Signing textiles authors needlework but also amplifies individual voices, voices that might be forgotten. To resist anonymity people have embroidered their signatures on textiles to register their existence or record a common trauma in indelible sewing which leaves a lasting impression. Such stitched signatures are the physical marks of individual or collective insistence on being recognised. Mary, Queen of Scots, declared her rightful sovereignty, again and again, in her needlework through her embroidered coat of arms, monogram and emblem; the suffragettes in Holloway gaol smuggled out handkerchiefs bearing their stitched autographs as avowals of undiminished resolve; the women in Changi prison sewed their signatures to name themselves, over and over, as survivors, as individuals in a system where their identity was reduced to a mere number. And the signing of cloth is also a way to represent those who cannot speak for themselves: the victims in Mexico's war against drugs still have a presence through others embroidering their names on handkerchiefs displayed in public places; the makers of AIDs quilts humanised lost loved ones who were anonymised as statistics. In the state of Chihuahua on the Mexican and U.S. border, where over two thousand women have been murdered since the early 1990s, many of them garment workers – the artist Mandy Cano Villalobos restores the identity of forgotten victims by sitting in a performative exhibition surrounded by piles of shirts and T-shirts onto which she sews their names.

Needlework can also be a way to give voice to those who might otherwise go unheard. In South Africa, the *Amazwi Abesifazane* memory cloth programme collects the autobiographical testimonies of women's experiences under apartheid. It has established an embroidered archive of over three thousand individual stories and statements on discrimination, forced removals, police brutality, imprisonment, rape, faction fighting, murder and other atrocities. In a country of many different dialects and a high level of female illiteracy, written evidence is partisan, unrepresentative of most and inaccessible to many. But, through needlework, sewn pictorial re-enactments of racism, abuse and discrimination are being documented in a common language, ensuring that what might have gone unregistered is recorded. The Advocacy Project based in Washington, D.C., with the support of American quilters, supports damaged communities elsewhere in the world to speak of their trauma. It has made quilts with the Roma people of the Czech Republic, the Bosnian survivors of the Srebrenica massacre, freed domestic slaves in Nepal and the waste-pickers of Chintan in India.

But the most prolific relic of the suppression of voices lies in the samplers sewn by schoolgirls in the eighteenth and nineteenth century. As early as 1631, John Taylor in his *The Needles Excellency*, a compendium of designs for embroidery, advised the tempering of women's speech through their needlework:

> And for my countries quiet, I should like
> That Woman-kinde should use no other Pike
> It will increase their peace, enlarge their store
> To use their tongues lesse, and their Needles more.

Taylor's exhortation was zealously seized upon by the educators of schoolgirls, as an effective way to temper the supposedly febrile female spirit. These small rectangles of linen, originally designed as aide memoires for embroiderers to record stitches and patterns before they had access to printed guides, had little artistic purpose in educational establishments. Instead, they were devised as tools of discipline to inculcate in students an understanding of the attributes expected of them as women: the 'feminine' qualities of humility and reticence.

The schoolroom making of samplers wasn't just an exorcism of creative expression but the literal physical limitation of needlework itself. Fabric was no longer softly held in a sewer's hand but stretched taut over a frame; scaled down to a small rectangle of cloth: colours were limited, the type of stitches and imagery prescribed. The first sewn task demanded of a schoolgirl was to produce serried rows of letters or numbers – alphabets, multiplication tables, almanacs – basic literacy practised in an exactitude of stitches. From there she graduated to longer text, moral platitudes or biblical quotations, corrective in nature. Content was restricted to a uniform template: a central house or school building surrounded by symmetrically arranged pairs or rows of stylised stock motifs.

We have such a sampler, handed down through my husband's family, typical for its time: a handsome house, stylised trees, a dog sleeping on the fenced front lawn and two sentinel peacocks in open tail-feathered splendour strutting below. There are twins of pineapples, bluebirds, crowns and flowering shrubs. The border is wreathed in blossom and a stretch of regimented thistles confirms a Scottish provenance. The text is suitably Calvinistic:

Wealth and titles are the only gifts of fortune, but peace and content are the peculiar endorsement of a well-disposed mind, a mind that can bear affliction without a murmur, and the weight of a plentiful fortune without vainglory.

The sampler is signed and dated: 'Jean McMorron, 1829'. And while no one in the family can recall how Jean fitted into family history, her sampler still echoes her voice, translated through her needlework.

Many of the samplers wrought by schoolgirl hands centuries ago were valued as family heirlooms: archiving not just the name and age of their maker, the date of completion but often including their place or school of origin and the initials of family members. They have become collectors' pieces, displayed in museums, sold as antiques, valued as echoes of a bygone age. But their value is dubiously nostalgic, a sentimental attachment to a time when girls were schooled in domestic and moral duty, when their creative voices were dulled by duty-bound stitchery. While samplers are undoubtedly pretty, their exacting stitches, strict arrangements and small sermons speak more of silent perseverance than of pleasure. Moreover, the signing and dating of samplers, while they represent the first pieces of needlework, of any quantity, to authenticate a female provenance, were not authored to mark a girl's talent. Instead these restrictive rectangles of sewing were school certificates. Their naming executed in the same tightly controlled cross-stitch employed on the sampler itself. Framed, hung on walls, they boasted a school's credentials, not a girl's presence.

Through the centuries needlework became increasingly domesticated. It was hidden from public view and, as it started to be replaced by manufactured goods and its traditional forms were truncated or lost, its complex language faced extinction. It was feminist artists of the 1960 and 70s who reclaimed its potency and visibility. The art world they entered still considered painting and sculpture to be the highest forms, and disparaged any other mediums, including needlework, as lesser. The representation of women by women themselves, through mediums like needlework, in which they were familiar, barely existed in the public realm. Artists like Miriam Schapiro, Faith Ringgold and Judy Chicago, active in the newly-forged women's liberation movement, recognised that their own reticence to be associated with a gendered women's craft – knitting and sewing and others – was a prejudice handed down by men and dishonoured their own female heritage. They committed themselves to the reinstatement of women's craft traditions, and the values inherent in them, as relevant and potent artistic expressions of women's lives. Faith Ringgold made quilts that incorporated deliberate allusions to techniques of sewing and pattern-making and used the nuances of different kinds of fabric to interpret her African story-telling heritage and confront issues of racism and sexism. Miriam Schapiro used diverse materials associated with women's domestic work – aprons, tea towels, sewing – to make contemporary, textured, abstract art which transformed functional fabrics into an articulation of women's experiences.

In 1970 Judy Chicago set up a Feminist Arts program at the California Institute of the Arts and with Miriam Schapiro and her students took over a dilapidated mansion in 1972 to renovate it and transform it into an exhibition space for women artists where they could curate their own work uncompromised by being juxtaposed with male-made art. In the house's seventeen rooms they created art installations which claimed the themes of domesticity, childbirth and female sexuality as viable subjects for art. They called the project Womanhouse.

Textiles featured in many of the rooms: a row of aprons in the kitchen, a stitched chandelier in the dining room, opulent miniscule furnishings in the bedroom of a doll's house, quilts on the stairwell, the train of a wedding dress trailing down the stairs – all created as metaphors for the reality of women's domesticity. The aprons had false breasts attached to them to suggest that, in their removal, a woman was divested of all a man required of her – housekeeping and sex. The wedding dress train changed from white to grey as it neared the hallway of home to symbolise the drabness of life as a wife, the tiny sewn luxury in the bedroom of the doll's house made it harem-like, a site for male desire not female pleasure. Ten thousand people came to see Womanhouse. For women, it was one of the first times they had seen exclusively female art set within a domestic context, art which used explicit female imagery and reflected their own experiences. Men had the novel experience of being spectators of a world in which for once they were the outsiders.

The project, Judy Chicago declared, 'allowed women to feel that their lives had meaning.' It was a revelation.

In 1974 Chicago embarked on what became a five-year project, to involve women in the creation of a monumental multimedia artwork which interpreted the experiences and achievements of women through history. The Dinner Party was conceived as a response to Leonardo da Vinci's painting of The Last Supper, reinterpreted by Chicago with a triangular table on which place settings were laid out chronologically for thirty-nine women who, in different ways and in a variety of spheres, had made their mark on the world. Each of the three sides represented a historical period: Pre-History to Rome, Christianity to the Reformation; the American Revolution to the Women's Revolution. Each table had settings for thirteen women, the number of men present at The Last Supper but, by making her table triangular, Chicago arranged them democratically. There was no focal point, no central figure. The floor beneath the table was inscribed with the names of another nine-hundred and ninety-nine women who represented the support they had had from other women's endeavours as a foundation for the artwork itself.

The research was extensive. At a time when there was little in the way of historical research into women's history and no women's study courses to draw on, few images or texts were available. Twenty researchers worked for two years unearthing the stories of women since the beginning of time, and before that, into mythology. The thirty-nine women chosen were selected not because they were the most celebrated in their field but because their lives and work best revealed the circumstances of women's achievement at a particular time and the nature of their struggle to progress women's status and role in society. Already experimenting with china-painting as an art medium Chicago decided to have a ceramic plate at each woman's place featuring stylised vaginas, symbolising the wellspring of birth and creation, each customised to reflect individual experiences:

three-dimensional representations of each woman's personality. Each plate incorporated a butterfly, the ancient symbol of liberation, but in different stages of metamorphosis, becoming more fully formed as women gained social independence and more prominent as women garnered creative power.

But Chicago also became fascinated by needlework and decided to use it to embed additional cultural and biographical information at each setting. She studied textiles and different kinds of embroidery. Aware that until now she had dismissed women's craft from her own practice, she decided not just to include sewing in the Dinner Party, but to exploit and demonstrate the rich visual potential of traditional needlework to signify progress or restriction. She introduced large fabric runners to each place setting which referenced – symbolically and pictorially – each woman's chronological place in history and provided greater insight to their narratives. On the front was the flourish of each woman's name, stitched in a thick lustre of gold thread, the initial of her first name elaborately worked as a symbol to define her contribution to society – for the physician Elizabeth Blackwell (1821–1910) a stethoscope, for the biblical heroine Judith, a sword, for the composer Ethel Smyth (1858–1944) a metronome. And, collectively, the runners traced the status and circumstances of the women themselves through the changing nature of the needlework of their time: the early creativity of medieval embroidery becoming more constrained as women became sequestered at home or, in the eighteenth century, as samplers became tools of education.

A wide variety of needlework techniques was embraced. This was no tokenistic application of sewing to enhance the Dinner Party's visual effect. Each runner was thoroughly researched, carefully considered and exquisitely executed: stitchers translating Chicago's graphic designs to texture and colour through myriad sewing techniques, painstakingly finding ways to overcome technical challenges. It took two years to complete the runner for

Hatshepsut (1503–1482 BCE), the female Egyptian pharaoh of the XXVIII dynasty, made from the finest linen and embroidered with hieroglyphic characters in praise of her reign. The eleventh century Italian gynaecologist Trotula's runner featured a tree of life worked in trapunto quilting, a form of Italian quilting, its soft white fabric mimicking a baby's swaddling cloth. For Christine de Pizan (1363–1431) the first professional woman author in France, a technique called bargello was adopted, its jagged pattern suggestive of the hostile climate in which she wrote and, for the artist Artemisia Gentileschi (1590–1652), a sumptuous three-dimensional runner fashioned from deep folds of velvet. Different fabrics, methods, colours and motifs were all purposefully chosen to provide tangible interpretations of individual experiences. Sometimes the design on a runner would be an extension of that on a plate to signify a woman who had temporarily broken down the barriers between herself and the world to which she was trying to contribute. In others, a rigid constraint signalled enforced limitations. This was the multi-layered language of needlework harnessed to offer a textural and, at times, an emotional background to these women's lives. Hundreds of women were involved in the creation of the Dinner Party, their names embroidered into the backs of the table runners.

Five thousand people attended the opening of the Dinner Party at the San Francisco Museum of Modern Art in March 1979 and one hundred thousand came to see it during its three-month run, many queuing for hours. An American tour had been planned when, inexplicably, one by one each venue pulled out and it proved impossible to find alternatives. The Dinner Party, which Chicago had designed to make women's voices heard, to ensure – through scale and popularity – that a lasting imprint of women's lives would persevere in the public arena, was made invisible, silenced. It went into storage and the people who had created it went their separate ways.

It did go on tour in the early 1980s, to fourteen venues in six countries, garnering public interest, media support and an over-whelmingly hostile and negative response from the art world from its critics and mainstream curators. The focus of the negativity was on the plates separated in art reviews from the context of their place settings and the needlework on which they stood. The Dinner Party was called pornographic and obscene. In 1990 a plan to house it permanently in the proposed new multicultural art centre at the University of the District of Colombia was shelved under pressure from staff and students with a Republican Congress announcing that it was 'offensive to the sensitivities and moral values of our various related communities.' It moved back into storage, in danger of damage and disintegration. In 2002 it finally found a permanent home at the Elizabeth A. Sackler Center for Feminist Art in Brooklyn, twenty-three years after it had been seen for the first time and after it had been visited by over one million people.

The history of art is awash with graphic and stylised representations of male genitalia. But when Judy Chicago put vaginas on her plates the critics and curators of the art world were aghast. She had stepped across an invisible threshold of gendered taste, its male gatekeepers appalled that such a normal feature of woman's physicality should feature within an artwork dedicated to women' lives. It is curious to consider what the reaction might have been if her images had been executed in paint or sculpture, whether the prejudice directed at them was solely because of their subject matter or because they were realised through craft? Rather than being hailed as a pioneer of contemporary women's art, Chicago was pilloried as an opportunist, using shock tactics to gain attention for her work. The exquisite needlework – the embroidery, beading, quilting, ribbon-work – which exemplified each woman's story in such thoughtful textured interpretations was all but ignored. Its neglect epitomised a conflicted response to sewing itself: a prac-tice from which men were largely excluded and in which they had no experience to proffer a critical voice. They could not interpret its vocabulary nor judge its quality. Access to its physicality, to its nuances of style and technique had long been denied them. Male critics avoided the pit-fall of opinion.

Alongside women men, too, had been the skilled embroiderers of medieval Europe – messaging faith and the promoters of the powers of emperors in China and the Ottoman and Moghul Empires. These male embroiderers had the skill, dexterity and imaginative understanding of needlework's properties to embroider the finest of textiles to promulgate religious and political advancement. But societal change began to exclude them from its sensory language, and decreed that men should be apportioned the 'harder' materials of wood and metal, seen as more representative of their gender. Some men, made vulnerable by physical or mental infirmity, *had* reclaimed sewing to speak of worlds in which they had once been active: John Craske re-spooling his stories of the sea in embroidery; invalided soldiers of the Crimean War revisiting military triumphs on their quilts; the Pow Clifford Gatenby embroidering his experience of the Second World War. There may have been many more men who were closeted embroiderers; their voices never heard, their stories never told. For all we know there could be examples of male needlework which are as yet unaccounted for, or go unrecognised, presumed to have been worked by female hands. But for most men the world of needlework was elusive. They were denied access to its language by dictum of an educational system that deemed it inappropriate for a constructed myth of masculinity to be tainted by an equally constructed myth of femininity. So men remained, by and large, unexpressed in sensory materiality, not just uncertain but prejudiced against a language which had excluded them.

This was precisely what Judy Chicago exploited in her continued use of needlework to drive forward a feminist arts agenda. The Dinner Party had made her realise just how much sewing could convey to women through its techniques and properties. In her next artwork, The Birth Project, she pushed needlework further, expanding its traditions and technical boundaries to create images of creation myths, women's own experiences of pregnancy and childbirth, of miscarriage and the state of motherhood. For Birth Tear quilting was used to capture an image of a woman lying in agony, her head thrown back, her hands clasping her spread legs and a long jag of red embroidery depicting the tear itself. Quilting allowed for the fabric to become skin-like – soft, puckered, rounded – emphasising the indent of the tear. Smocked Figure depicted the simple shape of a pregnant woman weeping. Her body was made from cream linen, the outline of her pregnancy framed in a closely-stitched band of rainbow thread to mark out isolation. The cream back cloth was worked in smocking, the tight pleating of fabric, to suggest compression, the emotional ambivalence some women feel on becoming pregnant. This was Chicago using all the armoury needlework had to offer – the form it took, the techniques involved, the nature of fabric, the different effects embroidery could produce, its physicality – to articulate emotion.

But, of all her work, it is the Dinner Party which has been hailed as her masterpiece. Judy Chicago might chafe against the fact that among her varied and extensive portfolio of artworks in different media, it is this work which has not just been now accepted by the art world but given an iconic status. Its elevation is not only because of its scale and the controversy which surrounded its exhibition but because it accelerated the accepted status of both women's art and women's craft. It recalibrated needlework's value and demonstrated how an underrated medium was a potent form through which women, using its visual and textural language, its historical connotations, could better describe and communicate the world they experienced. I went to see it when it came to Edinburgh in 1984 but I had not expected the seriousness of it, the darkened room, the table lit like a sacrificial altar, the silence of its audience as they tiptoed around its edges, their reverence. Chicago had wanted to echo the sacramental, and create an artwork where the women it represented were honoured, and in the silence which accompanied its viewing, had their voices heard.

With these feminist artists, textile art came of age and has remained a central element of contemporary art, made by men as well as women. It has become an art form in its own right, written about, critiqued, analysed, collected and exhibited. Its creators are now legion, experimentation continuing to push back the boundaries of what fabric and sewing can express, the materials it can encompass, the different ways others can be involved in its genesis. Today textile artists can connect online, share techniques, show their work and are no longer dependent on a gallery system to curate and disseminate their work. They can also, unlike the feminist artists of the 1960s and 70s, access a sewn heritage through the digital archives of museums and galleries, or at least access what remains of it and what is available to tell of its purpose and cultural meaning.

Needlework which remained within families or tribal groups was cherished as emotional and cultural connectors between generations. But these were private treasures, only precious to those who safeguarded them. Most historical needlework collected by or donated to public institutions is divorced from its social and emotional purpose. It has no voice. With no provenance, beyond where and when it was bought or found, it is displayed, if at all, in isolation as an example of a specific technique or a marker of a specific culture. The identity and motive of its maker are immaterial and what is meant by it goes largely un-investigated. The nuanced stitching of its creators, like that of the Bayeux Tapestry, is of little interest. It is the object itself which matters. The Victoria and Albert Museum in London has over seventy thousand textiles, the National Museum of Scotland over twenty thousand and there are millions of textiles worldwide languishing in museum storerooms. Most have scant information on who made them. The word most commonly attached to their descriptions is 'anonymous.' Designated as 'orphan' objects, most of the textiles in global collections remain unseen with their stories unheard.

Our needlework heritage is vulnerable. Their very portability makes them more likely to be folded away and forgotten. The fabric and thread is susceptible to damage by light and dust. Lack of care can equate with lack of perceived value. If their significance is not recognised they are put away in attics, or drawers or simply discarded. Much has been lost already. The Bayeux Tapestry lay unseen, apart from a short annual outing at the Feast of Relics, for five hundred years; most of the embroideries of Mary, Queen of Scots were lost, sold or destroyed; one of Lorina Bulwer's long stitched scrolls was found in a local market, another abandoned in an attic, both discovered and identified one hundred years after their making; the beautiful cloth embroidered by veterans of the First World War for St Paul's Cathedral was thought to have been destroyed in the bombing of the church and rediscovered seventy years later in an old chest in the cathedral. The British patchwork quilt made in Changi prison languished in a drawer of the Red Cross for decades before its historical value was recognised. The tray cloth, a unique first-hand account of the women's arrival at the prison ended up at a jumble sale and many of the embroideries of John Craske, as his biographer Julia Blackburn discovered, lie invisible in the storerooms of museums.

But, perversely, abandonment can lead to survival for some. Rare medieval embroideries, were found at the start of the millennium, wrapped in an old blanket, by a house-clearer in Mayfair; the only surviving piece of clothing in Queen Elizabeth I's vast wardrobe was discovered in 2016, refashioned from a skirt to a wall hanging for a church in Norfolk; a seventeenth century depiction of a bare-breasted Mary Magdalene was unearthed from the Victoria and Albert Museum's 'orphan' objects in 2006, providing a tantalising anomaly to what women were thought to be sewing at the time. In 2011 a trove of embroideries was found in the wine cellar of Edinburgh College of Arts, where it had lain unseen for fifty years. It was part of the Needlework Development Scheme, a study loan scheme of historical and contemporary textiles set up by Scotland's four art schools, the textiles distributed amongst them when the scheme came to an end in 1961. And, in a charity shop in Leeds in 2017 a textile which had lain neglected in the shop for ten years, was re-discovered and was confirmed as a historically important banner, possibly the backdrop to the suffragette leader Emmeline Pankhurst's public meetings. In 2018 a large patchwork with the embroidered names of sixty First World War soldiers, made by them while convalescing in North Staffordshire Infirmary, was found folded inside a pillowcase at the death of its owner, a hundred years after it was made.

Where people have left little textual evidence of their lives, their embroideries gain greater significance as insights into their domestic and social worlds. How such material evidence is interpreted and displayed is of vital importance to its reinstatement. As lost or abandoned objects, their currency is diminished, even if we have reports of them. Descriptions, as those of the now lost autobiographical bed hangings Mary, Queen of Scots left to her son, Prince James, cannot convey more than scale and content. They cannot replace the interpretation of the eye: the emotional presence of the sewer's voice translated through needlework. Visibility heightens their understanding.

But it is not only the loss of visibility of textiles that we should mourn, but the visibility of the process of sewing, too. Needlework is no longer a common activity in people's homes or something we see women doing on the sunny doorsteps of rural villages. It is no longer an integral part of our lives. The act has become separate from the object, the maker from what they have made, and with it we have lost its emotional and social potency: its currency as a form of human communication. Patterns, stitches and techniques have become so dislocated from their original cultural messages that their meaning no longer resonates.

Voice

There is now, however, a growing interest in the material history
and culture of those whose lives have been least represented in our
museums and, until recent decades, neglected by historians and an
increased emphasis on researched and archived needlework. The
Quilt Alliance was established in the United States in 1993 to
document and preserve the history of quilts and quiltmakers and
has recorded interviews with over one thousand quilters and collectors. Its three-minute video oral history project *Go Tell It* continues
to gather information from quilt enthusiasts. When the Quilters'
Guild organised a Heritage Project in the U.K. between 2014 and
2017, over four thousand unknown quilts were recorded. There are
archives of campaign banners at the Peoples' History Museum in
Manchester, both actual and digital, and at the Peace Museum in
Bradford; the London's Women's Library has a collection of
suffrage banners with documentation on their designers and makers
and there are, increasingly, more detailed online archives of the
needlework collections of the Victoria and Albert Museum and
other significant museums around the world. These at least, are
preserving the voices and experiences of those who sewed, through
the images of their needlework which persist. For those that are
irretrievable, unconventional methods of rescuing information
are being adopted. Bridget Long of the University of Hertfordshire
turned to the records of the Old Bailey court in London to inves-
tigate the use and value of quilts between 1610 and 1820. For her
2014 thesis, *Anonymous Patchwork*, she studied the quantitative
and qualitative data available through the recording of trials for
the theft of quilts. Through this she could establish a much clearer
picture of their financial and cultural value and level of ownership
in seventeenth and eighteenth-century England.

But, while those which are lost are seldom retrieved, the store
of meaningful textiles is being replenished through projects which
seek to involve people in translating their voices into fabric and
thread. One of the most inspiring took place on 10th June 2018
when thousands of women gathered in Britain's capital cities to

process through their streets in honour of the suffragettes who had similarly gathered there one hundred years before them.

In an event called *Processions*, the performance art organisation Artichoke created a living portrait of women in the twenty-first century with four simultaneous processions of thousands of women in Belfast, Cardiff, Edinburgh and London. For *Processions* they wanted participants to make their own banners and, to help them make them, they needed a banner advisor – and so, they invited me to take on that role. On June 10th 2018, the mobilisation of thousands of women created moving rivers of colour and imagery in banners that voiced who they were and what mattered to them. Women literally walked in the footsteps of their great grandmothers, processing the same routes the suffragettes had taken for their rallies at the start of the twentieth century.

I joined the procession in Edinburgh with thousands of other women. When I reached the top of the Mound, a high point in the city, I looked down its curve to Princes Street, Edinburgh's main thoroughfare, and all I could see were streams of women wearing the violet, white and green scarves the organisers had provided, now choreographed into thick bands of each colour in one ribbon of marchers. Amongst them were throngs of banners, pennants and decorated staffs. This was a camaraderie of women of all ages, cultures and backgrounds, vital and energetic, collectively, visually, proclaiming their presence.

I carried the banner I had made for the day: Mary, Queen of Scots, dancing, resplendent in a gown of cream and purple inscribed with embroidered words to encapsulate her life: 'betrayal, miscarriage, power, defeat, friendship'. I walked with her on the route she last took as a humiliated prisoner, after her defeat at Carberry Hill in 1567, a defeat which led to her long-term captivity and ultimately to her execution. This, in my mind, was an act of restoration, ensuring her triumphant return to Holyrood Palace accompanied by a phalanx of women who no longer considered their place to be lesser, their power diminishable or their voices unheard.

Later, I asked one of Scotland's national co-ordinators of *Processions*, what she felt the project had achieved. She cited the vast presence of women in a public space, the democracy of the project being open to anyone who wanted to take part. The process of banner-making, sitting around a table together, working collectively brought people together, some as unlikely collaborators, in shared creativity. The material presence of the banners added another layer to the event as a representation of the social fabric of women's lives, as varied in size, shape, character as the participants themselves. She felt that the level of response to the invitation to use needlework to express individual and collective lives was both surprising and overwhelming. When I asked Janet, who runs my local village shop and who, with fourteen other local women, made a banner to carry on the day what she thought, she said how important it was to her, as a sewer, that the project had enabled sewing skills to be passed on to a younger generation. And she had been surprised by how emotional she had found the day itself. She hadn't expected to feel such a strong sense of belonging, both to the women in her own group and to the unknown women around her. It was the respect shown to the women present and their respect for the struggles of women in the past – manifested in their coming in their thousands to pay homage – which she will remember, that and the glorious spectacle of their banners held high above them. But claiming a presence, a voice, through needlework need not always be done through such large-scale demonstrations. Sometimes it is the least remarkable, the simplest form, that has most to say: Jan Ruff-O'Hern's handkerchief, the headscarves of Les Madres de Plaza de Mayo and, in South Africa, the lapel of Ruth First's dressing gown.

During apartheid in South Africa, in 1963 the resistance fighter Ruth First was incarcerated in solitary confinement for 117 days, the first white woman to be detained without charge under the

Ninety-Day Detention Law. She maintained her identity through her embroidery. Secretly, under the lapel of her dressing gown, she began to mark down each day of her imprisonment by stitching row upon row of black lines in groups of six, and on the seventh day she sewed a stroke. Then she realised that, through her sewing, she could control time. Some days she wouldn't sew at all leaving two or three days to mark down later in the week thereby gaining time. Or she would unpick a day and redo it again to regain time. Stitching this self-made calendar became an act of unofficial recording, a diary of sorts. Refused the means to write by the guards, this simple needlework, hidden from view, was a small act of rebellion against her loss of freedom. In prison, when she had no power over her life or her death, she could still make time for herself. Even in this, through the most basic act of sewing, needlework could communicate her spirit and manifest her defiant voice. By the time she was assassinated in 1982 she had published a short autobiography in which she documented her days of sensory deprivation and the significance of her sewing to express her sense of self.

Needlework can record history, convey complex social information about people's status, relationships, beliefs, origin and allegiances. It can conserve memory, protecting and preserving personal and collective testimonies. It has a vital role to play in archiving tradition and telling people's stories in a medium that carries emotional and physical meaning. Fabric and thread can convey a prayer, trace out a map, proclaim a manifesto, send out a warning, bestow a blessing, celebrate a culture and commemorate lives lived and lost. Lives expressed not just through images but through texture and colour, different kinds of stitches, the various processes of piecing, patching, recycling, quilting to more clearly articulate the different layers of our humanity and manifest the fabric of our lives. Sewing is a way to mark our existence on cloth: patterning our place in the world, voicing our identity, sharing something of ourselves with others and leaving the indelible evidence of our presence in stitches held fast by our touch.

Ending

You cut a length of thread, knot one end and pull the other end through the eye of a needle. You take a piece of fabric and you think about what you are going to make, what you are going to say, who it will be for and what others will be able to read from it. And you consider what patterns and motifs you might use in this embroidery. Will it have a story or will its message be told in symbols – readable to future generations? Will it hold sewn promises of protection, blessings from the heart, warnings to spirits who might wish harm? You choose colours with care to convey specific emotions. You look through your collection of adornments, the tiny glittering sequins, the box of beads, the braid of jig jigging pompoms and select all or some to add when the embroidery is complete. Then you push your threaded needle in one side of the cloth and pull it out on the other, on and on in rhythmic sewing, until you have made something that matters: a thing of beauty and meaning, an embroidery that holds your spirit fast within its threads.

Bibliography

Threads of Life has involved extensive research and reading. It would be impossible to list every book where I have found a nugget of useful or illuminating information or insight. But there are some which either provide more in-depth study of specific subjects or that I found particularly interesting. Many are sadly out of print but they can be found through second-hand booksellers and libraries.

GENERAL

Ackerman, Diane. *A Natural History of the Senses*. Phoenix, 1996.

Arthur, Liz. *Embroidery 1600–1700 at the Burrell Collection*. John Murray in Association with Glasgow Museums, 1995.

Dhamija, Jasleen. *Asian Embroidery*. Crafts Council of India, 2004.

Gillow, John and Bryan Sentence. *World Textiles*. Thames & Hudson, 2004.

Gillow, John. *Textiles of the Islamic World*. Thames & Hudson, 2013.

Gordon, Beverly. *Textiles: The Whole Story*. Thames & Hudson, 2013.

Paine, Sheila. *Embroidered Textiles: A World Guide to Traditional Patterns*. Thames & Hudson, 2010.

Parker, Rozsika. *The Subversive Stitch: Embroidery and the Making of the Feminine*. The Women's Press, 1984.

Prichard, Sue. *Quilts 1700–2010: Hidden Histories, Untold Stories*. V & A Publications, 2012.

Quilt Treasures: The Quilters' Guild Heritage Search. The Quilters' Guild, 2010.

Rae, Janet. *The Quilts of the British Isles*. Deidre McDonald Books, 1996.

Rae, Janet. *Warm Covers: A Scottish Textile Story*. Sansom & Company, 2016.

Schoeser, Mary. *World Textiles: A Concise History*. Thames & Hudson, 2003.

Swain, Margaret. *Scottish Embroidery: Medieval to Modern*. B.T. Batsford, 1986.

UNKNOWN

Bernstein, David J.. *The Mystery of the Bayeux Tapestry*. Weidenfeld & Nicolson, 1986.

Henderson, Anna C. with Gale R. Owen-Crocker., *Making Sense of the Bayeux Tapestry*. Manchester University Press, 2016

Lemagnen, Sylvette. *The Bayeux Tapestry: A Step-by-Step Discovery*. OREP Editions, 2015.

Messent, Jan. *The Bayeux Tapestry Embroiderers' Story*. Madeira Threads UK, 1999.

Moffat, Alastair. *The Great Tapestry of Scotland*. Birlinn, 2013.

POWER

Arnold, Janet. *Queen Elizabeth's Wardrobe Unlock'd*. Routledge, 1988.

Bath, Michael. *Emblems for a Queen: The Needlework of Mary Queen of Scots*. Archetype Publications, 2008.

Browne, Clare and Glyn Davies. *English Medieval Embroidery: Opus Anglicanum*. Yale University Press, 2016.

Swain, Margaret. *The Needlework of Mary Queen of Scots*. Van Nostrand Reinhold Company, 1973.

FRAILTY

Blackburn, Julia. *Threads: The Delicate Life of John Craske*. Jonathan Cape, 2015.

Hornstein, Gail A.. *Agnes's Jacket: A Psychologist's Search for the Meaning of Madness*. PCCS Books, 2012.

Bibliography

Thesiger, Ernest. *Adventures in Embroidery*. The Studio, 1941.
Thesiger, Ernest. *Practically True*. William Heinemann, 1926.

CAPTIVITY

Archer, Bernice. *The Interment of Western Civilians under the Japanese 1941-1945*. Routledge Curzon, 2004.
Chevalier, Tracy and Fine Cell Work, *The Sleep Quilt*. Pallas Athene Publishers, 2017.
Materson, ray and Materson, Melanie. *Sins and Needles: A Story of Spiritual Mending*. Algonquin Books of Chapel Hill, 2002.
Ruff-O'Herne, Jan. *Fifty Years of Silence: Comfort Women of Indonesia*. William Heinemann, 2008.

IDENTITY

El-Khalidi, Laila.*The Art of Palestinian Embroidery*. Saqi Books, 2001.
Luciow, Johanna. *Ukrainian Embroidery*. Van Nostrand Reinhold Company, 1979.
Naughton, Jim. *Conflict and Costume: The Herero Tribe of Namibia*. Merrell Publishers, 2013.
Tarlo, Emma. *Clothing Matters: Dress and Identity in India*. The University of Chicago Press, 1996.
Weir, Shelagh *Palestinian Embroidery*. British Museum Press, 1979.

CONNECTION

Styles, John. *Threads of Feeling: The London Foundling Hospital's Textile Tokens, 1740–1770*. The Foundling Museum, 2016.

PROTECT

Frater, Judy. *Threads of Identity: Embroidery and Adornment of the Nomadic Rabaris*. Mapin Publishing Pvt., 1997.
Salomon, Kathryn. *Jewish Ceremonial Embroidery*. B.T. Batsford, 1988.

Bibliography

JOURNEY

Courtenay, P. P. and Maria Wronska-Friend. *Migrants of the Mountains: The Costume Art of the Hmong People of Mainland Southeast Asia.* James Cook University of North Queensland, 1995.

Smith, Ruth. *Miao Embroidery from South West China: Textiles from Gina Corrigan's Collection.* Occidor, 2005.

PROTEST

Corbett, Sarah. *A Little Book of Craftivism.* Cicada Books, 2013.

Corbett, Sarah. *How to be a Craftivist: The Art of Gentle Protest.* Unbound, 2017.

Gorman, John. *Banner Bright.* Allen Lane, 1973.

Greer, Betsy. *Craftivism.* Arsenal Pulp Press, 2014.

Pershing, Linda. *The Ribbon around the Pentagon: Peace by Piecemakers.* The University of Tennessee Press, 1996.

The Ribbon: A Celebration of Life. Lark Books, 1985.

Tickner, Lisa. *The Spectacle of Women: Imagery of the Suffrage Campaign 1907-14.* Chatto & Windus, 1987.

LOSS

Agosin, Marjorie. *Tapestries of Hope, Threads of Love: The Arpillera Movement in Chile.* Rowman & Littlefield, 2007.

Deacon, Deborah A. and Paula E. Calvin. *War Imagery in Women's Textiles: An International Study of Weaving, Knitting, Sewing, Quilting, Rug Making and other Fabric Arts.* McFarland & Company, 2014.

Nisenthal Krinitz, Ester and Berenice Steinhartdt. *Memoirs of Survival.* Hyperion Books for Children, 2005.

Otto Lipsett, Linda. *Elizabeth Roseberry Mitchell's Graveyard Quilt: An American Pioneer Saga.* Halstead & Meadows, 1995.

Ruskin, Cindy. *The Quilt: Stories from the Names Project.* Pocket Books, 1988.

COMMUNITY

Anderson, David. *Shamiana: The Mughal Tent.* V & A Publications, 1999.

Arthur, Liz. *Keeping Glasgow in Stitches.* Mainstream Publishing, 1991.

PLACE

Benberry, Cuesta. *A Piece of My Soul: Quilts by Black Arkansans.* The University of Arkansas Press, 2000.

Fry, Gladys-Marie. *Stitched from the Soul: Slave Quilts from the Antebellum South.* The University of North Carolina Press, 2002.

Tobin, Jacqueline L. and Raymond G. Dobhard. *Hidden in Plain View: A Secret Story of Quilts and the Underground Railroad.* Anchor Books, 2000.

Tyner, Judith A. *Stitching the World: Embroidered Maps and Women's Geographical Education.* Ashgate Publishing, 2015.

Witney Antiques, *Samplers – Mapped and Charted.* Witney Antiques, 2005.

VALUE

Hayden, Ruth. *Mrs Delany: Her Life in Flowers.* British Museum Press, 1980.

Laird, Mark and Alicia Weisberg-Roberts. *Mrs Delany and Her Circle.* Yale University Press, 2009.

Morris, Barbara. *Victorian Embroidery.* Barrie & Jenkins, 1962.

Roberts, Jane. *George III and Queen Charlotte: Patronage, Collecting and Court Taste.* Royal Collections Publications, 2004.

Srobel, Heidi A. *The Artistic Matronage of Queen Charlotte 1744-818: How a Queen Promoted both Art and Female Artists in English Society.* Edwin Mellen Press, 2011.

Bibliography

ART

Arthur, Liz. *Glasgow Girls: Artists and Designers* 1890-1930. Kirdcudbright, 2010.

Bilcliffe, Roge. *Charles Rennie Mackintosh and the Art of the Four.* Frances Lincioln, 2017.

Burkhauser, Jude. *Glasgow Girls: Women in Art and Design* 1880-1920. Canongate, 1990.

Connell, Linda. *Textile Treasures of the WI.* The National Needlework Archive, 2007.

Quinton, Rebecca. *Patterns of Childhood: Samplers from Glasgow Museums.* The Herbert Press, 2005.

Tarrant, Naomi E. A. *'Remember Now Thy Creator': Scottish Girls' Samplers,* 1700–1872. Society of Antiquaries in Scotland, 2014.

WORK

Adler-Milstein, Sarah and John M. Kline. *Sewing Hope: How One Factory Challenges the Apparel Inustry's Sweatshops.* University of Caifornia Press, 2017.

Burman, Barbara. *The Culture of Sewing: Gender, Consumption and Home Dressmaking.* Berg, 1999.

VOICE

Auslander, M., 2017. *Rose's Gift: Slavery, Kinship, and the Fabric of Memory.* Present Pasts, 8(1), p.1. DOI: http://doi.org/10.5334/pp.78.

Bryan-Wilson, Julia. *Fray: Art and Textile Politics.* University of Chicago Press, 2017.

Chicago, Judy and Susan Hill. *Embroidering Our Heritage: The Dinner Party Needlework.* Anchor Books, 1980.

First, Ruth. *117 Days.* Virago, 2010.

Prain, Leanne. *Strange Material: Storytelling through Textiles.* Arsenal Pulp Press, 2014.

Wellesley Smith, Claire. *Slow Stitch: Mindful and Contemplative Textile Art.* Batsford, 2015.

Images

Many of the textiles mentioned in this book are accessible online. Here are some websites where you can find them:

Bayeux Museum: bayeuxmuseum.com
Conflict Textile Collection: cain.ulster.ac.uk
Craftivist Collective: craftivist-collective.com
Embroiderers' Guild: embroiderersguild.com
Foundling Museum: foundlingmuseum.org.uk
Hunterian Museum: gla.ac.uk
Judy Chicago: judychicago.com
Peace Museum: peacemuseum.org.uk
People's History Museum: phm.org.uk
Quilt Museum: quiltmuseum.org.uk
Sewing Matters: sewingmatters.co.uk
Smithsonian Institution: si.edu
Smithsonian National Museum of African American History
   & Culture: nmaahc.si.edu
Textile Society: textilesociety.org.uk
Victoria and Albert Museum: vam.ac.uk
Visual Arts Data Service: vads.ac.uk